RACIAL ATTITUDES
IN THE
1990s

RACIAL ATTITUDES
IN THE
1990s

Continuity and Change

Edited by
Steven A. Tuch
Jack K. Martin

PRAEGER

Westport, Connecticut
London

Library of Congress Cataloging-in-Publication Data

Racial attitudes in the 1990s : continuity and change / edited by
   Steven A. Tuch and Jack K. Martin.
         p.   cm.
      Includes bibliographical references and index.
      ISBN 0–275–95015–8 (alk. paper). — ISBN 0–275–96037–4 (pbk. :
   alk. paper)
      1. United States—Race relations. 2. Whites—United States—
   Attitudes. 3. Afro-Americans—Attitudes. 4. Racism—United
   States. I. Tuch, Steven A., 1949–   . II. Martin, Jack K., 1949– .
   E185.615.R2137   1997
   305.8'00973—dc21   97–11075

British Library Cataloguing in Publication Data is available.

Library of Congress Catalog Card Number: 97–11075
ISBN: 0–275–95015–8
       0–275–96037–4 (pbk.)

First published in 1997

Praeger Publishers, 88 Post Road West, Westport, CT 06881
An imprint of Greenwood Publishing Group, Inc.

Printed in the United States of America

The paper used in this book complies with the
Permanent Paper Standard issued by the National
Information Standards Organization (Z39.48–1984).

10 9 8 7 6 5 4 3 2 1

In fond memory of

A. Wade Smith

Contents

Illustrations

FIGURES

Acknowledgments

As editors of this volume we owe many debts of appreciation. First, thanks are due to the University of Georgia's Survey Research Center, Institute for Behavioral Research, Department of Sociology, and African-American Studies Program for their financial support of the January 1993 conference that provided the motivation for this collection. We also appreciate the authors' efforts in preparing and revising their contributions to this volume. Gratitude is also due Paul Roman and Lee Sigelman for their many helpful insights that proved invaluable in moving the manuscript toward final production. We give special thanks to the administrative staff of the University of Georgia Survey Research Center. In particular, we appreciate the efforts of Linda White, Kathie Shinholser, Lori Ducharme, Eileen Harwood, and Andrea Dodas for their deft handling of the endless retyping of tables and chapters, and the handling of correspondence. Finally, we are grateful for the patience and support of our families during the many hours we devoted to this project.

Introduction

Jack K. Martin, E. M. Beck, and Steven A. Tuch

This volume had its beginning in a two-day conference on "Racial Attitudes in the 1990s" held at the University of Georgia in the winter of 1993. Sponsored by the University's Survey Research Center and the Institute for Behavioral Research, the conference brought together several leading researchers in the study of race and racial attitudes in the United States. Featured speakers at this conference were A. Wade Smith (late) of Arizona State University and Lawrence Bobo of Harvard University. Additional commentary was provided by E. M. Beck of the University of Georgia, Steven A. Tuch of The George Washington University, and Jack K. Martin of the University of Georgia.

The featured papers at the conference form the core of this original collection of chapters on racial attitudes. The only exception is the final chapter by Tuch, Sigelman, and Martin, which is reprinted from *Challenge*. The timeliness of such a collection finds emphasis in the fact that the January 1993 conference roughly corresponded with the fiftieth anniversary of Gunnar Myrdal's (1944) disturbing portrait of black-white relationships in post–World War II U.S. society, *An American Dilemma: The Negro Problem and Modern Democracy*, and by the fact that the conference followed closely on the heels of the civil unrest and racial tension generated by the Rodney King verdict in Los Angeles. Thus 1993 was a particularly opportune time to turn our attention to the issue of racial attitudes, and events since that time have done little to change this. Commentary and debate surrounding the state of race relations in the wake of the O. J. Simpson trial and the recent wave of racially motivated arson aimed at

African-American churches in the South reemphasize the need for continued scholarly attention to issues of contemporary U.S. race relations and racism.

The chapters that follow are organized around three broad themes: aggregate levels of white support for general principles of racial equality and of support for policies designed to realize the principles; sociodemographic distinctiveness in whites' racial attitudes; and the still underresearched question of African-American attitudes toward race and racism. Part I includes a prologue on the state of race attitudes theory and research adapted from A. Wade Smith's conference presentation and an overview of the transformation of Americans' attitudes regarding race is based on Lawrence Bobo's conference paper. Parts II, III, and IV are comprised of nine chapters solicited from leading researchers in the area.

Chapters 1 and 2 constitute Part I, "The Transformation of Racial Attitudes in the United States." Until his death in 1994, A. Wade Smith was one of the nation's leading researchers in the area of race relations. Wade's talk provided conference participants with a provocative assessment of the current state of theory and method in the area. As a tribute, inadequate as it is, to Wade and his numerous contributions to our understanding of racial attitudes and race relations, we are including his introductory remarks at the conference as Chapter 1 in this volume. Titled "Prologue: Reflections on Racial Attitude Research," these brief remarks constitute Wade's final writings.

As noted, more than 50 years have passed since the publication of Myrdal's landmark work, *An American Dilemma: The Negro Problem and Modern Democracy*. The ensuing years have witnessed a dramatic decline in overt expressions of antiblack and segregationist sentiments by white Americans. According to some commentators, however, this liberalizing trend may have moderated, or at least been transformed, in recent years. In Chapter 2, "Laissez-Faire Racism: The Crystallization of a Kinder, Gentler, Antiblack Ideology," Lawrence Bobo, James R. Kluegel, and Ryan A. Smith provide an overview of this transformation in the racial attitudes of white Americans.

The chapter by Bobo, Kluegel, and Smith argues that racial attitudes and beliefs are best understood within the overlapping contexts of the economics and politics of race in the United States. According to these authors, traditional, or Jim Crow, racism — which found its roots in the post–Civil War South and the Southern planter elite — disappeared from the scene as structural economic changes reduced the importance of traditional forms of agriculture to the economy. Thus, as traditional racist ideology lost its embeddedness in dominant economic and political institutions, its tenets came to be viewed as incompatible with U.S. values. These authors point to the progressive decline in white Americans' support for conventional racist attitudes and beliefs as support for their contention.

According to Bobo, Kluegel, and Smith, however, racist ideology did not disappear; it only changed. These authors outline a new form of racial antipathy, laissez-faire racism, which has its roots in black Americans' relatively disadvantaged position in U.S. society. Laissez-faire racism is an ideology that attributes black disadvantages to supposed characteristics of blacks themselves, such as lack of attachment to the work ethic, and denies the potency of structural determinants of conditions in black communities.

As an outline for understanding the transformation of white Americans' racial attitudes, the notion of laissez-faire racism provides a powerful analytic framework. Evidence of widespread laissez-faire racist attitudes and beliefs suggests that large numbers of white Americans will accept as much race-based inequity as an ostensibly free market and egalitarian polity creates.

Part II of this volume, "The Racial Attitudes of Whites," comprises two chapters, each focusing on aggregate levels of whites' endorsement of principles supportive of racial equality.

In Chapter 3, "Symbolic Racism, Old-Fashioned Racism, and Whites' Opposition to Affirmative Action," Michael Hughes provides an empirical evaluation of the utility of the concept of symbolic racism. Using data from the 1986 and 1992 American National Election Studies, Hughes assesses the correlates of both symbolic racism and attitudes toward affirmative action among white Americans.

Like the arguments developed by Bobo, Kluegel, and Smith in Chapter 2, Hughes argues that symbolic racism, like laissez-faire racism, is clearly distinguishable from traditional racist beliefs. Interestingly, he finds no evidence that this configuration of attitudes is simply an outcome of the combination of support for individualism and antiblack affect. Instead, Hughes finds that both group self-interest and symbolic racism have significant independent influences on whites' support for affirmative action; in a simple additive effects model, traditional prejudice is not associated with greater opposition to affirmative action programs, while symbolic racism is; and in a nonadditive model, at high levels of old-fashioned prejudice, symbolic racism has little or no influence on affirmative action attitudes, whereas at the lowest levels of old-fashioned prejudice, symbolic racism has a substantial negative impact on attitudes supportive of affirmative action programs.

Hughes's findings raise several important questions regarding the nature, sources, and consequences of symbolic racism. Although symbolic racism presumably has nothing to do with interests, Hughes's analyses and interpretations suggest the possibility that symbolic racism itself may be a reflection of group interest. His analyses, which are consistent with the idea that racial prejudice changes as the structural positions of various groups change, complement those of Bobo, Kluegel, and Smith and expand on H. Blumer's earlier argument that racial prejudice is a reflection of group position.

Aggregate levels of racial antipathy are also the focus of Chapter 4, "The Affective Component of Prejudice: Empirical Support for the New View," by Thomas F. Pettigrew. In this chapter Pettigrew contends that the tendency of theorists and researchers alike to focus almost exclusively on the cognitive components of prejudice (for example, stereotyping, causal misattributions, and so forth) results in the neglect of its affective component. Developing logic drawn from an emerging body of theory and research in the intergroup relations literature, Pettigrew presents evidence from two databases illustrating the situational and emotional specificity of prejudice and the importance of developing a group focus in prejudice research.

By explicitly incorporating the role of emotion in the study of prejudice, Pettigrew outlines a more comprehensive approach to the understanding of the sources of prejudice. As he points out, by emphasizing the way in which strong emotions act as a catalyst that magnifies intergroup processes, this more comprehensive model is capable of explaining both the positive and the negative extremes of intergroup relations.

Within the race attitudes literature there is a longstanding tradition of theory and research that addresses the determinants of whites' views of race and racial inequality. Many of these studies examine how one's position in the social structure, as defined by ascribed and achieved statuses, such as gender, age, schooling, wealth, and social class, condition the individual's perceptions of race and racism. The four chapters in Part III, "Sociodemographic Attributes and the Racial Attitudes of Whites," are located within this tradition, assessing whether distinctive racial attributions are associated with whites' sociodemographic characteristics.

In Chapter 5, "Status, Ideology, and Dimensions of Whites' Racial Beliefs and Attitudes: Progress and Stagnation," Lawrence Bobo and James R. Kluegel provide an empirical test of the laissez-faire racism thesis outlined in Chapter 2. Using data from the 1990 General Social Survey, Bobo and Kluegel examine four hypotheses relating whites' sociodemographic attributes and socioeconomic ideologies to measures of traditional and laissez-faire racism and attitudes toward racial policies.

Findings from their empirical tests provide support for each of their hypotheses. Sociodemographic characteristics, particularly age and schooling, are found to be predictive of traditional, or Jim Crow, racism. On the other hand, socioeconomic ideology — in the form of a denial of social responsibility for black disadvantage — is found to be an important correlate of contemporary stereotypes of blacks and perceptions of racial discrimination.

There are several important implications of these findings. First, the findings show clearly that support for traditional racist postures, especially among young and better educated whites, is low and declining. Unfortunately, this progress is offset by whites' general endorsement of newer, more subtle racist stereotypes that mitigate against the acknowledgment of societal responsibility for blacks' disadvantaged position.

Bobo and Kluegel's analyses demonstrate that although whites are now more in favor of egalitarian racial principles than they have been in the past, they continue to resist policies designed to ensure egalitarianism. According to the authors, this apparent paradox derives from the prevalent negative stereotypes of blacks as undeserving of any special treatment from government.

In Chapter 6, "Advance and Retreat: Racially Based Attitudes and Public Policy," Cedric Herring and Charles Amissah examine levels of social distance between white Americans and black Americans. In particular, these authors assess the social distance preferences of white ethnic groups in a variety of social contexts.

Using national survey data from the 1990 General Social Survey, Herring and Amissah compare ethnics and nonethnics with regard to their willingness to be integrated with blacks in neighborhoods, schools, marriage, and other contexts. Herring and Amissah's analyses show that despite the gains in racial integration observed over the past several decades, there is still substantial intolerance among nonblack Americans for African Americans, particularly among European whites and white nonethnics.

In discussing the implications of their research, the authors make a key observation: As long as large numbers of whites are unwilling to interact with blacks in these contexts, there will likely be continued difficulties in gaining widespread endorsement of social policies that require a pattern of routine social interaction among blacks and whites.

In Chapter 7, "White Ethnic Identification and Racial Attitudes," James E. Coverdill reports an innovative analysis of a question related to that of Herring and Amissah. Specifically, Coverdill derives and tests two hypotheses regarding the link between whites' ethnic identification and their racial attitudes. The first hypothesis suggests that white Americans' ethnic identification produces individualistic explanations for blacks' disadvantaged position in U.S. society; Coverdill's second hypothesis is that ethnics have a distaste for race-targeted policies designed to boost minority achievement.

Using data from the 1990 General Social Survey, Coverdill presents findings that are inconsistent with both of these hypotheses. His analyses demonstrate that ethnic identification has little effect on causal attributions of socioeconomic differences between blacks and whites and that ethnics and nonethnics are indistinguishable in terms of their racial policy attitudes.

In Chapter 8, "Regional Differences in Whites' Racial Policy Attitudes," the editors examine an enduring finding in the race attitudes literature: that residents of Southern states report the highest levels of racial antipathy. In a test of a notion drawn from mass society theory that regional distinctiveness in racial attitudes has effectively disappeared, Tuch and Martin explore regional variations in whites' attitudes toward policies aimed at eliminating race-based disadvantages.

Utilizing data from two national and two regional surveys, Tuch and Martin disaggregate responses to an array of racial policy questions by non-South, South, and Deep South residence. They find that whites' views of policy initiatives designed to combat racial discrimination and ameliorate its effects are characterized by marked regional distinctiveness. On most policy issues, Southerners — and those raised in the Deep South, in particular — are much less likely than residents of other regions to endorse race-targeted policies.

Tuch and Martin interpret these findings as providing no evidence of the kind of regional convergence in racial affect predicted by mass society theory. In spite of substantial demographic and economic changes in Southern social structure over the last 50 years, Southerners — particularly those raised in the regional core — continue to be more resistant than non-Southerners to policies designed to change the racial status quo.

Compared to what is known about the attitudes of white Americans regarding issues of race, our knowledge of black Americans' racial attitudes is fragmentary at best. There are several reasons for this disparity in the literature. To begin, because blacks represent only about 12 percent of the U.S. population, in most national polls African Americans are not found in large enough numbers to sustain meaningful statistical analyses. More troubling, however, is the fact that, historically, African Americans have been treated as a monolithic group; that is, their racial attitudes have been assumed to be uniform, reflecting shared norms, values, and experiences. Beyond the obvious naiveté of such a view, the end result of having ignored intragroup variation in black Americans' attitudes about race is that little reliable data on demographic, socioeconomic, or regional differences in blacks' racial attitudes exist today. Moreover, lacking evidence of variation among African Americans, the tendency has been to assume that such differences do not exist. In this way, the untested assumption of a unity of opinion underestimates the variability of attitudes and beliefs among African Americans, ultimately leading to an overestimation of the contribution of race per se to black Americans' racial outlooks.

In an attempt to provide a partial remedy to this situation, Part IV, "The Racial Attitudes of African Americans," contains three chapters that focus explicitly on analyses of variation in the racial attitudes of black

Americans. In the first of these, "Blacks, Whites, and the Changing of the Guard in Black Political Leadership," Lee Sigelman explores public evaluations of four prominent black leaders: Jesse Jackson, Douglas Wilder, Colin Powell, and Louis Farrakhan.

Using survey data from a 1991 *Newsweek* poll conducted by the Gallup organization, Sigelman analyzes the transformation of black political leadership and African-American and white attitudes toward black leaders. Several interesting findings stand out. First, among both blacks and whites, Jackson was the most visible of the four leaders, Wilder the least visible; Powell was the only one of the group who was more visible among whites than among blacks; blacks were most favorably disposed toward the idea of Jackson assuming a more prominent national leadership role, followed by Powell and Wilder (only Farrakhan was negatively evaluated by blacks in this regard); and whites were most favorable toward Powell. Nevertheless, blacks were significantly more likely than whites to report that an increased leadership role for any one of the four African-American leaders would benefit black Americans. As Sigelman points out, this view likely reflects African Americans' symbolic affirmation of a strong desire for an increased presence of black decision-makers on the national political scene.

On the other hand, particularly with regard to the endorsement of the two more salient black leaders, Jackson and Powell, Sigelman's analyses indicate a clear differentiation within the black rank and file. For example, Jackson found his strongest support among younger blacks, those of lower educational attainment, blacks who identified themselves as Democrats, and those who blamed black poverty on society rather than on poor blacks themselves. Among whites, however, the only predictor of support for Jackson was societal rather than individual attributions of the causes of black poverty. A different pattern emerged with respect to evaluations of Colin Powell. Among blacks who expressed an opinion about Powell, those who attributed black disadvantage to blacks themselves were more likely to endorse Powell's leadership role.

Thus, Sigelman's analyses, like others in this volume, cast further doubt on the notion of a monolith of attitudes and beliefs among black Americans. At least as far as support for increased leadership roles for black leaders is concerned, African Americans differ in important respects.

Previous research has clearly demonstrated that the structure of employers' racial attitudes has important effects on the employment patterns of African-American workers. Not known, however, is whether the attitudes of black employers toward black workers are similar to or different from those of their majority group counterparts. In Chapter 10, "African-American Employers' Attitudes toward African-American

Workers," Joleen Kirschenman speaks directly to this deficiency in the literature.

Using data from a sample of employers collected under the auspices of the University of Chicago's Urban Poverty and Family Structure Project, Kirschenman provides a qualitative analysis of in-depth interviews with 14 African-American employers in the Chicago metropolitan area. Surprisingly, these analyses suggest that, overall, these black employers harbor views of black workers that are nearly as negative as the views of white employers. Although there is evidence that black employers' attitudes are somewhat less pejorative than those of whites — and that, when asked, these employers invoke structural rather than individualistic explanations for the perceived deficiencies of African-American workers — Kirschenman argues that the result is the same: race-based discrimination in employment.

Kirschenman interprets these findings to provide support for the notion that it is class differences between black employers and workers and the tenuous position of the black middle class that account for African-American employers' prejudicial attitudes and discriminatory behavior.

In the final chapter of this volume, Chapter 11, "Fifty Years after Myrdal: Blacks' Racial Policy Attitudes in the 1990s," Steven A. Tuch, Lee Sigelman, and Jack K. Martin explore the attitudes of African Americans, particularly those in the middle class, toward policies designed to ameliorate racial disadvantage. This chapter was adapted from a paper originally presented at the 1994 Morehouse University conference commemorating the 1944 publication of Myrdal's *An American Dilemma: The Negro Problem and Modern Democracy* and first published in the journal *Challenge*.

Using national survey data drawn from a variety of sources, these authors examine race and class influences on attitudes toward a range of race-targeted public policies. As expected, Tuch, Sigelman, and Martin find that, compared to whites, African Americans demonstrate high levels of support for race-targeted policies. On the other hand, blacks are by no means uniform in their support. Most important, opinions about policies on which blacks tend to disagree (for example, preferential hiring) cannot be explained as a function of class position. Thus, there is little evidence of an emerging political divide between black members of the middle and working classes.

In Chapter 1 of this volume, A. Wade Smith noted that the mid-1990s can be characterized as a period in which racial attitude research reveals "discord on the important issues and much less than full agreement on the general direction of race relations in America." Each of the chapters in this volume highlights this issue, and each offers suggestions about its implications for furthering our understanding of contemporary race relations. As the end of the twentieth century approaches, the United States remains at a crossroads over the issue of race. It is imperative that we continue to identify those individual and structural processes that create or perpetuate barriers to meaningful improvement in black-white relations and racial equality or, alternatively, that offer opportunities for effective remedies to racism and its consequences. In one way or another, each of the contributions to this volume moves us further down this road.

I

THE TRANSFORMATION OF RACIAL ATTITUDES IN THE UNITED STATES

1

Prologue: Reflections on Racial Attitude Research

A. Wade Smith

Change is the most constant of all things.

— Anonymous

Tolerance evolves, like culture or language. In similar fashion, Americans' regard for racial others appears to be an ever-unfolding drama that, at some times more than others, tightens its grasp on our nation's conscience. We need not be in the midst of a racial crisis — although these seem to occur with increasing frequency — to be stricken with concern over race relations. Sometimes, as with Alexis de Tocqueville's (1966 [1835]) analysis, it is the measurement of our nation in relative tranquility that reminds us of the unique nature of race in U.S. society. Often, disrupting these periods of calm (or at least our perceptions of calm), racial issues press harder against other forces competing to weave our social fabric — sometimes bringing civil war, sometimes civil rights. Over the years, we have seen enough of this ebb and flow to understand that within many long-term social trends, there is an oscillation or vibration in the pace of change that may give the appearance of retrenchment or reversal but that is really short lived. Thus, we wonder about the future: Are the trends we observe today enduring or ephemeral? Where will race relations go from here?

This chapter is an edited version of notes prepared by the late A. Wade Smith for this volume.

Most early research on whites' racial attitudes focused on a narrow range of issues: questions about social distance preferences and principles of integration and nondiscrimination in public-sector domains, now usually referred to as old-fashioned or traditional prejudice. The concern with racial principles that so dominated early work meant that questions about policies that might be implemented to help realize the principles went largely unexamined. Recent research has focused attention on policy issues, although data on policy preferences remain less abundant and cover a shorter time span than do data on traditional racial attitudes. This change from a focus on indicators of traditional racial affect to a concern with racial policy marked an important transition in research priorities.

There is yet another kind of change in the study of race relations, bearing a different rhythm. Previously, the questions that are addressed in this volume would be asked and answered only from the context and perspective of the dominant group. As the structure of race relations has changed, however — sometimes fundamentally, more recently at the margins — so too have the kinds of people asking and answering the questions about race. While de Tocqueville yielded to Myrdal (1944), Du Bois (1961 [1903]), Drake and Clayton (1945), Frazier (1949), and other black scholars toiled in varying degrees of ignominy and anonymity among their contemporaries. Since then, although the majority of scholars wrestling with issues of race and racism remain white, African Americans and other minority scholars now hold prominent places in discussions of race and racial change. Perhaps the questions that we ask about race and race relations depend on who does the asking.

The study of racial attitudes is one of the longest running topics in the social sciences. Indeed, the advent of modern sampling and interviewing techniques has yielded more survey data on racial attitudes than on any other noncommercial topic. Simply put, since World War II more U.S. surveys have included questions on racial attitudes than on any other subject. Similarly, the enduring presence of racial attitude questions in surveys has allowed students of race to identify and catalogue a major contributor to social change. In the mid-1990s, however, we researchers find ourselves in some discord on the important issues and in much less than full agreement on the general direction of race relations in the United States. These issues and this direction form the thematic content of this book.

2

Laissez-Faire Racism: The Crystallization of a Kinder, Gentler, Antiblack Ideology

Lawrence Bobo, James R. Kluegel, and Ryan A. Smith

Studies of racial attitudes in the United States present a difficult puzzle. On the one hand, several recent studies point to the steadily improving racial attitudes of whites toward African Americans (Steeh & Schuman 1992; Firebaugh & Davis 1988). These attitudinal trends are reinforced by many more tangible indicators, most notably the size, relative security, and potentially growing influence of the black middle class (Dawson 1994; Landry 1987). On the other hand, a number of social policies put forward to improve the status of African Americans and other minorities, such as affirmative action, are often contested if not ubiquitously unpopular (Bobo & Smith 1994; Kluegel & Smith 1986). Again, signs of negative racial attitudes are borne out by a number of tangible indicators, such as the burgeoning evidence of racial discrimination experienced by blacks almost irrespective of social class background (Bobo & Suh 1995; Kirschenman & Neckerman 1991; Feagin & Sikes 1994; Braddock & McPartland 1987; Waldinger & Bailey 1991; Zweigenhaft & Domhoff 1991).

These contradictory patterns open the door to sharply opposed interpretations of the real state of racial attitudes and black-white relations. Some scholars argue that antiblack racism, although not completely dead, plays only a delimited and, more important, diminishing role in politics (Sniderman & Piazza 1993; Roth 1990) and other spheres of social life (D'Souza 1995). With equal plausibility, some scholars argue that antiblack racism lives on, powerfully influencing politics (Sears 1988; Kinder & Sanders 1996), a wide array of other social outcomes (Massey & Denton

1993), and day-to-day encounters between blacks and whites (Feagin & Sikes 1994).

We aim to bring greater theoretical coherence to the hotly debated question of whether the racial attitudes of white Americans reflect less racism now than was evident 40 — or even 20 — years ago. We argue that in post–World War II U.S. society, the racial attitudes of white Americans involve a shift from Jim Crow racism to laissez-faire racism. As part of this change, we witnessed the virtual disappearance of overt bigotry, of demands for strict segregation, of advocacy of government-mandated discrimination, and of adherence to the belief that blacks are the categorical intellectual inferiors of whites. The decline of full-blown Jim Crow racism, however, has not resulted in its opposite: a thoroughly antiracist popular ideology based on an embracing and democratic vision of the common humanity, worth, dignity, and place in the polity for blacks alongside whites. Instead, the institutionalized racial inequalities created by the long era of slavery followed by Jim Crow racism are now popularly accepted and condoned under a modern free market or laissez-faire racist ideology.

Laissez-faire racism involves persistent negative stereotyping of African Americans, a tendency to blame blacks themselves for the black-white gap in socioeconomic standing, and resistance to meaningful policy efforts to ameliorate U.S. racist social conditions and institutions. Jim Crow racism was at its zenith during a historical epoch when African Americans remained a largely southern, rural, agricultural workforce; when antiblack bias was formal state policy (that is, separate schools and other public accommodations); and when most white Americans comfortably accepted the idea that blacks were inherently inferior. Laissez-faire racism is crystallizing in the current period as a new U.S. racial belief system at a point when African Americans are a heavily urbanized, nationally dispersed, and occupationally heterogeneous population; when state policy is formally race neutral and committed to antidiscrimination efforts; and when most white Americans prefer a more volitional and cultural, as opposed to inherent and biological, interpretation of blacks' disadvantaged status.

Our purpose in this chapter is threefold. First, we seek to clarify the concept of laissez-faire racism and to distinguish it from related notions, such as "symbolic racism." Second, we assess the record of change in whites' racial attitudes in the light of our concept of laissez-faire racism. Third, we develop the historical and theoretical basis for understanding laissez-faire racism as the core thrust of the modern U.S. racial ethos. Our argument draws heavily on the framework for understanding racial prejudice developed in the work of Herbert Blumer.

RACISM IN THE MODERN ERA

Is Racism an Appropriate Label?

The social science literature has put forward many different definitions of racism (Chesler 1976; See & Wilson 1988). For our purposes, Wilson offers a particularly cogént specification when he argues that racism is "an ideology of racial domination or exploitation that (1) incorporates beliefs in a particular race's cultural and/or inherent biological inferiority and (2) uses such beliefs to justify and prescribe inferior or unequal treatment for that group" (Wilson 1973, p. 32). Jim Crow racism readily fits within this definition of a racist ideological system. The express aim of the ideology was the domination and exploitation of African Americans; it mandated inferior treatment across virtually all domains of social life; and all of this was justified on the premise that blacks were the inherent biological inferiors of whites (Fredrickson 1971). Thus, the ideology was manifest in institutional arrangements, such as separate schools and voting restrictions, a variety of collective behaviors, such as lynchings, and readily expressed individual beliefs.

It is less apparent that the modern period is as fittingly termed "racist." Race relations and the status of African Americans have changed markedly in the post–World War II period (Jaynes & Williams 1989). Nonetheless, a strong case can be made that the United States remains a racially dominative society: We believe it appropriate to continue to speak of a racist social order in the United States. We use the phrase "laissez-faire racism" to emphasize, however, that the forms and mechanisms of that domination are now far more loosely coupled, complex, and permeable than in the past.

The basis for retaining the term "racism" is twofold. First, African Americans remain in a unique and fundamentally disadvantaged structural position in the U.S. economy and polity. This disadvantaged position is partly the legacy of historic racial discrimination during the slavery and Jim Crow eras. Even if all direct racial bias disappeared, African Americans would be disadvantaged because of the cumulative and multidimensional nature of historic racial oppression in the United States. Furthermore, racial discrimination continues to confront African Americans, albeit in less systematic and absolute ways in its current form. Rather than relying on state-enforced inequality as during the Jim Crow era, however, modern racial inequality relies on the market and informal racial bias to re-create, and in some instances sharply worsen, structured racial inequality. Hence, laissez-faire racism.

The unique structural disadvantage of African Americans is manifested in several ways. Despite important relative gains on whites recorded during the 1940s and the 1960s, the black-white gap in socioeconomic status remains enormous. Black adults remain two-and-a-half times as likely as whites to suffer from unemployment. This gap exists at virtually each level of the education distribution (Jaynes 1990). If one casts a broader net to ask about "underemployment" — that is, falling out of the labor force entirely, being unable to find full-time work, or working full time at below poverty-level wage rates — then the black-white ratio in major urban areas has risen from the customary 2-to-1 disparity to very nearly 5-to-1 over the past two decades (Lichter 1988). Conservative estimates show that young, well-educated blacks who are matched in work experience and other characteristics with whites still earn 11 percent less annually (Farley 1984). Studies continue to document direct labor market discrimination at both low-skill, entry-level positions (Kirschenman & Neckerman 1991; Turner, Fix, & Struyk 1991; Waldinger & Bailey 1991) and more highly skilled positions (Feagin & Sikes 1994). A growing chorus of studies indicate that even highly skilled and accomplished black managers encounter glass ceilings in corporate America (Fernandez 1986; Jones 1986), prompting some analysts to suggest that blacks will never be fully admitted to the U.S. power elite (Zweigenhaft & Domhoff 1991). In contrast to an earlier era, however, black disadvantage in the modern labor market is more likely to flow from informal recruitment and promotion mechanisms than from a blanket racial exclusion or segmentation.

Judged against differences in wealth, however, black-white gaps in employment status and earnings seem absolutely paltry (Jaynes & Williams 1989; Oliver & Shapiro 1995). The average differences in wealth show black households lagging behind whites by a factor of nearly 12 times. For every one dollar of wealth in white households, black households have less than ten cents. In 1984 the median level of wealth held by black households was around $3,000; for white households, the figure was $39,000. Indeed, white households with incomes of between $7,500 and $15,000 have "higher mean net worth and net financial assets than black households making $45,000 to $60,000" (Starr 1992, p. 12). That is, whites near the bottom of the white income distribution have more wealth than blacks near the top of the black income distribution. Wealth is in many ways a better indicator of likely quality of life than earnings (Oliver & Shapiro 1995).

Blacks occupy a uniquely disadvantaged position in physical space, as well. Demographers Douglas Massey and Nancy Denton (1989) concluded that it makes sense to describe the black condition as hypersegregation — a condition wherein a group simultaneously scores as extremely racially isolated from whites on four of five standard measures of residential segregation. As contrasted to the conditions of Asian Americans and Latinos, African Americans are the only group, based on 1980 census data for large metropolitan areas, to rank as hypersegregated from whites

(Massey & Denton 1993). Although there was some modest decline in the level of racial residential segregation between 1980 and 1990 (Farley & Frey 1994), blacks remain hypersegregated (Denton 1994). What is more, housing audit studies show high levels of direct racial discrimination by realtors and landlords against African Americans (Pearce 1979; Turner 1992; Yinger 1996). There is mounting evidence that mortgage lenders discriminate against African Americans, with some of the more careful studies showing racial bias even after controlling for financial resources and credit history (Jackson 1994). Residential mobility has been a critical pathway to assimilation into the economic and social mainstream for other groups (Lieberson 1980). Yet it is clear that African Americans, including the black middle class, face formidable obstacles in the search for high-quality housing. Such segregation is consequential. Neighborhoods may vary greatly in services, school quality, safety, and levels of exposure to a variety of unwanted social conditions (Massey, Gross, & Eggers 1991). Indeed, a particularly troubling trend is the increasing overlap among suburban versus urban location, race, and distinct political jurisdictions. In the extreme case, a largely black inner city (for example, Detroit) is a municipal unit separate from the surrounding white suburban areas. This is a development that, if it continues, would weaken the basic structural interdependency presumed to exist between black and white communities (Massey & Hajnal 1995).

The problems of differential unemployment, wage differentials, disparities in wealth, and racial residential segregation place African Americans in a uniquely disadvantaged position in U.S. economy and polity. Adverse market trends, apparently race neutral in origin, have far more pronounced negative effects on African Americans as a result. Over the past two decades, the U.S. economy has undergone slow but modest growth, sharply rising inequality in wages paid to high- and low-skill workers (heavily favoring the former over the latter), and a generally sharp rise in the skill demands for workers made by employers (Danziger & Gottschalk 1995). These general trends, however, appear to have worsened the relative position of blacks in the labor force. The employment prospects of young black males relative to comparable white males declined during the 1980s, with the earnings of college-educated black males undergoing a particularly sharp drop during this period (Bound & Freeman 1992).

Similarly, the uniquely disadvantaged position of African Americans means that government policy retrenchments may also have disproportionate adverse effects. For example, it appears that the shift in federal support for higher education from outright grants and scholarships to loans hit African Americans particularly hard. There was a sharp decline, both absolutely and relative to whites, in the chances that a black high school graduate would go on to college beginning in about 1979 and continuing through the mid-1980s (Jaynes & Williams 1989; Hauser 1993a). This occurred for both black men and black women and occurred largely across the class spectrum in the black community. The trend runs against other evidence of rising black achievement scores relative to whites and persistently high aspirations (Hauser & Anderson 1991; Hauser 1993b).

Our second reason for retaining the term racism is that these racial inequalities exist in a social climate of widespread acceptance of notions of black cultural inferiority. In the wake of the civil disorders of the 1960s, H. Schuman (1971) called attention to the pronounced tendency of white Americans to view the race problem as flowing from the freely chosen cultural behaviors of blacks themselves. The tendency to deny the modern potency of discrimination and to see a lack of striving and effort on the part of blacks as the key issue in black-white inequality has been confirmed in a number of subsequent investigations based on regional data sources (Apostle, Glock, Piazza, & Suelzle 1983; Sniderman & Hagen 1985) and national data sources (Kluegel 1990; Kluegel & Bobo 1993; Tuch & Hughes 1996). (With the publication of works, such as R. J. Herrnstein and C. Murray's *The Bell Curve* (1994) and D'Souza's *The End of Racism* (1995), one could argue that an incipient biological racism, no longer plainly on the margins, is reasserting itself.) We review more fully below and in a later chapter the evidence on the prevalence of belief in black cultural inferiority. The critical point is that sharp and, in some instances, worsening racial inequalities exist. Rather than constituting a problem widely recognized as justifying ameliorative social intervention, however, these conditions are comfortably accepted, if not in fact actively justified and explained, by many white Americans as a reflection of the choices blacks themselves have made.

We try to use the term racism in a delimited sense. We argue neither that racial discrimination is the only factor constraining black opportunity in the modern period nor that race is as central a factor in the life chances for any given black individual as it was in the pre–civil rights era (Wilson 1978). Indeed, we have emphasized the role of the market, the formally race-neutral and antidiscrimination posture of the modern state, the shift away from biological racist ideas, growing class heterogeneity among African Americans, and the informal, complex, loosely coupled, and more permeable character of the modern color line. Nevertheless, we use the term racism to characterize the modern period and common patterns of attitudes and belief. We do so because African Americans remain in uniquely disadvantaged positions despite greater class differentiation within the black community; because racial discrimination of both historic and a variety of modern types plays a part in the social reproduction of distinctly racial disadvantage; and because a large segment of white America attributes black-white inequality to the failings of black culture.

Does Laissez-Faire Racism
Differ from Symbolic Racism?

We are not the first or only analysts to attempt to conceptualize the changing character of whites' attitudes toward blacks. One important line of research is that concerning symbolic racism. Although defined and ultimately measured in a variety of ways, the concept of symbolic racism proposes that a new form of antiblack prejudice has arisen in the United States. It is said to involve a blend of early learned social values, such as the Protestant ethic and antiblack fears and apprehensions. In a context where segregationist and biological racism are less in evidence, according to the symbolic racism researchers, it is this modern symbolic racism that plays a more formidable role (Sears & Kinder 1971; McConahay & Hough 1976).

Our concept of laissez-faire racism differs in two critical respects from the theory of symbolic racism as proposed by David Sears and colleagues (Kinder & Sears 1981). First, the theory of laissez-faire racism is explicitly based in a historical analysis of the changing economics and politics of race in the United States. Even in the most extensive theoretical statements offered after two decades of research (Kinder 1986; McConahay 1986; Sears 1988), the symbolic racism researchers have not satisfactorily explained why what they call old-fashioned racism went into decline or why symbolic or modern racism assumes the specific form and content that it now does. In some respects, this theoretical silence on the causes of the shift from old-fashioned to symbolic, or modern, racism is a virtual necessity of the logic of the theory. As originally formulated, the theory expressly denies that there is a significant material social basis to the formation of antiblack attitudes outside of processes of socialization and the operation of routine cognitive and emotional psychological processes (Kinder & Sears 1981; Sears, Hensler, & Speer 1979).

We argue that Jim Crow racist ideology reflected the economic and political needs, as well as the prevailing cultural ideas, of a specific historical period and set of actors. The setting was the post–Civil War South. The critical actors were the old Southern planter elite. The cultural trend was the rise and scientific legitimacy accorded notions of biological racism. As the economic and political power of these historic conditions and actors waned, as cultural trends turned against biological racism, and as the power resources of the black community rose, Jim Crow social structures and, ultimately, Jim Crow ideology were defeated. Rising from the collapse of Jim Crow racism, we argue, is laissez-faire racism. The latter set of ideas legitimates persistent black oppression in the United States, but now in a manner appropriate to a modern, nationwide, postindustrial free labor economy and polity. In effect, a significant segment of white America effectively condones as much black disadvantage and segregation as the legacy of historic discrimination and modern-day free-market forces and informal social mechanisms can reproduce or even exacerbate. Understood in this fashion, the labels Jim Crow racism and laissez-faire racism are both more concrete and historically well specified than the vague terms old-fashioned racism and modern racism used in the symbolic racism literature.

Second, our theory of laissez-faire racism is expressly rooted in a sociological theory of prejudice. Below we elaborate on H. Blumer's classic statement on prejudice as a sense of group position (Blumer 1958), which places a subjective, interactively and socially created, and historically emergent set of ideas about appropriate status relations between groups at the center of any analysis of racial attitudes. The framework is one that takes seriously the imperatives that derive from both the institutionalized structural conditions of social life as well as from the processes of human interaction, subjectivity, and interpretation that lend meaning to social conditions and thereby guide behavior. Symbolic racism, in contrast, was explicitly premised on a sociocultural theory of prejudice (Kinder & Sears 1981). Such theories place central importance on social learning and the psychological-affective nature of racial attitudes (Allport 1954; Katz 1991; Sears 1988).

Under the group position theory, the crucial factors are: first, a sense among members of the dominant racial group of proprietary claim or entitlement to greater resources and status and, second, a perception of threat posed by subordinate racial group members to those entitlements. Together, the feelings of entitlement and threat become dynamic social forces as members of the dominant racial group strive to maintain a privileged status relative to members of a subordinate racial group. From this vantage point, as the economic and political foundations of the Jim Crow social order weakened, white privilege had to be justified and defended on new and different grounds. Jim Crow racist ideology lost its structural supports and, therefore, eventually lost its persuasive appeal to the mass of white Americans. Whites still enjoyed a substantially greater share of economic, political, and prestige resources than African Americans, however, despite important changes in the magnitude and permeability of the color line. Furthermore, many whites perceived black demands as threatening incursions on their interests and prerogatives. Hence, in our argument, laissez-faire racist attitudes emerged to defend white privilege and explain persistent black disadvantage under sharply changed economic and political conditions. It is the sense of entitlement and threat, as delineated in Blumer's group position theory of prejudice, that we believe gives us the greatest theoretical leverage in accounting for changes in whites' racial attitudes in the United States. The full import of this position we develop below.

PATTERNS OF CHANGE IN RACIAL ATTITUDES

The longest trend data from national sample surveys may be found for racial attitude questions that deal with matters of racial principles, the implementation of those principles, and social distance preferences. Questions about principle ask whether U.S. society should be integrated or segregated and engage in equal treatment of individuals without regard to race. Such questions do not raise issues of the practical steps that might be necessary to accomplish greater integration or assure equal treatment. Implementation questions ask what actions, usually by government (and, especially, the federal government), ought to be taken to bring about integration, to prevent discrimination, and to achieve greater equality. Social distance questions ask about the individual's willingness to personally enter hypothetical contact settings in schools or neighborhoods where the proportions of blacks to whites vary from virtually all white to heavily black (Schuman, Steeh, & Bobo 1985).

The Decline of Jim Crow Racism

The gradual retreat of Jim Crow racism is seen most clearly in the trends for questions on racial principles. These types of questions provide the largest and most consistent pool of evidence on how the attitudes of white Americans toward blacks have changed. With crucial baseline surveys having been conducted in 1942, trends for most racial principle questions show a steady increase among whites in support for principles of racial integration and equality. Whereas a solid majority, 68 percent, of white Americans in 1942 favored segregated schools, only 7 percent took such a position in 1985. Similarly, 55 percent of whites surveyed in 1944 thought whites should receive preference over blacks in access to jobs, compared with only 3 percent who offered such an opinion as long ago as 1972. Indeed, so few people were willing to endorse the discriminatory response to this question on the principle of race-based job discrimination that it was dropped from national surveys after 1972. On both of these issues, then, majority endorsement of the principles of segregation and discrimination have given way to overwhelming majority support for integration and equal treatment (unless otherwise noted, all percentages are taken from Schuman, Steeh, & Bobo 1985).

This pattern of movement away from support for Jim Crow toward apparent support for racial egalitarianism holds with equal force for questions dealing with issues of residential integration, access to public transportation and public accommodations, choice among qualified candidates for political office, and even racial intermarriage. To be sure, the high absolute levels of support seen for the principles of school integration and equal access to jobs (both better than 90 percent) are not seen for all principle-level racial attitude questions. Despite improvement from an extraordinarily low level of support in the 1950s and 1960s, survey data continue to show substantial levels of white discomfort with the prospect of interracial dating and marriage.

Opinions among whites have never been uniform or monolithic. Both historical research (Fredrickson 1971; Jordan 1968) and sociological research (Turner & Singleton 1978) have pointed to lines of cleavage and debate in whites' thinking about the place of African Americans. The survey-based literature has shown that views on issues of racial principle vary greatly by region of the country, level of education, age or generation, and other ideological factors. As might be expected, opinions in the South more lopsidedly favored segregation and discrimination at the time baseline surveys were conducted than was true outside the South. Patterns of change, save for a period of unusually rapid change in the South, have usually been parallel. The highly educated are also typically found to express greater support for principles of racial equality and integration. Indeed, one can envision a multitiered reaction to issues of racial justice. At the more progressive and liberal end, one finds college-educated whites who live outside the South. At the bottom, one finds Southern whites with the least amount of schooling (Schuman, Steeh, & Bobo 1985).

Age plays a part, as well. Younger people are usually found to express more racial tolerance than older people. Differences in average levels of education across generations as well as socialization in more tolerant times help account for this pattern (Smith 1981).

The transformation of attitudes regarding the principles that should guide black-white interaction in the more public and impersonal spheres of social life has been large and sweeping. Those living outside the South, the well educated, and younger people led the way on these changes; however, change has usually taken place within all of these categories. H. Schuman, C. Steeh, and L. Bobo characterized this change as a fundamental transformation of social norms with regard to race. Robert Blauner's (1989) in-depth interviews with blacks and whites over nearly three decades led him to reach a very similar conclusion. He wrote: "The belief in a right to dignity and fair treatment is now so widespread and deeply rooted, so self-evident that people of all colors would vigorously resist any effort to reinstate formalized discrimination. This consensus may be the most profound legacy of black militancy, one that has brought a truly radical transformation in relations between the races" (Blauner 1989, p. 317).

In short, a tremendous progressive trend has characterized whites' racial attitudes where the broad principles of integration, equality, and discrimination are concerned. Those who believe that the United States is making progress toward resolving the "American Dilemma" point to this evidence as proof that Americans have taken a decisive turn against racism. As R. G. Niemi, J. Mueller, and T. W. Smith argue: "Without ignoring real signs of enduring racism, it is still fair to conclude that America has been successfully struggling to resolve its Dilemma and that equality has been gaining ascendancy over racism" (1989, p. 168). The potency of this trend is suggested by claims from the former Klansman, David Duke, in his failed run for the Louisiana Governor's office, that he was no longer a racist. Whether this claim is true is less important than the fact that Duke apparently felt constrained to take such a public position. In a more positive vein, the recent groundswell of support, more so among whites than blacks, for the prospect of General Colin Powell entering the 1996 presidential contest is further evidence of the reach of this change. Some ideas — state-imposed segregation, open support for antiblack discrimination, and claims that blacks are inherently inferior to whites — have fallen into profound disrepute. The reach of this change appears to include taking seriously the prospect of a black man as a presidential nominee.

Opposition to Progressive Social Policy

If trends in support for racial principles are the optimistic side of the story, then the patterns for implementation questions tell the first part of a more pessimistic story. It should be noted that efforts to assess how Americans feel about government efforts to bring about greater integration and equality or to prevent discrimination really do not arise as sustained matters of inquiry in surveys until the 1960s. To an important degree, issues of the role of government in bringing about progressive racial change could not emerge until sufficient change had taken place at the level of the basic principles involved.

There are sharp differences in level of support between racial principles and policy implementation. This is not surprising insofar as principles, viewed in isolation, need not conflict with other principles, interests, or needs that will often arise in more concrete situations. The gaps between principle and implementation, however, are large and consistent in the domain of race relations. For example, in 1964 surveys showed that 64 percent of whites nationwide supported the principle of integrated schooling; however, only 38 percent felt that the federal government had a role to play in bringing about greater integration. The gap had actually grown larger by 1986. At that time, 93 percent supported the principle, but only 26 percent endorsed government efforts to bring about school integration.

Similar patterns emerged in the areas of jobs and housing. Support for the principle of equal access to jobs stood at 97 percent in 1972. Support for federal efforts to prevent job discrimination, however, had only reached 39 percent. Likewise, in 1976, for housing, 88 percent supported the principle that blacks have the right to live wherever they can afford; however, only 35 percent of whites said they would vote in favor of a law requiring homeowners to sell without regard to race.

There are not only sharp differences in absolute levels of support when moving from principle to implementation, but also differences in trends. Most strikingly, there is a clear divergence of trends in the domain of school integration. From 1972 to 1986, when support for the principle of integrated schooling rose from 84 percent to 93 percent, support for government efforts to bring about integration fell from 35 percent to 26 percent. It should be noted that this decline is restricted almost entirely to individuals living outside the South. Indeed, this trend reverses the multitiered tolerance effect we described earlier. By 1978, the difference in support for federal efforts to help bring about school integration between college-educated whites outside the South and Southern whites who had not completed high school was virtually zero.

Several complexities are worthy of note. A couple of implementation issues do show positive trends. The most clear-cut case involves whether the government has a role to play in assuring blacks fair access to hotels and public accommodations. This may be the only instance in which parallel questions on principle and implementation undergo roughly parallel positive change. A somewhat similar pattern occurs in the case of residential integration and support for an open housing law; however, even as recently as 1988, barely 50 percent of white Americans endorsed a law that would forbid racial discrimination in the sale or rental of housing.

Antiblack animus is not the only source of opposition to government involvement in bringing about progressive racial change. H. Schuman and L. Bobo (1988) have shown that whites are equally likely to oppose open housing laws whether the group in question is blacks, Japanese Americans, or other groups. There appears to be a real element of objection to government coercion that influences attitudes in this domain. At the same time, Schuman and Bobo (1988) also found that whites express a desire for greater social distance from blacks than they do from other groups, a pattern confirmed in other recent examinations of attitudes on racial residential integration (Bobo & Zubrinsky 1996; Zubrinsky & Bobo in press).

Level of education, region, and age typically have much less to do with who supports or opposes implementation of racial change than is true of racial principles. Weak to nonexistent effects of education and age in particular suggest that we are unlikely to see much positive change in the future on these issues.

Comparatively few trend questions speak directly to affirmative action policies. Many different questions have been asked, beginning in the mid- to late 1970s. These results point to the complexity of affirmative action policies themselves and of public response to them. Support for affirmative action varies dramatically depending on exactly which type of policy is proposed (Kluegel & Smith 1986; Lipset & Schneider 1978). Policies that aim mainly to increase the human capital attributes of blacks are comparatively popular (Bobo & Kluegel 1993). Policies that lean toward achieving equal outcomes, preferences for minorities that ignore merit considerations, as powerfully symbolized by the term "quotas," elicit high levels of opposition among whites (Bobo & Smith 1994).

CONVENTIONAL EXPLANATIONS OF THE TRENDS

Several attempts to explain change in racial attitudes can be found in the research literature. For our purposes, these attempts can largely be grouped into one of three categories: demographic lag theories, the Myrdalian guilt hypothesis, and the cultural turn against biological racism argument.

Demographic Lag

Seen in descriptive rather than explanatory terms, the progressive trend in racial attitudes can be traced to one of two sources. First, part of the rise in racial liberalism on matters of principle can be credited to cohort replacement effects. As older, less tolerant individuals fall out of the population and are replaced by younger, more tolerant individuals, a progressive trend would result. Second, part of the progressive trend can be traced to individual change. Persons who once advocated segregation and discrimination might undergo soul-searching and a change of heart, coming instead to see the case for integration and equality.

Research suggests that the process of change itself may be changing. During the 1950s and 1960s, there is evidence of both a large measure of individual change and cohort replacement contributing to change. During the 1970s, the relative balance of the two began to change to a more even mixture of the two. In addition, the distance between younger and older cohorts began to narrow, strongly suggesting that the engines of change are cooling off. Analyses by G. Firebaugh and K. E. Davis (1988) show that the mixture of cohort replacement effects and individual change is increasingly issue specific and region specific. For example, on the issue of racial intermarriage there has been no evidence of individual change between 1974 and 1984. Furthermore, most of the change seen in the South after 1974 is attributable to cohort replacement effects. Whatever the mix of forces that propelled the progressive movement in whites' attitudes on racial principle issues, it appears to be slowing, particularly in the South.

Despite these patterns there is no evidence of a broad backlash in racial attitudes. Many have expressed special concern that young adults, those who underwent critical socializing experiences during the Reagan-Bush years, are the source of a racial backlash. Work by C. Steeh and H. Schuman (1992) indicates no distinctive backward movement among younger white adults, who continue to be a bit more liberal than their immediate predecessors. What evidence there is of backward movement is quite issue specific. During the 1980s, most whites, regardless of age, became less supportive of policies seeming to call for racial preferences for minorities.

There is also little sign that whites' understanding of the causes of black-white economic inequality will change in favorable ways. How whites perceive and explain the black-white socioeconomic gap is an important input to whether they will support or oppose policies designed to improve the position of blacks (Kluegel & Smith 1982, 1986). The more individualistic the attributions made for black-white inequality (for example, blacks do not try hard enough), the less open to supporting government intervention on behalf of blacks an individual is likely to be. The more structural the attributions made for black-white economic inequality (for example, blacks face racial discrimination), the more open to supporting intervention an individual may be. As Kluegel's cohort analyses (1990) have shown, however, there has been little or no change in the denial of discrimination or in the prevailing tendency to attach individual blame for the black-white socioeconomic status gap.

These cohort studies are valuable, but they are also limited. All of these analyses of cohort replacement or individual change as sources of the sweeping increase in support for racial equality and inequality are not explanatory. The analyses provide a statistical decomposition of trends, not substantive accounts of the roots of the change.

Myrdal's Hypothesis

One possibile explanation of the change is Myrdal's (1944) guilt hypothesis. He proposed that the discomfort and internal tension created by the ever-raging conflict in the hearts of white Americans would increasingly be resolved in favor of racial equality. Any number of direct efforts to test Myrdal's hypothesis have failed. Even in the 1940s and 1950s, few whites felt that blacks were unfairly treated (Hyman & Sheatsley 1956; Williams 1964). Those who acknowledged differences in treatment were quick to offer justifications for it (Westie 1963). Even more recent and novel tests of Myrdal's idea produced no support for it (Cummings & Pinnel 1978). The empirical research literature provides no support for the Myrdalian hypothesis at the individual level.

To reject Myrdal's guilt hypothesis does not mean embracing the position that in the main, whites' racial attitudes reflect undifferentiated hostility toward blacks. First, at a societal level, the American creed was clearly an important cultural and ideological resource used by civil rights activists in the struggle for social change. In this more societal but causally delimited sense, Myrdal's analysis seems more telling. Second, an argument closely related to Myrdal's formulation can be called the ambivalence hypothesis. There is evidence of internal complexity and ambivalence in the views on race held by many white Americans. Indeed, Katz and Hass (1988) proposed that whites' racial attitudes are profoundly ambivalent, mixing both aversive and sympathetic tendencies. The inclination that predominates in thinking is a function of immediately salient contextual factors. Using college student subjects in experimental settings, Katz and colleagues have shown that contextual cues that make individualism, hard work, and self-reliance salient will also incline whites to focus on blacks' shortcomings in these areas. Contextual cues that reinforce egalitarianism and humanism, in contrast, tend to elicit a more sympathetic response to blacks.

The ambivalence theory, however, fails to specify whether there is a predominant tenor to whites' racial attitudes, nor does it well specify how these ambivalent feelings are likely to play out in concrete social settings. Perhaps most important, the theory seems unable to explain the persistent and substantial opposition to a range of social policies aimed at substantially improving the material conditions of African Americans.

The Decline of Biological Racism

A second substantive explanation of the broad progressive trend is the possibility that key beliefs in the case for racial segregation and discrimination suffered a direct cultural assault and quickly eroded. Surveys showed that popular acceptance of the belief that blacks were less intelligent than whites went into rapid decline in the post–World War II period. In 1942, 53 percent of white Americans nationwide expressed the opinion that blacks were less intelligent. By 1946 this number had declined to 43 percent, a 10-percentage-point drop in only four years. By 1956, fully 80 percent of whites nationwide rejected the idea that blacks were less intelligent; this is rapid change. It is especially telling that this change occurred well before the height of the civil rights movement and thus presumably before the larger national climate shifted decisively in favor of protecting the civil rights of African Americans.

What seemed the bedrock belief in the case for a racially segregated and discriminatory social order had undergone a precipitous drop in acceptance. Consequently, it is less surprising that support for racial segregation and discrimination in schools, in housing, and the like would also gradually decline. Fighting a war against racism, the considerable contribution of blacks in the war effort, and the continued trend in academe away from accepting notions of biologically given and hierarchically ordered racial groupings all contributed to this process of rapid change (Bobo 1988b).

Yet, as an account of the larger progressive trend in racial attitudes, this explanation is lacking. It begs the question of why popular acceptance of biological racism, an attitude in its own right, went into decline. What is more, there are strong grounds to believe that negative stereotypes of African Americans remain widespread. In 1990 the General Social Survey employed a new set of questions intended to measure social stereotypes. Previously, the simple questions drawn from surveys first launched in the 1940s asked respondents to agree or disagree with blunt categorical statements. Now, respondents used bipolar trait-rating scales. Respondents were called upon to rate the members of several racial minority groups — blacks, Asian Americans, and Hispanic Americans — as to whether they tended to be rich or poor, hard working or lazy, intelligent or unintelligent, preferring to live off welfare or to be self-supporting, and so on. If a respondent wished to assert no difference between groups, he or she could do so. If an individual wanted to credit their own group with positive traits and out-groups with all negative traits, he or she could do so. Individuals could also offer more qualified views. Crucially, the format of the questions did not force one to merely accept or reject a simplistic statement. Measured in this manner, negative stereotypes of African Americans remain common among whites, and quite consensually so on some specific traits (Bobo & Kluegel 1991).

For example, some 56 percent of whites rated blacks as less intelligent than whites, using the bipolar trait-rating format (two-and-a-half times the rate suggested by older, closed-ended format survey items). Fully 78 percent rated blacks as more likely to prefer living off welfare than whites. Largely similar patterns — though not as extreme — were found in a recent survey in the Los Angeles County area (Bobo, Zubrinsky, Johnson, & Oliver 1994).

Whatever else one might say about the progressive trend in racial attitudes, it has not brought an end to negative stereotyping of African Americans. Instead, the character of the stereotypes has changed. What were once viewed as categorical differences based in biology now appear to be seen as differences in degree or tendency (Jackman & Senter 1983). Furthermore, these differences in degree appear to be understood as having largely cultural roots (Bobo 1988b). Thus, we do not accept the view of declining negative stereotypes about blacks as a crucial source of the broader shift in views on issues of racial segregation, discrimination, and the principle of equal treatment. Negative stereotypes persist.

THE EMERGENCE OF LAISSEZ-FAIRE RACISM

If these other explanations, including Myrdal's guilt hypothesis, are not convincing explanations, what then accounts for both the momentous positive changes in attitudes that occurred between the 1940s and the present and the persistence of negative stereotypes and opposition to social policies favorable to African Americans? We believe that structural changes in the U.S. economy and polity that reduced the importance of the Jim Crow system of exploited black agricultural labor to the overall economy lies at the base of the positive change in racial attitudes. In short, the structural need for Jim Crow ideology disappeared. Correspondingly, though slowly and only in response to aggressive and innovative challenge from the black civil rights movement and its allies, the political and ideological supports for Jim Crow institutions finally yielded. It is precisely the defeat of Jim Crow ideology and the political forms of its institutionalization (for example, segregated schooling and public facilities, voting hindrances) that are the principal accomplishments of the civil rights movement. The defeat of this particular form of social oppression, however, fell well short of elevating blacks to a status of genuine economic, political, and social equality.

We do not advance a purely materialistic interpretation that would, perforce, render popular racial attitudes of little social import. Such theorizing at once misunderstands the role of human agency and subjectivity and the highly contingent nature of the critical events and actions that helped to bring about the shift from Jim Crow racism to laissez-faire racism. Nor do we advance a purely ideational account of changing racial attitudes of the sort advanced in the symbolic racism research. The strictly material and the strictly psychological accounts are, we believe, needlessly extreme and flawed.

There are inevitable connections between economic and political structures, on the one hand, and patterns of individual thought and action, on the other hand. As the structural basis of longstanding group relations undergoes change, there is a corresponding potential for change in the ways of thinking, feeling, and behaving that had previously been commonplace and that had wrapped group relations in a cloth of social meaning and coherence. The collapse of Jim Crow ideology was not the inevitable outcome of the related demographic and economic shifts that foreshadowed changing patterns of belief. The political defeat of Jim Crow was a hard-fought struggle that required sustained collective action; it also involved deliberate efforts to transform consciousness in both the black and white communities.

Our analysis of the sources of change in racial attitudes rests principally on three important sociological works analyzing the emergence, dynamics, and impact of the civil rights movement. D. McAdam's book,

Political Process and the Development of Black Insurgency, 1930–1970 (1982), provides a rich analysis of how socioeconomic and demographic shifts fundamentally altered the level of power resources of the black community. Aldon Morris's *The Origins of the Civil Rights Movement: Black Communities Organizing for Change* (1984) reveals in detail the internal organizational dimensions of strategies used by black communities and leadership as they mobilized the growing resource base in their own communities for political and economic gain. J. M. Bloom's book *Class, Race, and the Civil Rights Movement* (1987) helps pinpoint the great success of the civil rights movement as the political defeat of the old planter aristocracy, whose economic fortunes were most dependent on the Jim Crow strictures that had locked many blacks in a condition of poverty and agricultural labor. Taken together, these works provide a rich sociological analysis of how the interweaving of the economy and polity resulted in changes in the status of blacks and set the stage for the emergence of a new U.S. ideology on race.

Growing Power Resources in Black Communities

As long as blacks remained a heavily oppressed, poorly educated, Southern and rural labor force, they were unlikely to be able to mount effective political resistance to the Jim Crow social order. According to McAdam, four factors presage the emergence of a sustained and potent civil rights movement. A series of reinforcing economic and demographic changes led to expanded political opportunities for blacks. These transformations increased the potential within black communities to develop stronger indigenous organizations. When coupled with a more receptive political climate at the national level in the post–World War II period, a major transformation of political consciousness within the black population took shape. The end result was a sustained and effective movement of protest for social change.

During the Jim Crow era, core institutions of the black community that would later become engines of the civil rights movement — the black church, black colleges and universities, and organizations such as the National Association for the Advancement of Colored People (NAACP) — were fledgling versions of what they would become. From roughly 1880 through 1930, not only did the black church espouse an other-worldly theology of waiting for better treatment in the afterlife, but also black congregations tended to be small, the churches were financially strapped, and ministers were often poorly educated. Black colleges at the time were sorely underfunded, providing little more than a high school–equivalent education. The NAACP, founded in 1909–10, was principally a Northern organization, still crafting its long-term legal strategy for change.

The position of blacks as an impoverished and heavily oppressed agricultural labor force began to shift decisively with the decline of "King Cotton." Increasing foreign competition, the introduction of new technologies and of synthetic fibers, the boll-weevil infestation, and the declining centrality of cotton to the U.S. export economy began to push more and more blacks away from the rural South in order to earn a living.

According to McAdam, "the factor most responsible for undermining the political conditions that, at the turn of century, had relegated blacks to a position of political impotence . . . would have to be the gradual collapse of cotton as the backbone of the southern economy" (1982, p. 73). When measured by the amount of cotton acreage harvested and the average seasonal price of cotton per pound, the decline in cotton as the backbone of Southern economy was enormous. The price of raw cotton took a nosedive "from a high of 35 cents per pound in 1919 to less than 6 cents in 1931" (McAdam 1982, p. 75). From 1931 to 1955, the price of raw cotton actually rose; yet during this same period, in an attempt to increase the demand for cotton, the total amount of cotton harvested significantly decreased.

In addition, with World War I and the cessation of heavy European immigration, there was a growing need for black labor in the industrial North. The combination of these and other forces led to one of the greatest internal migrations of all time. Upwards of 200,000 blacks migrated to the North in the first decade of the century, while the next decade saw the largest black outmigration at more than 500,000 (McAdam 1982, p. 74). The migration of blacks reduced the number of Southern black farm operators. From a high of slightly more than 915,000 in 1920, the number of black farm operators plummeted to a low of 267,000 by 1959 (McAdam 1982, p. 95). Blacks thus shifted from a largely rural and Southern population to a heavily urban and increasingly Northern population.

These changes had the concomitant effect of altering the resource base of critical black institutions, such as the church, black colleges and universities, and the NAACP. The rise in the numbers of blacks in urban settings had the effect of increasing black economic resources while reducing the level of intimidation and violence used to repress blacks. Urban black church congregations tended to be much larger and to have more substantial financial support, which facilitated the hiring of better trained and better educated ministers. These forces, coupled with greater political latitude afforded blacks in urban settings, contributed to a shift in the theological emphasis within many black churches toward an increasing concern for justice in the here and now.

The growing success of the NAACP legal strategy, which initially sought to force Southern states to live up to the doctrine of separate but equal, had led to important increases in the resource base at many historically black colleges and universities. Thus, more blacks began to receive better college-level educations. In addition, the number and size of NAACP chapters in Southern states rose as the number of blacks in the urban South rose. In sum, formidable changes in the power resources within black communities took place, particularly between the early 1900s and the early 1950s. The economic footing of black communities improved. The institutional base for political action also increased dramatically.

Mobilizing Black Power Resources for Change

Morris carefully documents the patterns of social networks and organization-building that existed in black communities. For example, he shows the lines of communication between the new, better educated group of black ministers, epitomized by Rev. Martin Luther King. Morris also reviews the high level of internal financing that supported organizations such as the Montgomery Improvement Association (MIA), which directed the historic 1955–56 bus boycott. Internal networks, a new indigenous leadership cadre, and internal financial support were essential to the type of local movement center, such as the MIA, that became a politicized umbrella organization linking a number of black ministers and their congregations. Morris points, moreover, to the mass base of the protest movement that King came to spearhead and the extent to which targeted nonviolent social protest became a genuine power resource in the struggle for racial change. Critically, Morris documents how the increasing persecution directed at the NAACP in much of the South impelled the development of new organizational forms such as the MIA and, subsequently, the Southern Christian Leadership Conference. Where McAdam identifies the broad demographic and economic trends affecting black institutions, Morris shows how these increasing power resources were translated into concrete organization-building and sustained, effective mass protest at the grassroots level within black communities.

The ability to mount effective campaigns at the grassroots level within Southern black communities reached its pinnacle after the Montgomery bus boycott of 1955. The boycott gave blacks a sense that they could effect political change through actions directed by preexisting black institutions and community organizations. According to Morris: "The Montgomery bus boycott was the watershed. The importance of that boycott was that it revealed to the black community that mass protests could be successfully organized and initiated through indigenous resources and institutions" (1981, p. 751).

Morris's discussion of the emergence and rapid spread of the sit-in strategy in the South during the late 1950s and early 1960s provides a clear picture of the intricate and deliberate formation of black political

networks. Dispelling myths that the sit-in tactic was an entirely sponta-
neous, student-run operation that originated in Greensboro, North Carolina, in 1960, Morris shows how such efforts actually grew out of preexisting institutions and organizations such as the black church. As such,
they drew on both veteran civil rights workers and student members.

Included in this new alliance were a host of black colleges, fraternities,
and sororities. The emergence and proliferation of the sit-in movement
involved interaction between black colleges and local movement centers
often based in the church. Many of the student leaders were also church
members and had learned about the civil rights movement and the tactic
of nonviolent protest from their local churches even before sit-ins were
instituted as a protest strategy. Thus, the organizational base to launch
and coordinate sit-ins stemmed from the church — with black college students, through their fraternities and sororities, serving as the foot soldiers.

The actual organization, financing, and spread of the sit-in clusters followed an elaborate pattern of coordination among a variety of groups.
Morris provides a vivid description of the sequence:

Organizers from SCLC, NAACP and CORE raced between sit-in points relaying
valuable information. Telephone lines and the community "grapevine" sent forth
protest instructions and plans. These clusters were the sites of numerous midday
and late night meetings where the black community assembled in the churches,
filled the collection plates, and vowed to mortgage their homes to raise the necessary bail-bond money in case the protesting students were jailed. Black lawyers
pledged their legal services to the movement and black physicians made their services available to injured demonstrators. Amidst these exciting scenes, black spir-
ituals calmed and deepened the participants' commitment. (Morris 1981, p. 759)

Throughout the South, activities such as these served to create, sustain,
and project the new-found power of a grassroots, church-based movement designed to dramatize and change the second-class citizenship status of African Americans.

Defeating Jim Crow

To this picture, Bloom (1987) adds critical information concerning the
old white planter aristocracy. He maintains that the principal political
accomplishment of the civil rights movements was the defeat of the
power of the old planter elite. This group benefited most directly from Jim
Crow ideology and practices and were the central actors in the erection of
Jim Crow social arrangements. Correspondingly, it was this group that
played a pivotal role in first launching the White Citizens Councils
(WCCs) in the wake of the NAACP's legal success in the *Brown v. Board of
Education* decision. As Bloom explains:

The impetus, the organization, the leadership, and the control of this movement rested in the hands of the traditional black-belt ruling class that had emerged after Reconstruction. That class was still centered in the black belt, though in most cases now in small towns. Its members were businessmen and bankers in these areas, as well as merchants and landlords. . . . It was the old Southern ruling class that set state policy. It was, moreover, the Deep South states of Georgia, Mississippi, Alabama, Louisiana, and South Carolina that, in addition to Virginia made up the core of the resistance. In these states the old Southern ruling class remained the strongest. In almost every single case where the White Citizens Council emerged, they were led and organized from the black belt. (1987, pp. 101–102)

It was this old planter elite, still heavily located in cotton-producing black-belt areas, that most depended on the Jim Crow social order for their livelihoods. As such, leadership of the WCCs was often drawn from the upper classes. The WCCs drew their leadership "primarily from the ranks of the white community's business, political, and social leadership. . . . These are the same people who made up the 'courthouse cliques' that ran the South, the 'banker-merchant-farmer-lawyer-doctor-governing class'" (Bloom 1987, p. 102).

The WCCs directed both economic and political intimidation at blacks who attempted to challenge their subordinate status. Indeed, although the leaders of the WCC were drawn from the ranks of the most respected leaders of the South, they were not above committing or sanctioning acts of violence against blacks to protect their interests. Although violence against blacks was more frequent in an earlier era and more commonly associated with the tactics used by the Ku Klux Klan, subsequent to the Brown decision, violence against blacks on the part of the WCCs became an effective tool, particularly in discouraging blacks from voting. Murders sprang up all over the South, most noticeably in places such as Mississippi, with the effect of causing terror in blacks throughout the region. After economic pressures failed, for example, a leader of the NAACP was wounded by a shotgun for not giving up his right to vote; a black minister who promoted black voting was murdered; and a black political leader who sought to teach blacks how to vote by absentee ballot to avoid violence at the polling booth was murdered. Perhaps the most noteworthy case was the murder of Emmit Till, the 14-year-old boy who was "kidnapped from his grandfather's home in the middle of the night, pistol whipped, stripped naked, shot through the head with a .45 caliber Colt automatic, barb-wired to a 74 pound cotton gin fan, and dumped into twenty feet of water in the Tallahatchie River" for having reportedly "wolf-whistled" at a white woman (Bloom 1987, p. 101).

Such extreme acts of violence meant that the eventual dismantling of Jim Crow loomed large in the minds of many whites. In desperation, some whites embarked upon a campaign of terror. As Bloom explains:

"These killings, by no means the only ones, were acts of terror designed to force blacks back into their place. They were part of the larger process of violence and intimidation in that period" (1987, p. 101). One study reported that upwards of 530 cases of murder against blacks occurred within a three-year period, between 1955 and 1958. The major effect of such terror was a precipitous drop in registered black voters throughout the South. For example, in Mississippi, prior to the Brown decision, "there had been 265 registered black voters in three black belt counties . . . by later summer in 1955 there were only 90. In the whole state the number of black voters declined from 22,000 to only 8,000 between 1952 and 1956" (Bloom 1987, p. 101).

The efforts of the WCCs and others committed to the Jim Crow social order did not succeed. The civil rights movement achieved pivotal victories — victories that crushed the institutionalized basis of the Jim Crow South. With the passage of the Civil Rights Act of 1964 and the Voting Rights Act of 1965, the Jim Crow social order, the political power of the older planter elite, and the arrangements they had created lay in ruins.

The Link to Mass Racial Attitudes

The declining importance of cotton to the larger U.S. economy and as a source of livelihood for blacks opened the door to tremendous economic and, ultimately, political opportunity for African Americans. These opportunities — stronger churches, colleges and universities, and political organizations — produced a sustained movement of protest for racial justice. The movement and the organizations it created had indigenous leadership, financing, and a genuine mass base of support. Through creative, carefully designed, and sustained social protest, this movement successfully toppled a distinct, epochal form of racial oppression; a system of oppression of African Americans that was no longer essential to the interests and needs of a broad range of U.S. political and economic elites.

Quite naturally then, widespread cultural attitudes endorsing elements of the Jim Crow social order began to atrophy and decay under a relentless attack by blacks and their white allies. Segregationist positions were under steady assault and increasingly lacked strong allies. We suggest the end product of these forces, the decline of Jim Crow racism, is seen in the broad pattern of improvement in the racial attitudes of whites in the United States. Public opinion shifted decisively against the principles of segregation, antiblack discrimination, and the bedrock premise of the Jim Crow social order that blacks were the innate intellectual inferiors of whites.

Although monumental accomplishments, the Brown decision, the Civil Rights Act of 1964, and the Voting Rights Act of 1965 primarily secured the basic citizenship rights of African Americans. The successes of the civil rights movement did not end racialized social identities among black or white Americans (Sheatsley 1966); they did not eradicate sharp black-white differences in social and economic status (Duncan 1968; Lieberson & Fuguitt 1967; Siegel 1970); and they did not undo nationwide patterns of racial residential segregation (Taeuber & Taeuber 1965). That is, the enormous and far-reaching gains of the civil rights movement did not eliminate stark patterns of racial domination and inequality that existed above, beyond, and irrespective of the specific dictates of the distinctly Southern Jim Crow system.

In the wake of the collapse of Jim Crow social arrangements and ideology, the new ideology of laissez-faire racism began to take shape. This new ideology concedes basic citizenship rights to African Americans; however, it takes as legitimate extant patterns of black-white socioeconomic inequality and residential segregation, viewing these conditions, as it does, not as the deliberate products of racial discrimination, but as outcomes of a free-market, race-neutral state apparatus and the freely taken actions of African Americans themselves.

LAISSEZ-FAIRE RACISM AND THE SENSE OF GROUP POSITION

This analysis casts studies of racial attitudes in a different light. Students of prejudice and racial attitudes may have misunderstood the real object of racial attitudes. The attitude object, or perceptual focus, is not really the social category of blacks or whites; it is not neighborhoods or schools of varying degrees of racial mixture. Instead, as Herbert Blumer (1958) argued, the real object of prejudice — what we really tap with attitude questions in surveys — is beliefs about the proper relation between groups. The real attitude object is relative group positions. This attitude of sense of group position is historically and culturally rooted, socially learned, and modifiable in response to new information, events, or structural conditions, as long as these factors contribute to or shape contexts for social interaction among members of different groups.

Attitudes toward integration or toward blacks are, fundamentally, statements about preferred positional relations among racial groups. They are not simply or even mainly emotional reactions to groups, group symbols, or situations. Nor are they best understood as statements of simple feelings of like or dislike toward minority groups and their members, although certain measurement approaches may fruitfully aim at such specific constructs. Nor, in addition, are they simply perceptions of group traits and dispositions, although stereotypes are also key dimensions of prejudice. Racial attitudes capture aspects of the preferred group positions and those patterns of belief and feeling that undergird, justify, and make understandable a preference for relatively little group differentiation and inequality under some social conditions, or for a great deal of differentiation and inequality under others.

By this logic, decreasing advocacy of the principle of segregated schooling does not mean a desire for greater contact with blacks or even a positive value attached to integrated education. From the vantage point of group position theory, it means declining insistence on forced group inequality in educational institutions. Declining support for segregated public transportation does not signal a desire for more opportunities to interact with blacks on buses, trains, and the like. Instead, it means a declining insistence on compulsory inequality in group access to this domain of social life.

Under the group position theory, change in political and economic regularities of social life decisively shape the socially constructed and shared sense of group position. The sources of change in attitudes — changes in preferred group positions — are not found principally in changing feelings of like and dislike. Changes in the patterns of mass attitudes reflect changes in the social structurally based, interactively defined and understood, needs and interests of social groups (Bobo & Hutchings 1996). To put it differently, in order to have meaning, longevity, and force in people's everyday lives, the attitudes held by individuals must be linked to the organized modes of living in which people are embedded (Rabb & Lispet 1962). As such, the demand for segregated transportation, segregated hotels, and blanket labor market discrimination increasingly ring hollow under an economy and polity that has less and less need — in fact may be incurring heavy costs — as a result of the presence of a super-exploited, racially identifiable labor pool. When the economic and political needs of a significant segment of a dominant racial group no longer hinge upon a sharp caste system for effective reproduction of the advantages of race for members of that dominant group, then the permeative acceptance and effects of that ideology will weaken and take new form.

A key link between changing structural conditions and the attitudes of the mass public are those significant social actors who articulate, and frequently clash over and debate, the need for new modes of social organization (Blumer 1958). The claims and objectives of the visible leadership elements of groups presumably spring from their conceptions of the identities, interests, opportunities, resources, and needs of the group at a particular time. That is, the direction and tenor of change are shaped in the larger public sphere of clash, debate, political mobilization, and struggle.

In that regard, following on the heels of the Reagan-Bush years, the new system and ideology of laissez-faire racism would now appear to be crystallizing. Although a full analysis of the current political context is beyond the scope of this paper, it is evident that the assault on affirmative action policies has intensified. The University of California Regents voted to eliminate their affirmative action efforts. Predictions are that this will result in a reduction in African-American and Latino undergraduate enrollments anywhere from a minimum of 50 percent to possibly as high as 80 percent. The effect on law school enrollments has been especially severe. The number of black students admitted to the UCLA law school declined by 80 percent, falling from 104 in the 1996–97 school year to just 21 for the 1997–98 school year. A similar decline ws recorded at UC-Berkeley, where black law school admissions fell from 75 students to 14 (Weiss 1997). After a highly racially polarized campaign, voters in California passed the California Civil Rights initiative effectively banning all affirmative action efforts by elements of state government. Parenthetically, these transformations immediately make it clear that there are real group and individual interests at stake in the politics of affirmative action, not merely symbolic resentments as some would maintain. Even a Democratic president, elected with substantial black support, has called for a reevaluation of and reduction in affirmative action commitments. Supreme Court rulings and other actions taken by the Republican-dominated Congress may soon reduce the number of blacks holding congressional seats. Funding for the Congressional Black Caucus has been eliminated. Fundamental reductions in the range of welfare state commitments are on the agenda of the new Congress. All of these events tend to signal the consolidation of a new understanding about race relations. We believe this new understanding is aptly described as laissez-faire racism because it stands in the face of substantial and widening racial economic inequalities, high levels of racial residential segregation, and persistent discrimination experienced across class lines in the black community.

CONCLUSIONS

The long and unabated record of sweeping change in racial attitudes that national surveys document cannot be read as a fundamental breakdown in racialized thinking or in antiblack prejudice. We have witnessed the disappearance of a racial ideology appropriate to an old social order: that of the Jim Crow post–Civil War South. A new and resilient laissez-faire racism ideology has emerged and has apparently begun to crystallize.

Jim Crow racism went into decline, in part, because of a direct and potent assault on it by the civil rights movement. Jim Crow practices and ideology were made vulnerable by an interlocking series of social changes — the declining importance of cotton production to the U.S. economy, limited immigration from Europe, black migration to urban and Northern areas — all of which dramatically increased the power resources available to black communities. The economic basis for Jim Crow had been weakened. Its political underpinnings were gradually undone by the Brown decision, the Civil Rights Act of 1964, the Voting Rights Act of 1965, and other political successes of the civil rights movement.

Because racial attitudes reflect the structural conditions of group life (Rabb & Lipset 1962), it is no surprise that Jim Crow attitudes in the mass public — such as near-consensus support for strict segregation and open discrimination — all premised on the assumed biological inferiority of blacks, would eventually and steadily ebb in popular acceptance. Jim Crow racism was no longer embedded in U.S. economic or political institutions with the centrality that it had once enjoyed. In response to the challenge posed by the civil rights movement and its allies, most of the ideological tenets of Jim Crow racism came to be widely understood as inconsistent with U.S. values.

African Americans, however, remain economically disadvantaged and racially segregated despite growing class heterogeneity within the black community and despite the successes of the civil rights movement. These social conditions continue to prompt many white Americans to feel both morally offended and apprehensive about losing something tangible if strong efforts are made to improve the living conditions of African Americans (Bobo 1983, 1988b). Furthermore, sharp black-white economic inequality and residential segregation provide the kernel of truth needed to regularly breathe new life into old stereotypes about putative black proclivities toward involvement in crime, violence, and welfare dependency. Viewed in this light, the gap between increasingly egalitarian racial principles and resistance to strong forms of affirmative action are not paradoxical at all. Both are the result of changes in U.S. social structure and politics that at once successfully deposed Jim Crow institutions but simultaneously left much of the black population in a uniquely disadvantaged position.

The end product of these conditions and processes is the emergence of a new racialized social order under a new racial ideology: laissez-faire racism. Under this regime, blacks are still stereotyped and blamed as the architects of their own disadvantaged status. The deeply entrenched pattern of denying societal responsibility for conditions in many black communities continues to foster steadfast opposition to affirmative action and other social policies that might alleviate race-based inequalities. In short, a large number of white Americans have become comfortable with as much racial inequality and segregation as a putatively nondiscriminatory polity and free market economy can produce: hence the reproduction and, on some dimensions, the worsening of racial inequalities. These circumstances are rendered culturally palatable by the new ideology of laissez-faire racism.

NOTE

The authors thank Howard Schuman for his comments on an earlier version of this paper. This research was partly supported by the Russell Sage Foundation and the National Science Foundation (SBR–9515183).

II

THE RACIAL ATTITUDES OF WHITES

3

Symbolic Racism, Old-Fashioned Racism, and Whites' Opposition to Affirmative Action

Michael Hughes

Despite considerable progress in prejudice research, questions persist about the nature of whites' racial attitudes and how they have changed over the past 50 years. Two facts are clear: traditional prejudice among whites has declined (Firebaugh & Davis 1988; Schuman, Steeh, & Bobo 1985; Taylor, Sheatsley, & Greeley 1978; Hyman & Sheatsley 1956, 1964), and support for policies that would reduce racial inequality has not increased (Steeh & Schuman 1992; Schuman, Steeh, & Bobo 1985; Bobo 1988a; Kluegel & Smith 1986). Controversy remains about the causes of this apparent inconsistency. One prominent explanation is that whites resist racial change because of symbolic racism. Symbolic racism differs from traditional racial prejudice not only in its content, but also because its source is presumably not the belief that blacks pose an economic, social, or political threat to whites. Symbolic racism represents the belief by whites that blacks violate traditional U.S. values and thus do not deserve any special help.

The concept of symbolic racism has been heavily criticized on theoretical and empirical grounds (Sniderman & Tetlock 1986a, 1986b; Pettigrew 1985; Bobo 1983, 1988b; Tuch & Hughes 1996b). Although research on symbolic racism is frequently cited, symbolic racism itself has not been the focus of recent studies of white racial attitudes (for example, Firebaugh & Davis 1988; Steeh & Schuman 1992; Bobo & Kluegel 1993; Monteith, Zuwerink, & Devine 1994; Taylor 1995; Tuch & Hughes 1996a). Using data primarily from the 1986 and 1992 American National Election Studies (ANES), this chapter evaluates the usefulness of the concept of symbolic racism, focusing specifically on features that make the theoretical argument about symbolic racism different from other arguments: the distinctiveness of symbolic racism from traditional prejudice; the definition of symbolic racism as the conjunction of antiblack affect and individualism; and the independence of symbolic racism from, and its supposed superiority over, interests as an explanation of white racial policy attitudes.

BACKGROUND

Symbolic Racism and Old-Fashioned Racism

If racial prejudice among whites has declined in the past 50 years to the point that only a small minority express prejudiced attitudes (Schuman, Steeh, & Bobo 1985), why do prejudiced reactions and discrimination by whites persist? One answer is that old-fashioned racism has been replaced by a new form of racism, symbolic racism, that "represents a form of resistance to change in the racial status quo based on moral feelings that blacks violate such traditional American values as individualism and self-reliance, the work ethic, obedience, and discipline" and is "rooted in deep-seated feelings of social morality and propriety and in early-learned racial fears and stereotypes" (Kinder & Sears 1981, p. 416). People who endorse the stereotypes and racial prejudices inherent in symbolic racism need not adhere to the old-fashioned racist notions that are at the core of traditional prejudice: that blacks are inherently inferior to whites; that the races should be separate; or that racial discrimination is, in principle, justifiable (Kinder & Sears 1981).

Clearly, some of the aspects of symbolic racism — particularly the notion that blacks violate traditional values of hard work and self-reliance — are a part of traditional racism (Bobo 1988b). Sears (1988, n. 15; see also Kinder 1986) argues that these notions are peripheral to old-fashioned racism, whose focus has traditionally been social distance and formal discrimination. In contrast, they are at the core of symbolic racism, which expresses resentment of the "special treatment" that blacks get and, according to J. B. McConahay (1982), denies continuing discrimination. In addition, symbolic racism functions independently of, and has a stronger political impact than, old-fashioned racism (Kinder & Sears 1981; McConahay 1982; Kinder 1986; Sears 1988).

The Definition of Symbolic Racism

Kinder and Sears (1981, p. 416) define symbolic racism as "a blend of anti-black affect and the kind of traditional American moral values embodied in the Protestant Ethic." The values in question are best expressed by the notion of individualism (Kinder & Sears 1981; Kinder 1986). Thus, prejudicial attitudes against blacks learned in childhood emerge as generalized antiblack affect (negative feelings toward blacks) and combine with traditional American individualism to form an adult attitudinal complex: symbolic racism.

McConahay, who uses the term "modern racism" to refer to essentially the same concept as symbolic racism, argues that underlying its expression are the beliefs that racial discrimination has disappeared, that blacks are pushing too hard in making illegitimate demands, and that they are receiving undeserved sympathy and benefits (McConahay & Hough 1976; McConahay 1982).

In summary, symbolic racism is "a joint function of two separate factors: anti-black affect and traditional values" (particularly the values of individualism, self-reliance, and hard work), and has a core content that is twofold: antagonism against blacks for "pushing too hard" and "moving too fast" and resentment because of the special treatment blacks receive through various government programs to improve their economic position (Sears 1988, p. 56). Resentment would appear to be the critical dimension underlying symbolic racism. Indeed, Kinder and Sanders (1996) now use the term "racial resentment" instead of symbolic racism.

Symbolic Racism and Self-Interest

The concept of symbolic racism was formulated in opposition to the idea that whites resist racial change because of the concrete threat that black progress poses to individual white interests (Kinder & Sears 1981). The focus on moral resentment and antagonism makes symbolic racism distinct from major sociological perspectives on prejudice, which assume that white opposition to racial change results from whites perceiving blacks as a threat and acting to protect the privileged position of whites in the racial hierarchy (Bobo & Kluegel 1993; Pettigrew 1985; Bobo 1983, 1988b; see also Quillian 1995; Bonacich 1972; Blalock 1957, 1967; Blumer 1958; Bernard 1951).

Symbolic racism is a moral orientation, rather than a self- or group-interested orientation, which generates white opposition to black political candidates, affirmative action, and busing because of moral outrage — not because whites believe that their children will be bused, that they will lose out to blacks in the job market or university admissions, that blacks will move into their neighborhoods and cause their property values to fall, or that they will be criminally victimized by blacks.

Empirical Findings in Symbolic Racism Research

Symbolic racism has been operationalized in survey research using attitudinal items that have varied widely from study to study (see Sniderman & Tetlock [1986] for an analysis and critique of this pattern). Frequently used items ask whether blacks have gotten more economically than they deserve (for example, McConahay 1982); if the government and news media treat blacks with more respect than they deserve (for example, McConahay 1982); if blacks are too demanding in their push for equal rights (Kinder & Sears 1981); if public officials pay more attention to blacks than to whites (Kinder & Sears 1981); if blacks on welfare could get along without it if they tried (Kinder & Sears 1981); and if blacks have gained more than they are entitled to (Kinder & Sears 1981). These kinds of items tap racial prejudices and stereotypes that differ from those typically measured by indices of old-fashioned racism.

Factor analyses that combine symbolic racism items with old-fashioned racism items find two distinct factors corresponding to the two kinds of racism (McConahay 1986; Bobo 1983; McClendon 1985). Although this well-established finding suggests that there are two empirically distinct dimensions underlying the indices that can be constructed with the two kinds of items (Sears 1988), these same researchers also report substantial correlations between the two indices.

Symbolic racism is a moderate-to-strong predictor of opposition to black political candidates (Kinder & Sears 1981; McConahay & Hough 1976), busing (McConahay 1982; Sears & Allen 1984), and affirmative action (Kluegel & Smith 1983; Jacobson 1985). In spite of the strong correlation between symbolic racism and old-fashioned racism, most studies of the impact of symbolic racism have not included measures of old-fashioned racism. Kinder and Sears's (1981) justification for not including old-fashioned racism in their study is that the level of support for old-fashioned racism among whites is so low that it could not be a major determinant of white policy attitudes.

In the few studies that have included both symbolic racism and old-fashioned racism (or equivalent variables not labeled as such) as predictors of racial policy attitudes, symbolic racism has usually emerged as the stronger predictor (McConahay n.d. [cited in Sears 1988]; Bobo 1983; Jacobson 1985; McClendon 1985 found no difference in the impact of the two variables).

Researchers have paid much more explicit attention to the issues of self-interest and group interest, often conceptualized as racial threat (Kinder & Sears 1981; Sears 1988). The major finding, replicated a number of times, is that objective or perceived interests, measured with reference to neighborhood desegregation, busing, school integration, job competition, or black crime, has little or no impact on white racial policy attitudes or voting behavior, whereas symbolic racism, as noted above, has a substantial impact (see Sears [1988] for a review). A good example is the often-cited finding that, although symbolic racism very strongly predicts opposition to busing, white parents of school-aged children (even white parents of children who were being bused) are no more likely to oppose busing than are whites without school-aged children (McConahay 1982 [who uses the term "modern racism" instead of "symbolic racism]; Bobo 1983).

Findings of a null impact of self-interest in symbolic racism studies do not appear to be a special case of racial self-interest having no effect on racial policy attitudes. Sears and Funk (1991), in a detailed review of the literature, demonstrate that self-interest has very little effect on social and political attitudes generally — the only exceptions being when the stakes are large and very clear and when there is a specific policy in question that is narrowly linked to self-interest. For example, taxpayers who expect their taxes will increase greatly are likely to express themselves against, and vote against, such a policy; likewise, smokers tend not to favor smoking restrictions. Generally, racial policy issues do not involve explicit threats to white self-interest analogous to these examples.

Criticisms

Group Conflict

The major criticism of the symbolic racism approach is that its proponents have drawn an unrealistically sharp distinction between symbolic racism and approaches that emphasize racial threat and group conflict. For example, as Bobo (1983) noted, Kinder and Sears (1981) have too narrow a focus on individual objective interests. If whites oppose racial policies because they feel their individual interests are linked to the fate of their group, then the important variable should be subjectively felt group interests.

Bobo (1983) also argues that some of the items typically used in symbolic racism indices (for example, items concerning civil rights leaders pushing too hard for change, and dislike for black militants) reflect not only resentment and antagonism but also realistic group conflict. Bobo demonstrates that these items, compared to other items in a symbolic racism index, are better predictors of white attitudes toward busing.

Bobo (1983) concludes his critique of symbolic racism by arguing that opposition to busing does not symbolize an abstract moral resentment, rather, "If anything, school busing is a symbol to whites, a concrete and clear cut instance, of how the demands and political activities of blacks can produce *real* changes in aspects of their lives, changes that may not always be restricted to schools (e.g., open housing laws and affirmative action)" (p. 1209). Thus, the oppositional stance that whites take on issues of racial policy constitutes a defense of whites' powerful and privileged position in society — a position they believe they deserve.

Measurement

Symbolic racism research also is criticized for not using a standard set of items to measure symbolic racism in surveys (Sniderman & Tetlock 1986; Pettigrew 1985). Critics charge that items tap not only the antagonism and resentment discussed above, but also policy attitudes about busing and affirmative action that symbolic racism presumably explains (Sniderman & Tetlock 1986; Pettigrew 1985). In one symbolic racism index, a researcher included items that tapped the belief that admissions practices of colleges and hiring practices of employers favored blacks over whites (Jacobson 1985) — appearing to make group interest an explicit part of symbolic racism.

Sears (1988) and Kinder (1986) respond that their critics have failed to distinguish symbolic politics (for example, Sears, Hensler, & Speer 1979) from symbolic racism. Studies of symbolic politics require general indices of racial attitudes that may include a variety of kinds of items; studies of symbolic racism (for example, Kinder & Sears 1981; Sears & Allen 1984) have refined indices of symbolic racism. Sears (1988) argues that using measures of busing and affirmative action attitudes as both dependent and independent variables in studies of symbolic racism is reasonable because these issues have become highly symbolic. The strategy of researchers has been to demonstrate this by examining them first, as dependent variables and, second, as independent variables, in a carefully laid-out analytic strategy (for example, Kinder & Sears 1981). In sum, although measurement has not been entirely consistent, variation in measurement also has not been entirely without reason. Nonetheless, the meaning of some findings remains in question, particularly when items containing policy issues and group interest are used as measures of symbolic racism.

The Confounding of Old-Fashioned Racism and Symbolic Racism

P. M. Sniderman and P. E. Tetlock (1986) have sharply criticized symbolic racism researchers for measuring symbolic racism so that it is highly correlated with old-fashioned racism or so that it includes old-fashioned racism items, thus confounding symbolic racism and old-fashioned racism. At the same time, Sniderman and Tetlock (1986) charge that the study of symbolic racism omits the concept of racial prejudice.

Kinder's (1986) response to these critiques was to drop the term "antiblack affect," and replace it with the term "racial prejudice." According to Kinder, symbolic racism is the "conjunction of racial prejudice and traditional American values. Symbolic racism is neither racism, pure and simple, nor traditional values, pure and simple, but rather the blending of the two" (Kinder 1986, p. 154; see also Kinder & Sanders 1996, pp. 291–294). Perhaps Kinder means that symbolic racism exists when both racial prejudice and individualism occur together, and the effects of symbolic racism occur when both variables act together. This interpretation could imply an additive model but appears most consistent with an interactive model in which the effect of one variable depends on the level of the other.

Kinder's response blurs the distinction between old-fashioned racism and antiblack affect and raises two obvious, but important and related, questions. If antiblack affect is strongly associated with, or the same thing as, old-fashioned racism, then does not the definition of symbolic racism as the blending of antiblack affect and individualism nullify the principle that symbolic racism and old-fashioned racism are distinct? Similarly, if symbolic racism is the main cause of white racial policy attitudes, how can one now argue that old-fashioned racism is no longer important?[1]

A main conclusion of Sniderman and Tetlock's (1986) critique is that, in fact, old-fashioned racism still exists and may have a powerful effect on white racial policy attitudes. To the degree that symbolic racism is racism, it is old-fashioned racism. Furthermore, Sniderman and Tetlock (1986) continue, another ingredient in symbolic racism — adherence to individualistic values — may affect white racial policy attitudes because it represents conservative political attitudes independent of racism. This conclusion implies that the concept of symbolic racism is meaningless because the important components appear to be old-fashioned racism and individualism, operating independently of each other. We need no special theory to understand the effects of these variables.

These questions about symbolic racism, old-fashioned racism, and individualism persist because, as noted above, few studies have included measures of both symbolic racism and old-fashioned racism. Researchers have failed to examine a full range of questions about how the two types of racism are related and whether they have similar effects. Furthermore, no studies that have looked at old-fashioned racism and symbolic racism have attempted to distinguish antiblack affect learned in childhood (an emotional response that presumably is still operative in adults) from old-fashioned racism (a set of beliefs).

THE PROBLEM

In summary, three interrelated questions about symbolic racism remain: Is symbolic racism distinct from old-fashioned racism? Is symbolic racism the conjunction of antiblack affect and the individualistic values embedded in the Protestant ethic? Is symbolic racism independent from, and superior to, self-interest as an explanation of white racial policy attitudes?

In the analyses that follow, I empirically examine the above questions by using data on whites primarily from two national studies — the 1986 and the 1992 ANES — that provide measures of affirmative action attitudes, old-fashioned racism, symbolic racism, antiblack affect, individualism, equalitarianism, self-interest regarding affirmative action, and socioeconomic and demographic variables.

Question 1: Symbolic Racism and Old-Fashioned Racism

If symbolic racism and old-fashioned racism are measures of the same thing, identical except for measurement error, we should observe four outcomes: We should not be able to distinguish the two dimensions through factor analysis. If we construct variables representing the two dimensions and regress each on a set of predictors, predictors of one of these variables should be identical to predictors of the other. If we put one of these two variables in an equation predicting the other, the effect of this predictor variable should be much greater than all other predictor variables in the equation, even accounting for the associations of all other predictors with the dependent variable. If we put both symbolic racism and old-fashioned racism in the same equation predicting attitudes about affirmative action, then the individual effects of both of these predictors should be sharply attenuated.

Four subsidiary questions can be answered when we put symbolic racism and old-fashioned racism in the same equation predicting whites' attitudes about affirmative action: Are these variables somewhat independent in their effects and equal in their impact, as McClendon (1985) found? Does symbolic racism explain the effect of old-fashioned racism? Does old-fashioned racism explain the effect of symbolic racism? Are old-fashioned racism and symbolic racism so intimately connected in their effects on whites' attitudes toward affirmative action that symbolic racism has its strongest effect when old-fashioned racism is high?

Question 2: The Definition of Symbolic Racism

If symbolic racism is the conjunction of antiblack affect and individualism, then antiblack affect and individualism, measured separately from symbolic racism, should be particularly strong predictors of symbolic racism. In fact, their effects should dwarf those of all other predictors. There may be a particularly strong interaction between antiblack affect and individualism such that the effect of antiblack affect is particularly strong when individualism is high, and vice-versa.

Question 3: Self-Interest

If symbolic racism is independent of, and superior to, self-interest as an explanation of white racial policy attitudes, then when we put both symbolic racism and self-interest in an equation predicting whites' attitudes about affirmative action, symbolic racism should emerge as the stronger predictor — and the effects of self-interest should be nonsignificant or quite negligible.

THE DATA

The Samples

The data used in this study come mainly from the 1986 and 1992 ANES. Some data from the 1988 and 1990 ANES are also used.[2]

All four samples are national probability samples designed to be representative of the noninstitutionalized adult population of the United States. More information on the data and sampling methodology is found in Miller (1987, 1989) and Miller, Kinder, and Rosenstone (1992, 1993). The present analyses are limited to data from white respondents, a minimum of 630 cases with complete data from the 1986 ANES and a minimum of 1,894 cases with complete data from the 1992 ANES. The relatively small number of cases with complete data (the ANES typically include data from 2,000 or more respondents per survey) results from the fact that different forms of the questionnaire were used, and many of the most important items for the present analyses were included only on one of these forms.

The survey from 1990 includes a measure of the critical dimension of individualism absent in the 1992 survey. A panel of 1990 respondents was included in the 1992 ANES. For analyses of 1992 affirmative action attitudes that include individualism as a predictor, data for all predictor variables except for individualism come from the 1992 ANES. Individualism was measured in 1990. In these analyses, a minimum of 443 cases is used because the panel was a subset of the 1992 sample. Using data collected in different survey years is not ideal. The reader should note that the estimates of the effects of individualism in the 1992 ANES analyses are conservative.

Data from 1988 and 1990 are also used as a check of the robustness of some major findings. In these analyses, there are a minimum of 1,360 cases for 1988 and 690 cases for 1990.

Measures

Symbolic Racism

Symbolic racism in the 1986 ANES was measured with the five items presented below. These items do not measure explicit group conflict motives (as noted in Bobo's [1983] critique of Kinder & Sears [1981]), evaluation of any explicit racial policy, or traditional prejudice (for example, belief in racial inferiority). These items had five response categories: strongly agree, agree, neither agree nor disagree, disagree, and strongly disagree. All items were coded so that a high score indicated symbolic racism.

1. Most blacks who receive money from welfare programs could get along without it if they tried.
2. Over the past few years, blacks have gotten less than they deserve.
3. Irish, Italians, Jewish, and many other minorities overcame prejudice and worked their way up. Blacks should do the same without any special favors.

For items 4 and 5, respondents were asked to agree or disagree with possible reasons why "white people seem to get more of the good things in life in America — jobs and money — than black people do."

4. It's really a matter of some people not trying hard enough; if blacks would only try harder, they could be just as well off as whites.
5. Generations of slavery and discrimination have created conditions that make it difficult for blacks to work their way out of the lower class.

The alpha reliability coefficient for this scale is 0.75.

The symbolic racism index used in analyses of the 1988, 1990, and 1992 ANES includes all of the items in the 1986 study, except for item 1. Reliability coefficients for these three surveys are 0.72, 0.76, and 0.75, respectively.

To deal with a frequent criticism of the measurement of symbolic racism — that items often allude to or ask about policies that may benefit blacks, and then use these items to predict policy preferences — models are included below in which the measurement of symbolic racism is reduced to item 4, which taps the essential notion in symbolic racism that blacks violate the principles of the Protestant ethic by not "trying hard" enough.

Old-Fashioned Racism

Two items from the 1986 ANES measure old-fashioned racism. These items had the same agree-disagree response format as the symbolic racism items above and were coded so that a high score indicated old-fashioned racism. They were also introduced with the same phrase as were items 4 and 5 in the symbolic racism index.

1. Blacks come from a less able race and this explains why blacks are not as well off as whites in America.
2. The differences are brought about by God; God made the races different as part of His divine plan.

The correlation between these items is 0.37, and the alpha reliability coefficient for the index is 0.54.

In the 1992 ANES, respondents rated white people and black people on a seven-point scale with regard to how intelligent or unintelligent they were, how violence prone or not violence prone they were, and how lazy or hard-working they were. For each of these dimensions, the rating for blacks was subtracted from that for whites, resulting in three variables, coded so that a high score on each variable indicates that the respondent rated blacks as less intelligent, more violent, or lazier, respectively, than whites. The reliability coefficient for this three-item index of old-fashioned racism in the 1992 ANES is 0.75.

Opposition to Affirmative Action

The ANES included two items in 1986, 1988, 1990, and 1992 that are used here as the measure of opposition to affirmative action, the dependent variable in part of the analysis. Respondents were asked whether they were for or against affirmative action policies in hiring and college admissions, and responded in one of four ways: for — strongly, for — not strongly, against — not strongly, and against — strongly. A high score indicates opposition to the policy.

1. Some people say that because of past discrimination blacks should be given preference in hiring and promotion. Others say that such preference in hiring and promotion of blacks is wrong because it gives blacks advantages they haven't earned. What about your opinion — are you for or against preferential hiring and promotion for blacks?
2. Some people say that because of past discrimination it is sometimes necessary for colleges and universities to reserve openings for black students. Others oppose quotas because they say quotas give blacks advantages they haven't earned. What is your opinion — are you for or against quotas to admit black students?

The alphas for this two-item index are 0.73, 0.68, 0.72, and 0.71 in 1986, 1988, 1990, and 1992, respectively.

Self-Interest

There are four items in the 1986 ANES that are used to measure perceived self-interest regarding affirmative action. Unfortunately, the 1992
ANES has no self-interest items. Substantial evidence exists in the symbolic racism literature that individual self-interest has little impact on
racial policy attitudes, whereas self-oriented group interest may be
important, although this has not been fully established (for example,
Sears & Kinder 1985; see Sears & Funk 1991, for a review). Items in the
1986 ANES tap both the respondent's perceived group interest (items 1
and 2 below) and perceived individual self-interest (items 3 and 4) with
regard to affirmative action. In factor analyses not reported here (but
described in Tuch & Hughes 1996b), I attempted to differentiate group
from individual self-interest with these items. Using a method assuming
orthogonal factors, only one strong factor emerged, and no other factor
had an eigenvalue greater than 1. Both the self-interest and the group-
interest items strongly loaded on this factor. Using a method that allowed
factors to correlate provided a slightly better fit to the data and yielded
two factors with a correlation of 0.82. I concluded that it is not possible to
differentiate individual self-interest from group interest in these data.
Therefore, the measure is one of self-oriented group interest, which I refer
to below with the term "self-interest."

The response categories for the self-interest items were perceived like-
lihoods that interests would be damaged, from very likely to not very
likely. A high score indicates a greater perceived threat to interests.

1. What do you think the chances are these days that a white person won't get
    admitted to a school while an equally or less qualified black person gets
    admitted instead?

2. What do you think the chances are these days that a white person won't get
    a job or a promotion while an equally or less qualified black person gets one
    instead?

3. What do you think the chances are these days that you or anyone in your
    family won't get admitted to a school while an equally or less qualified black
    person gets admitted instead?

4. What do you think the chances are these days that you or anyone in your
    family won't get a job or a promotion while an equally or less qualified black
    person gets one instead?

The alpha for this index is 0.85.

Antiblack Affect

Antiblack affect is measured in both the 1986 and the 1992 ANES using
the "feeling thermometer" rating for blacks. Respondents were asked to
rate political figures — and some demographic and political categories of

persons — on a thermometer. Ratings between 50 and 100 degrees mean that the respondent feels favorable and warm toward the person or category of persons. Ratings between 0 and 50 degrees mean that the respondent does not feel favorable toward, or care much for, the person or category of persons. Respondents were asked specifically to rate "blacks" according to this scale. Responses were coded so that a high score indicates antiblack affect.

Individualism

Six items in the 1986 ANES constitute a measure of individualism. The items all have an agree–disagree format as described for the symbolic racism items above. A high score indicates a high level of individualism.

1. Most people who don't get ahead should not blame the system; they have only themselves to blame.
2. Hard work offers little guarantee of success.
3. If people work hard they almost always get what they want.
4. Most people who do not get ahead in life probably work as hard as people who do.
5. Any person who is willing to work hard has a good chance of succeeding.
6. Even if people try hard they often cannot reach their goals.

This scale has an alpha reliability coefficient of 0.59.

Eight items, different from the 1986 individualism items, were included in the 1990 ANES to measure individualism and are used here to predict 1992 affirmative action attitudes (because no individualism items were asked in 1992). In a factor analysis, only three items were highly correlated enough to constitute an index:[3]

1. One, the main reason the government has become bigger over the years is because it has gotten involved in things that people should do for themselves; or two, government has become bigger because the problems we face have become bigger.
2. One, we need a strong government to handle today's complex economic problems; or two, the free market can handle these problems without government being involved.
3. One, the less government the better; or two, there are more things that government should be doing."

Respondents indicated which of the paired choices came close to their own opinions. A high score on the index represented greater individualism. The alpha reliability coefficient for this index is 0.70.

Equalitarianism

There are six items in each of the four ANES surveys that tap the respondent's belief in the abstract principle of equality. These items have the same agree–disagree format used in the symbolic racism items presented above. All items have been coded so that a high score indicates greater agreement with the principle of equality.

1. Our society should do whatever is necessary to make sure that everyone has an equal opportunity to succeed.
2. We have gone too far in pushing equal rights in this country.
3. One of the big problems in this country is that we don't give everyone an equal chance.
4. This country would be better off if we worried less about how equal people are.
5. It is not really that big of a problem if some people have more of a chance in life than others.
6. If people were treated more equally in this country, we would have many fewer problems.

In the 1986 analyses, only items 2 through 4 were used because the inclusion of item 1 reduced the reliability of the index. The alphas for this index are 0.60, 0.65, 0.60, and 0.71 for 1986, 1988, 1990, and 1992, respectively.

Socioeconomic and Demographic Variables

Age and education are measured in years. Gender is a dummy variable, where 0 = male and 1 = female. Southern residence is a dummy variable, where 1 = a residence in Alabama, Arkansas, Delaware, the District of Columbia, Florida, Georgia, Kentucky, Louisiana, Maryland, Mississippi, North Carolina, Oklahoma, South Carolina, Tennessee, Texas, Virginia, or West Virginia, and 0 = residence outside the South. Employment status is a set of dummy variables for unemployed, housekeeping, retired, and student. Employed is the contrast category. Urban is a dummy variable, where 1 = urban (resident in a city with 50,000 population or greater, or in a suburb of such a city) and 0 = nonurban. Income is a set of categories from 1 to 22, corresponding to categories of income from less than $3,000 to $75,000 or more.

FINDINGS

In this section, I first present factor analyses of old-fashioned racism and symbolic racism items. Next, old-fashioned racism and symbolic racism are regressed on a set of demographic predictor variables. Demographic variables, old-fashioned racism, and other attitudinal variables are then used to predict symbolic racism. Finally, opposition to affirmative action is regressed on symbolic racism, old-fashioned racism, other attitudinal variables, and demographic variables. Findings are then summarized in terms of questions 1, 2, and 3 in the section that follows.

Symbolic Racism and Old-Fashioned Racism

Table 3.1 presents the results of factor analyses (orthogonal factors; varimax rotation) for symbolic racism and old-fashioned racism items

TABLE 3.1
Factor Analyses of Symbolic Racism and Old-Fashioned Racism Items in the 1986 and 1992 American National Election Studies

	Factor Loadings	
	Symbolic Racism	Old-Fashioned Racism
1986		
Blacks could get along without welfare	0.68	0.29
Blacks got less than they deserve*	0.74	−0.07
Irish . . . overcame prejudice, blacks . . . same	0.74	0.29
If blacks would try harder . . .	0.72	0.34
Slavery and discrimination . . . difficult*	0.73	−0.13
Blacks come from a less able race	−0.03	0.84
Races different . . . His divine plan	0.19	0.75
Eigenvalue	2.90	1.30
Percent of variance explained	42.00	18.40
1992		
Blacks got less than they deserve*	0.77	0.15
Irish . . . overcame prejudice, blacks . . . same	0.73	0.24
If blacks would try harder . . .	0.71	0.25
Slavery and discrimination . . . difficult*	0.75	0.03
Blacks rated less intelligent than whites	0.05	0.83
Blacks rated more violent than whites	0.21	0.80
Blacks rated lazier than whites	0.24	0.73
Eigenvalue	3.00	1.30
Percent of variance explained	43.30	18.00

Notes:
 Items indicated here are with abbreviated descriptions. See text for the full wording of each item.
 *Direction of item was reversed before analysis

from the 1986 ANES and the 1992 ANES. As in results of previous studies (McConahay 1986; Bobo 1983; McClendon 1985), symbolic racism and old-fashioned racism constitute separate dimensions that can be empirically differentiated but are not completely distinct. For example, items that load high on the symbolic racism factor do not always have negligible loadings on the old-fashioned racism factor (for example, the item, "If blacks would try harder . . ." has a strong 0.72 loading on the symbolic racism factor in 1986, but a 0.34 loading on the old-fashioned racism factor). Also, the correlations between the indices constructed from the two kinds of items are not small (0.28 in the 1986 data and 0.41 in the 1992 data).

Table 3.2 presents regressions of old-fashioned racism and symbolic racism on various sets of predictor variables. Models 1 and 2 for each set of data regress old-fashioned racism and symbolic racism on identical sets of predictors. It is clear that the size and significance of coefficients predicting old-fashioned racism and symbolic racism are very similar but not identical. The major difference is that older respondents score higher on old-fashioned racism than younger ones, but age is not associated with symbolic racism.

In model 3 for each year, I enter old-fashioned racism in the equation predicting symbolic racism. In 1986, the effect of old-fashioned racism is moderate and significant (0.14), but education is the strongest predictor (−0.26). In 1992, the effect of old-fashioned racism is much stronger (0.38) and is the strongest predictor, being more than twice the size of the effect of education (−0.16).

How much of the difference we observe across the years is the result of differences in operationalization of old-fashioned racism, and how much is the result of changes over time is not clear; however, it is likely that a substantial amount of the difference is the result of differences in measurement. The 1986 measure taps belief in the inherent racial inferiority of blacks, whereas the 1992 items measure whites' belief that blacks are less intelligent, more violent, and lazier than whites.

It is important to emphasize that in both equations, variables other than old-fashioned racism are significant predictors of symbolic racism (education, being a student [in 1986], and being from the South [in 1986], income [in 1992], and being from an urban area [in 1992]).

To summarize briefly, the findings do not suggest that symbolic racism and old-fashioned racism are identical dimensions. Rather, it appears that they are different attitudes that are fairly strongly related.

TABLE 3.2
Regressions of Old-Fashioned Racism and Symbolic Racism on Sociodemographic and Attitudinal Variables, 1986 and 1992: Standardized Coefficients

	ANES 1986				ANES 1992			
	1 Old-Fashioned Racism	2 Symbolic Racism	3 Symbolic Racism	4 Symbolic Racism	1 Old-Fashioned Racism	2 Symbolic Racism	3 Symbolic Racism	4 Symbolic Racism
Age	0.12†	-0.03	-0.04	-0.08	0.08†	0.00	-0.03	-0.07
Female	-0.01	-0.07	-0.06	0.00	0.00	-0.03	-0.02	0.06
Education	-0.35**	-0.30**	-0.26**	-0.23**	-0.12**	-0.21**	-0.16**	-0.22**
Income	-0.06	0.01	0.01	-0.06	0.08†	0.14**	0.11**	0.08
Occupation								
Unemployed	-0.02	-0.06	-0.06	-0.06	0.01	0.00	0.00	0.04
Homemaker	0.01	0.03	0.03	0.04	0.03	0.04	0.03	0.01
Student	-0.04	-0.11†	-0.10†	-0.07*	0.00	-0.03	-0.03	-0.12†
Retired/Disabled	0.00	0.07	0.07	0.05	0.04	0.04	0.02	0.08
Urban	-0.02	-0.06	-0.05	-0.03	-0.04	-0.09**	-0.08**	0.06
South	0.14**	0.16**	0.14**	0.06*	0.00	0.02	0.01	0.07
Old-fashioned racism	—	—	0.14**	0.03	—	—	0.38**	0.27**
Equalitarianism	—	—	—	-0.21**	—	—	—	-0.21**
Individualism	—	—	—	0.23**	—	—	—	0.01
Antiblack affect	—	—	—	0.12**	—	—	—	0.13†
Self-interest	—	—	—	0.29**	(na)	(na)	(na)	(na)
R-squared	0.23**	0.17**	0.19**	0.44**	0.03**	0.05**	0.20**	0.29**

*p ≤ .05
†p ≤ .01
**p ≤ .001
— = variable not in model
(na) = data not available

The Definition of Symbolic Racism as the
Conjunction of Antiblack Affect and Individualism

Model 4 for each data set in Table 3.2 adds three other variables to each equation: antiblack affect, individualism, and equalitarianism. In the equation for the 1986 data, model 4 also adds self-interest. Although antiblack affect and individualism are both part of the definition of symbolic racism, these two variables are not clearly the most important predictors of symbolic racism in either the 1986 or the 1992 data. In 1986, although both individualism (0.23) and antiblack affect (0.12) have significant effects, education (−0.23), equalitarianism (−0.21), and self-interest (0.29) are also strong predictors. With these variables in the equation, old-fashioned racism no longer predicts symbolic racism. Self-interest is the strongest predictor in this equation. In the 1992 data, individualism is not significant; and although antiblack affect (0.13) is a significant predictor, it is clearly not the strongest, with old-fashioned racism (0.27), education (−0.22), and equalitarianism (−0.21) all being stronger.

In analyses not presented here, an interaction term of individualism x antiblack affect was added to each of the model 4 equations in Table 3.2. In both cases, this interaction term was nonsignificant and negligible. Thus, the blend of antiblack affect and individualism (Kinder & Sears 1981, p. 416) represented by the interaction of these two variables is not a strong predictor of symbolic racism.

In view of Kinder's replacement of antiblack affect with racial prejudice, I also did analyses in which the interaction term was individualism x old-fashioned racism. Interestingly, in this analysis for the 1986 data, this interaction was significant but was in the "wrong" direction. The effect of old-fashioned racism is lower when individualism is high, and the effect of individualism is lower when old-fashioned racism is high. Thus, in the 1986 data, the conjunction of old-fashioned racism and individualism (Kinder 1986, p. 154) decreases adherence to symbolic racism. In the 1992 data, the interaction term is not significant but is in the same direction.

How robust are these findings presented in Table 3.2? Analyses of data from the 1988 and 1992 ANES presented in Table 3.3 provide a partial answer. Findings with these data are distorted to an unknown degree by the absence of old-fashioned racism and self-interest. However, these analyses confirm the negative independent effects of education and equalitarianism on symbolic racism, the null effect of individualism (in 1990), and the effect of antiblack affect on symbolic racism. Also, in analyses not shown, I again investigated the effect of the interaction between individualism and antiblack affect (in 1990) in predicting symbolic racism and found that it was indistinguishable from zero.

TABLE 3.3
Regressions of Symbolic Racism on Sociodemographic and Attitudinal
Variables, 1988 and 1990: Standardized Coefficients

	1 ANES 1988	2 ANES 1990
Age	−0.07*	−0.06
Female	−0.05	0.06
Education	−0.15**	−0.20**
Income	0.01	−0.01
Occupation:		
Unemployed	0.01	−0.07*
Homemaker	0.01	−0.02
Student	−0.03	−0.04
Retired/Disabled	0.02	0.00
Urban	0.02	−0.05
South	0.07†	0.08
Old-fashioned racism	(na)	(na)
Equalitarianism	−0.41**	−0.37**
Individualism	(na)	−0.03
Antiblack affect	0.19**	0.22**
Self-interest	(na)	(na)
R-squared	0.26**	0.30**

* $p \leq .05$
†$p \leq .01$
**$p \leq .001$
(na) = data not available

In summary, although symbolic racism has been defined as a blend of antiblack affect and individualism (Kinder & Sears 1981, p. 416), the power of these two variables to predict symbolic racism is not extraordinary. In the 1986 and 1992 models, the effect of antiblack affect is not strong in either case, and individualism has no impact on symbolic racism in 1992. In 1988 and 1990 (where we have no controls for old-fashioned racism or self-interests), the impact of antiblack affect is a little stronger. In 1990, however, the impact of individualism is nil.

The interaction between antiblack affect and individualism in predicting symbolic racism is essentially zero. If we replace antiblack affect with old-fashioned racism, we find that, if anything, individualism decreases the impact of old-fashioned racism on symbolic racism.

It appears that if symbolic racism has its roots in a blending of, conjunction of, or interaction between antiblack affect and individualism, or in the interaction between old-fashioned racism and individualism, these are not strong roots. Other factors, such as egalitarianism, self-interest (vis-à-vis affirmative action), old-fashioned racism or antiblack affect (without regard to individualism), and low education appear to be stronger.

Self-Interest and Symbolic Racism

Table 3.4 presents a series of regressions of opposition to affirmative action on demographic and other variables. In model 1 for each data set, demographic variables, self-interest, and symbolic racism are entered into the same equation. In the 1986 data, education (0.20) has a positive effect, indicating that those with higher education oppose affirmative action more than those with less education. The unemployed (–0.12) and those from urban areas (–0.06) are more favorable to affirmative action. Notably, in the 1986 data, both self-interest (0.22) and symbolic racism (0.35) moderately to strongly increase opposition to affirmative action.

In model 2 for the 1986 data, old-fashioned racism is entered into the equation. Its effect (–0.13) is negative, indicating that higher levels of old-fashioned racism are associated with less opposition to affirmative action. This is a counterintuitive finding for which I offer no explanation. Suffice it to say that old-fashioned racism does not increase opposition to affirmative action in the 1986 data (its zero-order relationship with opposition to affirmative action is nonsignificant and negligible [–0.03]).

The same conclusion emerges from analysis of data from 1992. Model 2 shows that with symbolic racism and demographic variables in the equation, old-fashioned racism has no impact on opposition to affirmative action (its statistically significant zero-order relationship of 0.17 with opposition to affirmative action is completely explained by entering only symbolic racism into the equation; analysis not shown). In contrast, symbolic racism (0.50) is an extremely strong predictor. As in 1986, education (0.16) also significantly increases opposition to affirmative action as does income (0.13). In model 3 for each year, equalitarianism, individualism, and antiblack affect are entered, and the effect of symbolic racism (and that of self-interest in the 1986 data) is essentially unchanged.

The findings in models 1, 2, and 3 in Table 3.4 demonstrate three important points. First, symbolic racism affects affirmative action attitudes more than any other predictors in the equations. Second, old-fashioned racism does not have a proximate additive effect of increasing opposition to affirmative action. Third, the effects of symbolic racism are not due to its correlations with individualism (measured differently in each sample), equalitarianism, or antiblack affect. Fourth, in the 1986 sample, independently of other variables, self-interest increases opposition to affirmative action.

TABLE 3.4
Regressions of Attitude against Affirmative Action on Sociodemographic and Attitudinal Variables, 1986 and 1992: Standardized Coefficients

	ANES 1986				ANES 1992			
	1	2	3	4	1	2	3	4
Age	0.05	0.07	0.05	0.06	—	0.07	0.12*	0.11
Female	-0.07*	-0.07	-0.06	-0.05	—	-0.02	-0.04	-0.02
Education	0.20**	0.16**	0.15**	0.10*	—	0.16**	0.18**	0.14†
Income	0.04	0.04	0.02	0.02	—	0.13**	0.09*	0.13*
Occupation								
Unemployed	-0.12**	-0.12**	-0.12†	-0.12†	—	-0.01	-0.08*	-0.07
Homemaker	0.03	0.04	0.02	0.03	—	0.02	0.04	0.04
Student	0.00	0.00	0.00	-0.02	—	0.04	0.03	0.02
Retired/Disabled	0.02	0.01	0.00	0.01	—	-0.01	-0.06	-0.06
Urban	-0.06*	-0.07*	-0.07	-0.08*	—	-0.03	-0.07	-0.09*
South	0.05	0.07*	0.08*	0.10†	—	0.02	0.04	0.06
Old-fashioned racism	—	-0.13**	-0.15**	-0.16**	—	—	0.01	0.08
Egalitarianism	—	—	-0.09*	-0.14**	—	—	0.02	-0.08
Individualism	—	—	0.02	0.05	—	—	0.06	0.06
Antiblack affect	—	—	0.05	0.08*	(na)	(na)	-0.06	-0.01
Self-interest	0.22**	0.23**	0.21**	0.27**	—	0.50**	0.49**	(na)
Symbolic racism	0.35**	0.36**	0.31**	—	—	(na)	(na)	0.26**
Symbolic racism (1 item)	—	—	—	0.12†	—	0.28**	0.32**	0.20**
R-squared	0.27**	0.28**	0.29**	0.24**	—	0.28**	0.32**	0.20**

*p ≤ .05
†p ≤ .01
**p ≤ .001
— = variable not in model
(na) = data not available

Regarding the last point about self-interest, it is also notable that education (and income in the 1992 data) has the effect of increasing opposition to affirmative action. Because affirmative action programs that involve admissions to college, hirings, and set-asides tend to favor minority group members who already have some status resources, whites with more status resources (that is, moderate to high education and income) may be more negatively affected by affirmative action. Education and income may therefore constitute measures of objective interests in opposition to affirmative action whose impact is independent of subjective interests. In any event, these findings support M. R. Jackman's (Jackman & Muha 1984) hypothesis about education being associated with a superficial tolerance.

In models 1 and 2 in Table 3.5, I use data from the 1988 and 1990 ANES to replicate as closely as possible models 1 through 3 of Table 3.4. These models (which should be viewed with caution because they lack old-fashioned racism and self-interest [and individualism in 1988]) confirm that individualism and antiblack affect do not explain the impact of symbolic racism on opposition to affirmative action; that income and particularly education are positively associated with opposition to affirmative action; and that symbolic racism is the most important predictor of opposition to affirmative action.

Additional Questions

Are findings for opposition to affirmative action the result of symbolic racism item content? As noted above, objections have been raised that the questions included in symbolic racism indices are inappropriate for various reasons. For that reason, model 4 is included for each year in Table 3.4, and model 3 is included in Table 3.5. In these models, the symbolic racism index has been reduced to the single item about the belief that blacks would be just as well off as whites if they would only try harder. This item tacitly expresses the core notion in symbolic racism — that blacks violate the individualistic values of hard work and self-reliance. In these analyses, the effect of symbolic racism remains significant but is sharply weakened. Much of its weakness is probably the result of the limitations of a single-item measure. Symbolic racism is not always the strongest predictor in these analyses, but it is among the strongest predictors. All other major conclusions noted above remain intact.

Does old-fashioned racism increase the effect of symbolic racism? The findings presented above, indicating that symbolic racism but not old-fashioned racism is an important predictor of whites' attitudes about affirmative action, support an important conclusion of symbolic racism research: that traditional prejudice has little effect on white racial policy attitudes. These findings, however, assume that the effects of old-fashioned racism

TABLE 3.5

Regressions of Opposition to Affirmative Action on Sociodemographic and Attitudinal Variables, 1988 and 1992: Standardized Coefficients

	ANES 1988			ANES 1992		
	1	2	3	1	2	3
Age	0.04	0.03	0.01	0.18**	0.13**	0.11*
Female	-0.04	-0.03	-0.04	-0.07*	-0.05	-0.04
Education	0.15**	0.15**	0.15**	0.14**	0.13†	0.08*
Income	0.13**	0.12†	0.13**	0.12†	0.09†	0.10*
Occupation						
Unemployed	-0.02	-0.02	-0.02	-0.03	-0.04	-0.07
Homemaker	0.02	0.02	0.02	0.03	0.02	0.02
Student	-0.07†	-0.07†	-0.08*	-0.04	-0.02	-0.02
Retired/Disabled	-0.01	-0.02	0.02	-0.10*	-0.08	-0.08
Urban	-0.06*	-0.05*	-0.04*	-0.02	-0.03	-0.04
South	0.04	0.04	0.03	-0.03	0.04	-0.02
Old-fashioned racism	(na)	(na)	(na)	(na)	(na)	(na)
Equalitarianism	—	-0.12†	-0.21**	—	-0.07*	-0.18**
Individualism	(na)	(na)	(na)	—	0.08*	0.08*
Antiblack affect	—	0.09†	0.13†	—	0.07	0.12**
Self-interest	(na)	(na)	(na)	(na)	(na)	(na)
Symbolic racism	0.44**	0.35**	—	0.48**	0.44**	—
Symbolic racism (1 item)	—	—	0.19**	—	—	0.22**
R-squared	0.24**	0.26**	0.20**	0.29**	0.31**	0.21**

*$p \leq .05$
†$p \leq .01$
**$p \leq .001$
— = variable not in model
(na) = data not available

and symbolic racism are additive. This model may mask an important interaction. The effects of symbolic racism may be particularly strong the more one agrees with the principles of old-fashioned racism. If this is true, it means that old-fashioned racism magnifies the effect of symbolic racism, and the two dimensions may not be so distinct in how they affect white policy attitudes. In analyses not presented here, models were estimated for 1986 and 1992 that were analogous to those under the heading "Model 3" in Table 3.4. For the 1992 ANES data, the individualism variable, which had no significant effect, was dropped so that we would not have to use the 1990–92 panel and would have more cases for the analysis. An interaction term was added to represent the joint effect of old-fashioned racism and symbolic racism. In the 1986 analysis, the interaction term was not statistically significant. Its direction indicated that the greater the old-fashioned racism, the less the effect of symbolic racism. In the 1992 analysis, the same pattern was discovered, and in these data the interaction term was statistically significant.

Remember that, in 1992, old-fashioned racism consists of whites' ratings of blacks as less intelligent, more violent, and lazier than whites. Specifically, the 1992 analysis indicates that the effect of symbolic racism is greatest among respondents who report no difference in their ratings of whites and blacks on these stereotypes (or who give blacks the advantage). The effect of symbolic racism is less among those who rate blacks more stereotypically, and this difference is statistically significant.

Similar analyses analogous to those in model 4 of Table 3.4 were done but with interaction terms included. As noted above, in model 4 symbolic racism has been reduced to a single item. In both the 1986 and the 1992 analyses, the interaction term of the single-item symbolic racism measure x old-fashioned racism is a statistically significant predictor of white opposition to affirmative action. Again, the effect of symbolic racism is greater when old-fashioned racism is low and less when it is high. Again, the effect of symbolic racism is strongest for those who indicate no agreement with the principles of old-fashioned racism, and there is no effect of symbolic racism for respondents who are highest on old-fashioned racism.

In summary, there is a significant interaction between old-fashioned racism and symbolic racism, but it is not in the direction that indicates that old-fashioned racism is important because it increases the impact of symbolic racism. The opposite is true. Symbolic racism has its most important effect among those who would not admit to being prejudiced.

SUMMARY OF FINDINGS

Question 1: Symbolic Racism and
Old-Fashioned Racism

Symbolic racism and old-fashioned racism appear as separate but cor-related factors in factor analyses. Although they are moderately correlat-ed, they do not function as if both variables are measuring a common underlying dimension. Regressions indicate that old-fashioned racism is a significant predictor of symbolic racism, but other attitudinal dimen-sions, when added to the equations, are also important (in the 1986 data, far more important).

When both variables are used to predict opposition to affirmative action, symbolic racism is far more important than old-fashioned racism; in fact, old-fashioned racism has no proximate effect of increasing oppo-sition to affirmative action. In the 1986 data, symbolic racism does not explain the effect of old-fashioned racism because old-fashioned racism has no effect to explain. In the 1992 data, symbolic racism explains all of the 0.17 correlation of old-fashioned racism with opposition to affirmative action.

High levels of old-fashioned racism do not magnify the impact of sym-bolic racism. The interaction analyses indicate the opposite: The effect of symbolic racism is greatest among those who report no racist beliefs on old-fashioned racism indicators.

In summary, old-fashioned racism and symbolic racism are distin-guishable but related dimensions. According to the 1992 data, old-fash-ioned racism may be one of several causal factors in symbolic racism (which is consistent with Kinder's 1986 assertion that symbolic racism is rooted in prejudice), and symbolic racism may act as an intervening vari-able, explaining the impact of old-fashioned racism on opposition to affir-mative action.

Question 2: The Definition of Symbolic Racism

Antiblack affect and individualism, the two dimensions that are pre-sumably the source of symbolic racism, are not distinguished in their abil-ity to predict symbolic racism. Individualism has a moderate impact in the 1986 data and none in the 1992 analysis (but using a different mea-sure). Antiblack affect has a weak but significant impact in both years. In addition, these two variables do not interact in predicting symbolic racism. In summary, the evidence strongly suggests that more important sources of symbolic racism are education, the abstract belief in equalitar-ianism, and, in the 1992 data, old-fashioned racism.

Question 3: Self-Interest

The measure of self-interest in this analysis, which was available only in 1986 and which combined perceived self-interest and group interest regarding affirmative action, has a substantial impact on symbolic racism. Because there are cross-sectional data, of course we cannot rule out the hypothesis that it is actually symbolic racism that has the impact on perception of self-interest. People who, for various reasons, score high on symbolic racism may come to believe that affirmative action threatens their interests. In models 1 through 3 in Table 3.4, where both symbolic racism and self-interest are used to predict opposition to affirmative action, both have a significant effect. The effect of symbolic racism is greater than that of self-interest, but both effects are of at least moderate size. In summary: Symbolic racism does not explain the effect of self-interest; there is an effect of self-interest that is independent of symbolic racism; and the effect of self-interest does not pale in comparison to that of symbolic racism in this analysis.

CONCLUSIONS

The Importance of Symbolic Racism

Symbolic racism emerges from these analyses as the most important predictor of white opposition to affirmative action. It is far more important than old-fashioned racism, antiblack affect, individualism, equalitarian ideology, and demographic variables.

The symbolic racism concept has been mired in controversy over its meaning and its origins. Indeed, the present study indicates that the theoretical grounding of symbolic racism in individualism and antiblack affect is weak. There should, however, be little controversy over its power as a predictor of white opposition to affirmative action. Although the evidence presented here indicates that there are multiple causes of white attitudes about affirmative action (see also Tuch & Hughes 1996a), findings here also suggest that symbolic racism is a principal dimension that organizes white opposition to policies designed to bring about racial equality.

P. M. Sniderman and P. E. Tetlock (1986) concluded that if symbolic racism were racism, it was old-fashioned racism. Furthermore, opposition to racial policies by whites, if not the result of old-fashioned racism, was a principled opposition based in conservative individualistic ideology, untainted by racism. Findings in this paper do not support these notions.[4]

Symbolic racism and old-fashioned racism, although related, have distinct associations with opposition to affirmative action. Although symbolic racism may explain some of the association between old-fashioned racism and opposition to affirmative action, symbolic racism is by far the more important variable and is far more than a simple reflection of old-fashioned racism. Furthermore, individualism is not a critical predictor of symbolic racism and is unrelated to white attitudes about racial policy. This latter finding replicates those in a number of other studies (Kluegel & Smith 1983; Sears, Huddy, & Shaffer 1984; Bobo & Kluegel 1993; Tuch & Hughes 1996a). In addition, the impact of symbolic racism on opposition to affirmative action is not explained, moderated, or affected by individualism.

Symbolic Racism Among People Who Are Nonprejudiced

One intriguing finding in the present study that underscores the importance of symbolic racism as a dimension distinct from old-fashioned racism is that symbolic racism has its greatest effect, not among those subscribing to old-fashioned racist principles, but among those who fully disagree with old-fashioned racism. One possible explanation of this pattern is suggested by research in social cognition (see Monteith, Zuwerink, & Devine [1994] for a review of the social cognition approach to prejudice).

In one important line of work, Devine (1989) has shown that both prejudiced and unprejudiced people are aware of, and have their responses affected by, common racial stereotypes. Because such stereotypes are internalized through a long history of socialization and have been frequently activated in the past, Devine argues that they are automatically activated in the presence of stimuli symbolizing the stereotyped group. The difference between prejudiced and unprejudiced persons is not the presence or activation of stereotypes, but the deactivation of stereotypes in a process whereby nonprejudiced persons actively counter the content of the activated stereotypes with their belief that the stereotypes are not true. The "default" response, however, is consistent with the stereotype and will influence the reactions of even nonprejudiced persons if they do not have the time, the cognitive ability, or the awareness to counter the stereotype.

M. J. Monteith and others (1994) argue that the persistence of prejudiced responses among those who are low in prejudice occurs "because many low-prejudiced people have not progressed far enough in the prejudice reduction process in order to be efficient and effective at generating non-prejudiced responses that are consistent with their non-prejudiced beliefs" (p. 335). Similarly, perhaps some nonprejudiced persons do not regard symbolic racism attitudes as reflective of racial stereotypes. It is possible, therefore, that the stereotypes of blacks as welfare dependent, as undeserving but desiring special favors, and as no longer impeded by racial inequality are simply not deactivated by large numbers of nonprejudiced people, and these stereotypes remain the basis for white responses to racial policies. If so, educational programs that emphasize the structured nature of racial inequality and the persistence of discrimination and its effects could have some positive impact on this process.

Another interpretation is suggested in the work of Irwin Katz and his colleagues (Katz & Glass 1979; Katz, Wackenhut, & Hass 1986). Katz argues that whites may have both positive and negative attitudes about blacks and that such ambivalence leads to amplified positive and negative responses. Perhaps the interaction between symbolic racism and old-fashioned racism noted above reflects an amplified negative reaction of ambivalent (that is, high symbolic racism, low old-fashioned racism) whites to affirmative action policy. If so, perhaps educational programs designed to resolve ambivalence by promoting attitudinal consistency in line with individuals' established egalitarian beliefs would promote more white support for egalitarian racial policies.

Individualism and Antiblack Affect

Although the findings in the present paper give me no reason to dispute the original idea of Kinder, Sears, and McConahay that symbolic racism is a new ideology that is critical in understanding whites' contemporary racial policy attitudes, their original formulation of symbolic racism as a blend of antiblack affect learned in childhood and the traditional U.S. values embedded in the Protestant ethic receives little support in the present analysis. Other variables emerged as much more important. This soft spot in symbolic racism theory seems to have been acknowledged by Kinder (1986), who dropped antiblack affect from his discussion in favor of the term "racial prejudice" and by Sears (1988), who, citing evidence that individualism might not be relevant to symbolic racism, concluded that, if correct, this evidence would cause us to alter our view of symbolic racism. I agree and suggest in the final paragraphs how our view of symbolic racism might be changed.

Self-Interest

The finding that self-interest regarding affirmative action significantly predicts opposition to affirmative action strikes at the heart of the symbolic racism approach; however, several caveats are in order. First, this result occurred in only one data set, the measure being unavailable in the other. Second, the measure combines self-interests and group interests and thus closely approximates "self-oriented group-consciousness," which Sears and Kinder (1985) and Sears and Funk (1991) have acknowledged may strongly influence white racial policy attitudes. Third, the questions about self-interest refer specifically to affirmative action policy, reflecting a narrow interest in affirmative action that should increase the likelihood that interests would have an effect (Sears & Funk 1991).

So, perhaps narrowly defined self-oriented group interest has a modest impact on racial policy attitudes, independent of symbolic racism. As the next section explains, however, the importance of group interests and group conflict may be greater than this conclusion implies.

Thinking about Symbolic Racism in a New Way

The main question that now remains unanswered is why symbolic racism is such an important determinant of white opposition to affirmative action. If the answer is not that the roots of symbolic racism are in individualism and antiblack affect, what is it?

In Chapter 2 of this volume, Bobo, Kluegel, and Smith remind us of the usefulness of Blumer's definition of racial prejudice as something that "exists basically in a sense of a group position rather than in a set of feelings," as a "way in which the identified groups are conceived in relation to each other" (Blumer 1958, p. 3). The source of prejudice is located in social structure. Prejudice is a way people have of describing, justifying, and understanding their structural relations with people in other groups that emerge from those structural relations. If this is true, the content of racial prejudice should reflect the nature of the relations between groups. As the nature of group relations changes, then the content of prejudice should change. If groups become equal and boundaries dissolve, prejudice should disappear.

The nature of whites' and blacks' group positions in the United States 50 years ago was quite different than it is today, dominated by de jure segregation in the South and fully separate social institutions throughout the country. Today, de jure segregation is gone, barriers to full participation by blacks are falling, and blacks are slowly moving into the mainstream.

Given these structural changes, the nature of racial prejudice should have changed, and beliefs in inherent racial inequality — which justify structural segregation and can be sustained by low rates of interracial exposure and interaction — should decline. At the same time, as blacks continue to be integrated into mainstream institutions, threatening whites' claim to status and privilege, it is not surprising that new racial attitudes would emerge reflecting the nature of this threat.

Survey items that measure symbolic racism clearly reflect subjective states associated with status anxiety and status defense. Items inquire about whether the respondent believes that blacks violate the Protestant ethic (that is, individualism and the values of hard work and self-sufficiency) and are getting attention and rewards from the government that they do not deserve. Affirmative responses by whites to these items imply that whites are working hard, are conforming to traditional values, and risk losing out to those who are getting a "free ride." Thus, symbolic racism represents a status and life style defense, and appears to link the symbolic politics of Kinder and Sears and the status politics in the work of Joseph Gusfield.

Gusfield argued in his *Symbolic Crusade* (1963) that the nineteenth- and early twentieth-century temperance crusaders were drawn from the old Protestant middle class and were primarily motivated by a need to defend their status and lifestyle from social changes brought about by industrialization (the focus of much of their wrath being Catholic immigrants). Similarly, the ideology represented by symbolic racism is a defense of the white middle class lifestyle and status from the threat posed by the structural changes that would accompany actual racial equality.

In short, symbolic racism may, in itself, constitute self-oriented group interest in the sense of status defense (Bobo 1983). If hard work and self-reliance are symbols that whites use to define their status position and if whites believe that blacks can attain a similar status (that is, get special favors and benefits) when they do not deserve it, then whites may believe that their status has been devalued and express this sense or fear of devaluation as symbolic racism.

Symbolic racism researchers may be correct in arguing that the critical issues are not really busing, affirmative action, welfare, or black political candidates. The critical issue, however, is also not moral resentment and irrational antagonism: The issue represented by symbolic racism is status and power and whites' fear of losing them.

What Can Be Done?

A final question concerns what would increase white support for racial change. If symbolic racism, the strongest predictor of opposition to affirmative action, represents whites' sense of the tenuousness of their privileged position vis-à-vis blacks, this will be a difficult task. Education about the nature of racial discrimination and structured racial inequality may lead to modest gains. If, for example, whites come to believe that the stereotype of blacks as being dependent on welfare is as racist as the stereotype of blacks as inherently unintelligent, then there may be some change. However, old-fashioned racism declined primarily because the structure of society changed, then, perhaps symbolic racism will decline only as we approach actual racial equality. Thus, if what we really want is racial equality, we should try to directly change the structure of the society and let attitudes follow.

NOTES

Thanks to Jill Kiecolt and Steven Tuch for very helpful comments on a previous draft of this chapter.

1. Actually, Kinder (1986) has conceded that it was a mistake to conclude that old-fashioned racism was no longer important. This new understanding is apparently what stands behind his dropping of antiblack affect in favor of racial prejudice.

2. These data were made available by the Inter-University Consortium for Political and Social Research. Data for the ANES were originally collected by the Center for Political Studies of the Institute for Social Research, University of Michigan. The 1986 and 1988 studies were directed by Warren E. Miller. The 1990 and 1992 studies were directed by Warren E. Miller, Donald R. Kinder, and Steven J. Rosenstone. Neither the original collectors of the data nor the Consortium bears any responsibility for the analyses or interpretations presented here.

3. The other five items that I did not use each asked the respondent which of two statements came closer to their own opinion:

1. One, it is better to fit in with people around you; or two, it is better to conduct yourself according to your own standards, even if that makes you stand out.

2. One, people should take care of themselves and their families and let others do the same; or two, people should care less about their own success and more about the needs of society.

3. One, it is more important to be a cooperative person who works well with others; or two, it is more important to be a self-reliant person able to take care of oneself.

4. When raising children, which is more important: One, to encourage them to be independent-minded and think for themselves; or two, to teach them obedience and respect for authorities?

5. One, most poor people are poor because they don't work hard enough; or two, they are poor because of circumstances beyond their control?

I did analyses analogous to those presented in Tables 3.2 and 3.4 but that included these other five individualism items in various combinations. These analyses did not indicate that these other five items were better predictors than the three-item index used or that they were more theoretically relevant.

4. One thing that the analyses presented in this chapter do not contradict is the claim that symbolic racism is, in itself, not racism. This issue goes beyond the scope of this chapter. I refer interested readers to the original statements of Kinder and Sears (1981) and McConahay (1982) and to the responses of Kinder (1986) and Sears (1988) to critics. The present study rests on the assumption that the attitudes tapped by the kind of symbolic racism index used here do constitute racial prejudice — that is, that symbolic racism is a form of what is commonly referred to as racism.

4

The Affective Component of Prejudice: Empirical Support for the New View

Thomas F. Pettigrew

Social psychology's approach to prejudice has traditionally stressed both affect and cognition. Thus, G. W. Allport (1954, p. 9), in *The Nature of Prejudice*, made both essential components of his definition: "Ethnic prejudice is an antipathy based upon a faulty and inflexible generalization."

Yet until recently, the study of this critical intergroup phenomenon over past decades has focused almost exclusively on the cognitive component of prejudice. We now know far more about stereotypes, causal misattributions, and other natural cognitive processes that relate to prejudice than when Allport penned his classic in the early 1950s. These have been major advances; without detracting from their significance, however, it is now clear that this near-exclusive focus on cognition led to a distorted view of prejudice, unbalanced by its neglect of affect.

In recent years, the overdue correction has begun. Two seminal volumes on stereotypes, both edited by David Hamilton, highlight the dramatic shift. In *Cognitive Processes in Stereotyping and Intergroup Behavior* (Hamilton, 1981), the "push-cognitive-explanations-to-the-max" strategy was still in full force. Affect receives brief mention, motivation a bit more, and mood and emotion are not even in the index.

In sharp contrast, the volume *Affect, Cognition and Stereotyping: Interactive Processes in Group Perception* edited by Dianne Mackie and D. L. Hamilton (1993) centers on the topic. Intergroup relations specialists, like me, are far more comfortable with this new view because it is more congruent with our nonexperimental data on prejudice and group conflict. In this brief chapter, I will offer empirical support for the intriguing contentions advanced by those who now stress affect as a critical component of intergroup attitudes.

Abelson and his colleagues (Abelson, Kinder, Peters, & Fiske, 1982) pointed the way. Using survey data, they noted that positive and negative feelings toward politicians are virtually independent of each other. They also found these affect reports are less semantically filtered and less subject to consistency pressures than trait judgments. Moreover, summary feelings scores strongly predicted political preferences. This striking effect was independent of and more robust than that of trait judgments.

More recent research supports this special character of affect-based attitudes. For example, K. Edwards and W. von Hippel (1995), working with a person perception paradigm, found affect-based attitudes are more effectively altered by affective persuasion appeals. Moreover, subjects express these attitudes with greater confidence than cognitive-based attitudes.

Studies using prejudice as the dependent variable replicate these findings. M. P. Zanna and his colleagues (Zanna, Haddock, & Esses, 1990; Esses, Haddock, & Zanna, 1993) find that subjects' reports of emotions experienced during intergroup encounters relate to attitudes toward minorities. Similarly, A.J.M. Dijker (1987), interviewing respondents on the streets of Amsterdam, obtains strong relationships between specific affective states experienced during intergroup contact and attitudes toward minorities. Dijker also notes that the conditions of the intergroup contact shape the affective responses — as Allport (1954) predicted. Finally, C. Stangor, L. A. Sullivan, and T. E. Ford (1991) compare the predictive value of emotional responses with that of stereotypical beliefs. For a range of groups, the emotional indicators prove stronger and more consistent predictors of both intergroup attitudes and social distance.

Eliot Smith (1993), in his compelling chapter in the Mackie-Hamilton volume, takes the next step. He combines insights from both self-categorization theory (Turner, Hogg, Oakes, & Reicher, 1987) and appraisal theories of emotion (Roseman, 1984; Frijda, 1986; Frijda, Kuipers, & ter Schure, 1989; Scherer, 1988) to outline a fresh approach to intergroup prejudice. He defines prejudice as "a social emotion experienced with respect to one's social identity as a group member, with an outgroup as a target" (p. 304).

Smith's approach accounts for phenomena firmly established in the intergroup literature: the situational and emotional specificity of prejudice and the greater importance of a group than an individual focus in prejudice. Using results from two different, rich data sources, this chapter adds further evidence for these revived emphases.

AFFECT AND GROUP RELATIVE DEPRIVATION

First, from a meta-analysis of relative deprivation research (Smith, Pettigrew, & Vega, 1996), we see the critical role of affect in the relationship between relative deprivation and prejudice. Figure 4.1 shows the effect sizes reported by 15 studies that used 24 independent samples and 280 tests of the link between relative deprivation and dependent variables involving prejudice, discrimination, nationalism, and the like. When only a cognitive index measures relative deprivation, statistically significant but small effects occur. When affect is also involved, however, substantial effects arise — as Smith predicts.[1] Two points specify this effect further. First, we find far greater effects of relative deprivation measures with affective components in the meta-analysis for a wide range of dependent variables — not just those involving prejudice. Second, the cognitive-affective differences shown in the histogram are even larger for those tests with high-quality measures of relative deprivation (that is, multiple items): $d = 0.093$ for cognitive measures versus 0.432 for those with both cognitive and affective components. Hence, important effects of relative deprivation require an affective reaction, not just the perception of differences.

In addition, group-level comparisons are critical for the effect sizes between relative deprivation and prejudice. In Figure 4.2, we see for both cognitive only and affective measures of relative deprivation that the effects are significantly larger for ingroup-outgroup comparisons than for

FIGURE 4.1
Affect as Relative Deprivation Component of Prejudice
(15 Studies, 24 Samples, 280 Tests)

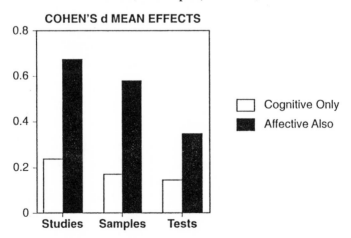

FIGURE 4.2
Group Comparisons Are Critical
(Tests only — 237)

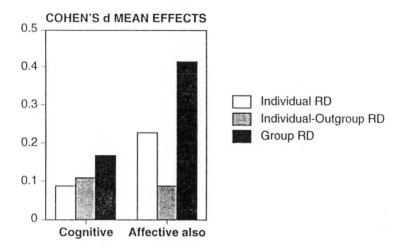

COHEN'S d MEAN EFFECTS

Individual RD
Individual-Outgroup RD
Group RD

Cognitive   Affective also

comparisons that involve the individual. By far, the largest effect is for group-relative deprivation that involves affect — again, as Smith's model predicts.

THE POWER OF INTERGROUP FRIENDSHIP

To test this newest "new look" further, we consider data from seven probability surveys conducted during 1988 in France, the Netherlands, Great Britain, and then-West Germany (Pettigrew & Meertens, 1995; Pettigrew, 1997). We removed minority respondents from the data.

Turkish immigrants serve as the target outgroup for the West German sample. Otherwise, the study drew two separate samples in each country so two minorities could serve as target outgroups. In France, one sample focused on North Africans, one on Asians. In Great Britain, one focused on West Indians, one on Pakistanis and Indians. In the Netherlands, one focused on Surinamers, one on Turks.

We developed 10-item Likert scales to measure blatant and subtle prejudice. Table 4.1 shows the scales in their English form. We used standard Likert-scale scoring. Thus, item responses were scored 1, 2, 4, and 5 on a strongly disagree, somewhat disagree, somewhat agree, and strongly agree dimension, with higher scores indicating greater prejudice. Five items were reversals in which disagreement was scored in the prejudiced direction (items 2, 3, and 4 of the intimacy subscale and the two items of the affective prejudice subscale). We assigned "don't know" responses

TABLE 4.1
The Blatant and Subtle Prejudice Scales and Their Five Subscales

---

Threat and Rejection Factor Items: The Blatant Scale

1. West Indians have jobs that the British should have.
   (strongly agree to strongly disagree)

2. Most West Indians living here who receive support from welfare could get along without it if they tried.
   (strongly agree to strongly disagree)

3. British people and West Indians can never be really comfortable with each other, even if they are close friends.
   (strongly agree to strongly disagree)

4. Most politicians in Britain care too much about West Indians and not enough about the average British person.
   (strongly agree to strongly disagree)

5. West Indians come from less able races and this explains why they are not as well off as most British people.
   (strongly agree to strongly disagree)

6. How different or similar do you think West Indians living here are to other British people like yourself — in how honest they are?
   (very different, somewhat different, somewhat similar, or very similar)

Intimacy Factor Items: The Blatant Scale

1. Suppose that a child of yours had children with a person of very different color and physical characteristics than your own. Do you think you would be very bothered, bothered, bothered a little, or not bothered at all, if your grandchildren did not physically resemble the people on your side of the family?

2. I would be willing to have sexual relationships with a West Indian.
   (strongly agree to strongly disagree) (Reversed scoring)

3. I would not mind if a suitably qualified West Indian person was appointed my boss.
   (strongly agree to strongly disagree) (Reversed scoring)

4. I would not mind if a West Indian person who had a similar economic background as mine joined my close family by marriage.
   (strongly agree to strongly disagree) (Reversed scoring)

Traditional Values Factor Items: Subtle Scale

1. West Indians living here should not push themselves where they are not wanted.
   (strongly agree to strongly disagree)

2. Many other groups have come to Britain and overcome prejudice and worked their way up. West Indians should do the same without special favor.
   (strongly agree to strongly disagree)

3. It is just a matter of some people not trying hard enough. If West Indians would only try harder they could be as well off as British people.
    (strongly agree to strongly disagree)

4. West Indians living here teach their children values and skills different from those required to be successful in Britain.
    (strongly agree to strongly disagree)

Cultural Differences Factor Items: Subtle Scale

How different or similar do you think West Indians living here are to other British people like yourself . . . (very different, somewhat different, somewhat similar, or very similar)

1. in the values that they teach their children?

2. in their religious beliefs and practices?

3. in their sexual values or sexual practices?

4. in the language that they speak?

Affective Prejudice Items: Subtle Scale

Have you ever felt the following ways about West Indians and their families living here? (very often, fairly often, not too often, or never)

1. How often have you felt sympathy for West Indians and their families living here?
    (Reversed scoring)

2. How often have you felt admiration for West Indians living here?
    (Reversed scoring)

the individual's mean on those scale questions answered. This procedure was used only for those answering at least four of the scale's ten questions. Removing respondents with fewer than four answers to the blatant or subtle scales resulted in sample losses of less than 3 percent.

From a pool of more than 50 separate items, we chose 10 items to measure each type on the basis of our conceptualization of the two forms and factor analyses. Using principle components analyses, exploratory factor analyses yielded remarkably similar results across the seven samples. For the blatant prejudice scale, two primary factors emerged after varimax rotation in each sample (eigenvalues > 0.98): the four intimacy items and the six threat and rejection items listed in Table 4.1. A weaker third factor also appeared in each analysis (eigenvalues between 0.79 and 1.09) and centered on the honesty question (item 6 of the threat and rejection factor). Together these factors explained from 54 percent to 62 percent of the variance across the samples.

For the subtle prejudice scale, three primary orthogonal factors emerged after varimax rotation in each sample (eigenvalues > 1): four traditional values items, four cultural differences items, and two affective prejudice items, as listed in Table 4.1. Together these factors explained from 49 percent to 56 percent of the variance of each of the samples.

The median alphas for these two main scales and their five subscales across the seven samples reach either adequate or marginal levels: blatant (median alpha = 0.90), subtle (0.77), threat and rejection (0.77), intimacy (0.81), traditional values (0.63), cultural differences (0.66), and affective prejudice (0.67). (For further psychometric details on these scales, see Pettigrew and Meertens [1995]).

Following self-categorization theory, Smith maintains that identification with the ingroup is the central locus of a person's prejudice against outgroups. The European surveys include an item that asks how proud the respondent is to be British, Dutch, French, or German. Figure 4.3 indicates that national pride relates to prejudice subscales with or without controls for four variables that covary with pride and prejudice (age, city size, education, and political conservatism). Using this as an indicator of national identity, Smith's prediction is confirmed — especially for the threat and rejection, intimacy, and traditional values indicators of prejudice.

Turning to intergroup contact (Pettigrew, 1997), these surveys also asked whether the respondents had any friends of a different culture, nationality, race, religion, or social class. As shown in Figure 4.4, this measure relates strongly and negatively with the five prejudice subscales with

FIGURE 4.3
Ingroup Pride and Prejudice
(Mean effects: Seven Samples, N = 3,806)

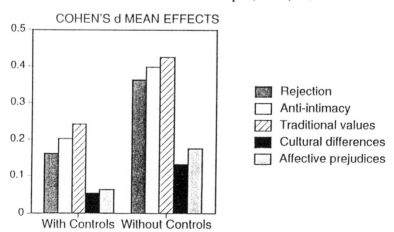

Controls: Education, Age, City Size, Conservatism

FIGURE 4.4
Intergroup Friendship and Prejudice
(Mean Effects: Seven Samples, N = 3,806)

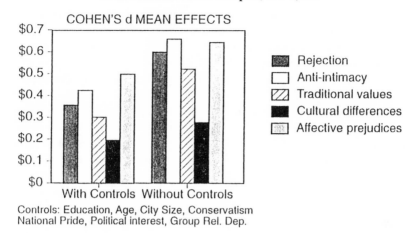

COHEN'S d MEAN EFFECTS

Rejection
Anti-intimacy
Traditional values
Cultural differences
Affective prejudices

With Controls Without Controls

Controls: Education, Age, City Size, Conservatism
National Pride, Political interest, Group Rel. Dep.

or without seven covarying controls (age, city size, conservatism, education, group relative deprivation, national pride, and political interest). Note that intergroup friendship relates most strongly with the two most affect-laden subscales of prejudice — opposition to intimacy with the outgroup and affective prejudice.

Inspired by the work of Dijker (1987) and J. F. Dovidio, J. Mann, and S. L. Gaertner (1989), the affective prejudice measure has high scorers who report never having experienced either sympathy or admiration for the outgroup. Even with seven controls, this measure relates strongly with intergroup friendship. This result, however, immediately raises the causal sequence question that plagues all cross-sectional studies of intergroup contact: Does intergroup friendship reduce prejudice? Or is it that the prejudiced avoid, and the unprejudiced seek, intergroup friends?

A simple nonrecursive model using the 3,806 respondents from all 7 samples provides maximum likelihood estimates. Figure 4.5 shows the standardized path coefficients among three latent variables: mixed neighborhood (with different cultures, races, and religions), intergroup friends (from different social classes, cultures, nationalities, races, and religions), and affective prejudice (no reported sympathy or admiration). Mixed neighborhoods increase the chance of having intergroup friends but do not relate with affective prejudice. The two coefficients between intergroup friends and affective prejudice are both significant; however, the friends-reducing-prejudice coefficient is larger than that of the selection bias of the prejudiced avoiding intergroup friends.[2]

To explore this difference between these two coefficients further, we compare this basic model with three competing models: one with the two coefficients equal in strength; one with only the friends-to-reduced-prejudice path; and the last with only the prejudice-to-fewer-intergroup-friends path. Although all four obtain adequate comparative fit indices, Table 4.2 shows that the basic model with a stronger friends-to-less-prejudice path is significantly better than the others. The next best model contains only the friends-to-reduced-prejudice path; the poorest model has only the prejudice-to-fewer-intergroup-friends path. So, while the selection bias of who has intergroup friends does operate, the power of intergroup friendship to reduce prejudice, especially affective prejudice, remains the stronger phenomenon.

TABLE 4.2
Comparisons of Friends — Affective Prejudice Models

	Chi-Square	df	Diff.	p	Comp. Fit
Basic model	846.25	32	—	—	0.948
With equality constraints	856.48	33	10.23	< .002	0.947
Only friends-prejudice path	852.19	33	5.94	< .02	0.947
Only prejudice-friends path	859.91	33	13.66	< .001	0.947

More surprising, given social cognition theory, is the generalization of this effect to policy preferences and other groups not directly involved in the initial contact. Figure 4.6 shows the effect sizes across the seven samples between intergroup friendship and attitudes concerning immigration policy. With the same seven controls, intergroup friendship consistently relates with more favorable immigration attitudes — immigration is a good thing, all immigrants should be allowed to stay, immigration rights should be extended, and citizenship should be made easier. Note that these attitudes apply to immigrants of all groups, not just those represented among one's friends.

Figure 4.7 reveals that mean intergroup friendship effects extend to a wide variety of groups, from Arabs and Turks to Jews and southern Europeans. Inspection of the effect sizes for individual samples further supports the conclusion that these data reflect wide generalization of reduced prejudice across groups. Turks, for example, are a major minority in Germany and the Netherlands but not in France and Great Britain. In the latter two countries, then, it is highly unlikely that respondents would have

FIGURE 4.5
Affective Prejudice Model
(Standardized Paths: Total Sample, N = 3,806)

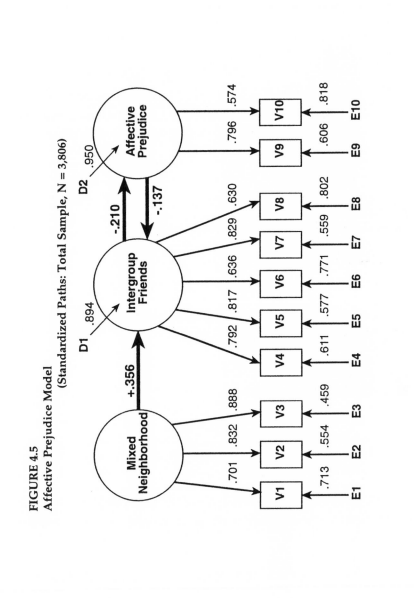

FIGURE 4.6
Intergroup Friendship and Immigration Policy Preferences
(Mean Effects: 7 Samples, 7 Controls)

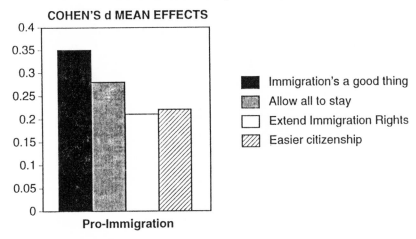

friendships with Turks. Yet the mean effect for the four French and British samples on ratings of Turks is identical to that of the three German and Dutch samples. North Africans are not as significant a group in Germany and Great Britain as they are in France and the Netherlands, but the mean

FIGURE 4.7
Intergroup Friendship and Outgroup Ratings
(Mean Effects: 7 Samples, 7 Controls)

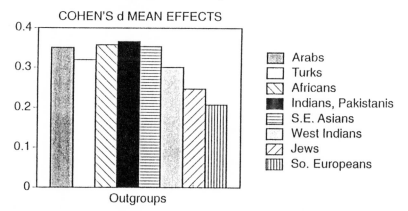

effects of these two sets of samples are also the same. Similarly, black Africans are far less common in Germany and the Netherlands than in Britain and France; however, the mean effects of these two sets are also the same.

We must consider two plausible alternative explanations for these results. First, all the outgroup ratings use the same 0-to-100 favorability rating format, so a strong response set could be involved; however, this possibility is unlikely for three reasons.

First, we just saw that similar effects occur for immigration attitudes, all four items of which use contrasting response formats.

Second, we constructed a measure of such a bias from three other questions that use the same 0-to-100 rating format. When we control for this independent measure of response set in the group ratings, the results shown in Figure 4.7 are virtually unchanged.

Third, when factor analyzed, the favorability ratings divide into two clear, orthogonal factors: one for those of non-European origin, the other for Europeans. The generalization effects apply to groups in both factors. This is a highly unlikely outcome if a strong response set were operating.

More fundamentally, the selection bias of the tolerant seeking and the prejudiced avoiding intergroup friends discussed earlier could be an explanation. Figure 4.8 provides the same basic nonrecursive model to test this possibility. This time we use the ratings of Arabs and Asians to measure the latent dependent factor of generalized prejudice.[3] Again, both the maximum likelihood estimates of the standardized path coefficients of interest are significant. Furthermore, the friends-to-prejudice standardized coefficient is larger than that of the prejudice-to-friends coefficient.

Table 4.3 compares the same four models as discussed previously. All four attain adequate comparative fit indices, yet the basic model is superior, rivaled only by the recursive model with just the friends-to-prejudice path. Thus, the selection process of prejudiced people avoiding intergroup friends emerges once more; however, it does not explain the generalization effects of intergroup friendships to new groups.

TABLE 4.3

Comparisons of Friends — Generalized Prejudice Models

	Chi-Square	df	Diff.	p	Comp. Fit
Basic model	856.59	32	—	—	0.952
With equality constraints	865.61	33	10.02	< .005	0.951
Only friends-prejudice path	864.33	33	7.74	< .01	0.951
Only prejudice-friends path	868.41	33	11.82	< .001	0.951

FIGURE 4.8
Generalized Prejudice Model
(Standardized Paths; Total Sample, N = 3,806)

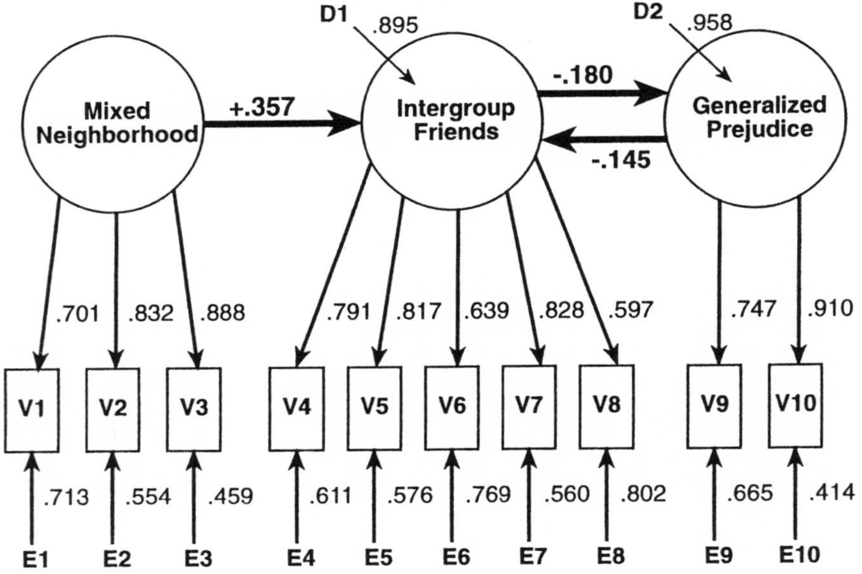

A FINAL WORD

To conclude, these results support the critical importance of affect in intergroup prejudice in general and Eliot Smith's new approach in particular. Furthermore, the wide generalization of positive feelings emanating from intergroup friendship challenges the current wisdom based exclusively on cognitive considerations.

Social psychology's overemphasis on cognitive factors focused on the problematic side of intergroup relations. Like other social sciences, the discipline concentrated on conflict. From a cognitive stance, we learned the natural human bases for prejudice and stereotypes, their appearance even in minimal situations, and their relative imperviousness to change.

I submit that these insights gleaned over the past generation are not wrong, just incomplete. Again, like other social sciences, social psychology has difficulty in explaining intergroup harmony, fair treatment, and tolerance (Pettigrew, 1991). Beyond the media headlines of bitter intergroup strife, however, most groups throughout the world actually live in relative peace. To be sure, some degree of prejudice and negative stereotypes prevails universally, but so does some degree of intergroup harmony and acceptance.

The reassertion of emotion into the study of prejudice represents a more comprehensive approach, one capable of explaining both the positive and negative extremes of intergroup relations. When strong emotions act as a catalyst, magnifying intergroup processes, the new approach may well explain the extremes — from the relative tolerance of the Dutch to the current butchery in Bosnia Herzegovina.

NOTES

This research is part of a larger project by the Working Group on International Perspectives on Race and Ethnic Relations. My project colleagues are James Jackson of the University of Michigan, Gerard Lemaine of l'Ecole des Hautes Etudes en Sciences Sociales, Roel Meertens of the Universiteit van Amsterdam, Ulrich Wagner of Marburg Universitat, and Andreas Zick of the Bergische Universitat, Wuppertal. I am deeply grateful for their help and intellectual stimulation.

1.   Cohen's d statistic, used in Figures 4.1–4.7, is a measure of effect size. Effect sizes assess differences largely independent of the size of the sample studied (significance test = effect size + sample size). More specifically, Cohen's d is the difference between the group means being compared given in standard score units, or z-scores. It is roughly twice the size of r ($d = 2r$ / square root of $1 - r^2$) (Rosenthal, 1991, pp. 16–20).

2.   A more elaborate, 12-variable model that uses five mixed neighborhoods variables yields the same conclusion as the 10-variable model shown here for simplicity.

3.   Again, a more elaborate, 18-variable model that uses five mixed neighborhoods and all eight generalized prejudice variables yields the same conclusion
as the 10-variable model shown here for simplicity.

III

SOCIODEMOGRAPHIC ATTRIBUTES AND THE RACIAL ATTITUDES OF WHITES

5

Status, Ideology, and Dimensions of Whites' Racial Beliefs and Attitudes: Progress and Stagnation

Lawrence Bobo and James R. Kluegel

For much of the past five decades, research on white attitudes toward blacks has focused on what is now often called traditional prejudice — or more appropriately, Jim Crow racism — involving open bigotry and support of legal and normative racial segregation and belief in the innate inferiority of blacks (Pettigrew 1982). When baseline national sample surveys were conducted in the 1940s, majorities of white Americans openly supported segregation and discrimination, believing that blacks were their innate inferiors (Hyman & Sheatsley 1956). The better educated held more positive attitudes. Those living outside the South, where more tolerant racial norms prevailed and where blacks were typically a smaller fraction of the population (Fossett & Kiecolt 1989), also held more positive attitudes. Younger people, especially the better educated among them, exhibited more tolerant outlooks.

This once openly racist pattern of belief has yielded over time to an increasingly egalitarian view (Smith & Sheatsley 1984). Most whites now endorse integration in principle and reject discrimination, preferring instead equal treatment regardless of race. Most whites also deny that blacks are innately inferior to whites (Schuman, Steeh, & Bobo 1985). The young, the better educated, and those living outside the South led the way on these changes.

Overall, this change represents a large and rapid societal shift, reflecting both change at the individual level and continued cohort replacement effects (Firebaugh & Davis 1988). Over the past three decades, a decline in traditional prejudice has resulted from people coming to reject Jim Crow attitudes they once held and from demographic change as older, more prejudiced people are replaced by younger, less prejudiced ones. Substantively, this positive trend has been read as a major normative transformation (Schuman, Steeh, & Bobo 1985). As R. A. Blauner explained, "The belief in a right to dignity and fair treatment is now so widespread and deeply rooted, so self-evident that people of all colors would vigorously resist any effort to reinstate formalized discrimination" (1989, p. 317). These patterns suggest that we are witnessing the steady decline of racial prejudice as classically understood.

Less sanguine, however, has been the relatively low and slowly changing levels of white support for any of a number of policies aimed at bringing about greater integration and equality (Jackman 1978). Surveys show widespread white opposition to school busing for desegregation (Sears, Hensler, & Speer 1979), to open housing laws (Schuman & Bobo 1988), and to strong affirmative action plans (Jacobson 1985; Kinder & Sanders 1987; Kluegel & Smith 1983; Lipset & Schneider 1978; Tuch & Hughes 1996a). Black candidates for political office also frequently encounter prejudice (Kinder & Sears 1981; Pettigrew 1972; Citrin, Green, & Sears 1990). To these attitudinal results we may add evidence of racial discrimination in access to housing and jobs that also casts doubt on the meaning of the decline in traditional prejudice (Jaynes & Williams 1989). These negative trends question whether factors that have brought about change in traditional antiblack prejudice affect other aspects of white attitudes about blacks as strongly or even at all.

How are we to best understand this pattern of progress and stagnation? In Chapter 2 of this volume, Bobo, Kluegel, and Smith propose that we can best understand this pattern in terms of a transition from Jim Crow racism to laissez-faire racism. In this chapter, we present a partial test of this thesis by examining the effects of sociodemographic status and socioeconomic ideology on indicators of Jim Crow and laissez-faire racism.

THEORY AND HYPOTHESES

Theory

Because the laissez-faire racism thesis is elaborated in Chapter 2, we will not present a detailed exegesis here; however, we think it useful to briefly summarize the thesis to provide context for the hypotheses we develop subsequently.

The laissez-faire racism thesis begins by asserting that racial beliefs and attitudes are best understood within the history of the economics and politics of race in the United States. Jim Crow racism, according to Bobo and colleagues, has its roots in the post–Civil War South and in the actions of the Southern planter elite. As structural changes in the U.S. economy reduced the importance of the Jim Crow system of black agriculture to the economy, the opportunity for an attack on Jim Crow ideology developed. The civil rights movement capitalized on this opportunity; through difficult struggle and sustained collective action, it achieved the political defeat of Jim Crow racism.

As Jim Crow racism lost its embeddedness in U.S. economic and political institutions, its ideological tenets increasingly came to be seen as inconsistent with U.S. values. Accordingly, support for Jim Crow items on national surveys progressively declined through the 1960s and 1970s. The large economic gap between whites and African Americans, however, persists.

Building upon H. Blumer's (1958) analysis of prejudice as reflecting the sense of relative group position in the United States, this thesis argues that a new form of racial ideology, laissez-faire racism, has emerged to defend white privilege. Laissez-faire racism encompasses an ideology that blames blacks themselves for their poorer relative economic standing, seeing it as a function of perceived cultural inferiority. This analysis of the bases of laissez-faire racism underscores two central components: contemporary stereotypes of blacks held by whites, and the denial of societal (structural) responsibility for the conditions in black communities.

In developing this thesis, Bobo and colleagues principally call upon "macro" data, or the aggregate, historical record of change and stagnation in racial beliefs and attitudes. This thesis, however, also has implications that may be tested through analyses of individual-level, or "micro," data. In particular, we may derive hypotheses from it about how sociodemographic characteristics and socioeconomic ideology affect indicators of Jim Crow and laissez-faire racism and how these forms of racism affect attitudes toward racial policy. Below we present and develop the reasoning for four such hypotheses.

Hypotheses

Hypothesis 1: Attitudinal and Belief Indicators of Jim Crow Racism, on the One Hand, and Contemporary Stereotyping and Perceived Social Responsibility for Black Conditions, on the Other Hand, Will Define at Least Two Separate Factors

Hypothesis 1 follows from the thesis that laissez-faire racism is a form of racial ideology distinct from Jim Crow racism. In other words, racial beliefs and attitudes are not the product of a single prejudice-like disposition toward blacks, but reflect forces from different eras in U.S. race relations. At the minimum, we expect to find a separate factor for Jim Crow racism items differentiated from a second factor underlaying the set of items used to measure laissez-faire racism; however, we also expect to find separate factors for stereotypes and perceived societal responsibility for blacks' conditions. As we have argued elsewhere (Kluegel & Bobo 1993), there is no logical reason to expect that denying individual blame alone — in this case, rejecting negative stereotypes of blacks — is sufficient to lead to endorsing social or structural causes of blacks' conditions. Indeed, W. Ryan (1976) notes that not only are people comfortable with denying individual blame without accepting structural explanations but also there may be a strong motivation to do so. Denying individual blame permits one to believe that he or she is racially sensitive and, in essence, is costless. Accepting structural explanations, on the other hand, may question the justice of one's own privilege and has potential costs if structural change is implemented.

Hypothesis 2: Sociodemographic Factors, Especially Age and Education, More Strongly Affect Jim Crow Racism than They Affect Stereotyping and Perceived Discrimination

Hypothesis 2 follows from the decline in the economic importance of Jim Crow racism. This decline was part of a long-term historical process of change that affected both prevailing modes of social organization and patterns of belief. Younger generations have been socialized in an era when Jim Crow racism no longer serves white privilege, as well as in a time when Jim Crow racism is considered inconsistent with U.S. values — or at least socially unacceptable. More highly educated persons are exposed more directly to the idea that Jim Crow racism is unacceptable (Jackman & Muha, 1984). On the other hand, because expressions of contemporary stereotypes and the denial of social responsibility for blacks' conditions are more clearly perceived to support white privilege, we expect to find that they are more broadly or consensually held across different sociodemographic groups.

Hypothesis 3: Socioeconomic Ideology More Strongly Affects Stereotyping and Perceived Discrimination than It Affects Jim Crow Racism

Hypothesis 3 also follows from the decline in the economic importance of distinctly Southern Jim Crow racism and the solidification of a U.S. national pattern of racial inequality that did not place an explicit premium on a racial division of labor. If Jim Crow racism is no longer seen to serve the defense of economic privilege, then there is no reason to expect that beliefs that justify the stratification order in general will affect it. If elements of laissez-faire racism are seen as defending white economic privilege, then justifications of economic inequality in general should motivate stereotyping and the denial of social responsibility for blacks' conditions — that is, people who see the stratification order in general as fair will be motivated to hold beliefs denying that blacks, as a specific case, are treated unfairly.

Hypothesis 4: Jim Crow Racism and Laissez-Faire Racism Each Affect Support for Policy to Improve Blacks' Economic Status, but Laissez-Faire Racism Plays a Stronger and More Persistent Role Over Time

Hypothesis 4 incorporates the explanation of the "principle-implementation gap" found in the laissez-faire racism argument. There is strong logical and empirical reason (Kluegel 1990) to expect that both Jim Crow and laissez-faire racism promote opposition to policy to improve blacks' economic status. The perceived biological inferiority of Jim Crow racism and the perceived cultural inferiority of laissez-faire racism both predispose the view that blacks are undeserving of help. Denying that there are social causes of blacks' economic conditions encourages opposition to policy to further racial equality on the grounds that such policy is not needed (Katz & Hass 1988; Kluegel & Smith 1983).

Support for policy to implement racial equality has not increased over the years with declining Jim Crow racism because laissez-faire racism has remained prevalent. Kluegel (1990) presents direct evidence for this claim in an analysis of trends in whites' explanations of the black-white economic gap in the period from 1977 to 1989. His analysis shows, consistent with the decline of Jim Crow racism, that among representative national samples of white Americans over this period, attribution of the black-white economic gap to innate black inferiority has substantially declined. The most prevalent attribution for the black-white economic gap throughout the period from 1977 to 1989 is to the lack of motivation on the part of blacks — that is, to blaming blacks for their own poorer economic standing. The percent of whites attributing this gap to the lack of motivation has remained virtually constant from 1977 to 1989, as has the (minority) percent who attribute it to discrimination.

DATA

To test these hypotheses we use data from the 1990 General Social Survey (GSS) (Davis & Smith 1990). The GSS is a full-probability sample of English-speaking adults living in households in the continental United States. There were a total of 1,372 respondents, with a response rate of 73 percent. Our analyses are based on data for the 1,150 white respondents. Further details on sample design can be obtained from Davis and Smith (1990).

There are numerous survey studies of Jim Crow racism, stereotyping, and perceived discrimination independently. The unique feature of the 1990 GSS permitting test of our hypotheses is its incorporation of questions about Jim Crow ideology, contemporary stereotypes, and perceived social responsibility for blacks' conditions in a single study. We thus are able to directly test hypotheses about the differential effects of status and socioeconomic ideology on different dimensions of racial beliefs and attitudes.

MEASURES OF RACIAL BELIEFS AND ATTITUDES

Stereotypes

Stereotypes were measured by five bipolar 1- to 7-trait rating scales. Respondents were asked to rank how each of five groups (Asian Americans, blacks, Hispanic Americans, Jews, and whites) stand, with "1" meaning "virtually all of the people" in a group have a given positive (negative) trait, "7" meaning "virtually all of the people" in a group have a given negative (positive) trait, and "4" meaning a group "is not toward one end or another." The trait dimensions we employ are patriotic or unpatriotic ("PATRIOTIC"), hardworking or lazy ("WORK HARD"), prefer to be self-supporting or prefer to live off welfare ("WELFARE"), unintelligent or intelligent ("INTELLIGENT"), and violence prone or not violence prone ("VIOLENT"). This set of traits was chosen because it covers critical social, political, and economic achievement-related characteristics. We focus here on the trait ratings for whites and for blacks.

We used trait rating scales because it is now widely accepted that measurement procedures that call for simple categorical judgments likely obscure the nature of stereotypes (Ashmore & Del Boca 1981; Jackman & Senter 1983; Jackman 1994). Simple agree-disagree statements and the Katz-Braly type checklist approaches force respondents to make categorical and blunt generalizations. To the extent many people hold more qualified views, such procedures will underestimate the level of stereotyping.

In subsequent analyses, we use difference scores formed by subtracting ratings on each trait for blacks from the respective rating for whites (trait ratings difference). Wealth, Work Hard, Welfare, and Patriotic ratings were reverse coded so that, overall, a positive score indicates that a white respondent perceives that a given trait is found more often among blacks than among whites, and a negative score means that it is found less often. We thus have a measure of whether whites evaluate blacks as inferior to themselves and of how big the gap between groups is perceived to be (see Jackman & Senter 1983). A critical question concerns whether our measures tap "stereotypes" or perceived behavior — that is, simply reflect respondents' perceptions of actual average group differences in levels of certain traits. In constructing these measures, we explicitly chose wording to call for judgments (evaluations) of group personality traits rather than assessments of social fact. For example, the "WELFARE" rating asked whether group members "prefer" to be self-supporting or live off welfare. Similarly, the "WORK HARD" rating called for evaluations in terms of being "hard working" or "lazy" — the latter term is clearly not value neutral but implies a pejorative judgment.

Discrimination

We employed three questions on perceived discrimination against blacks. The first asked about discrimination that hurts the chances of blacks to get good-paying jobs. The second question asked about discrimination that makes it hard for blacks to buy or rent housing wherever they want. The third question we used concerns the attribution of the black-white socioeconomic status gap "mainly" to discrimination. We use questions on discrimination to indicate perceived social responsibility for blacks' conditions because discrimination is popularly employed as a short-hand term for various "extra-personal" causes of blacks' disadvantage relative to whites in economic status and other areas. It is possible, of course, that some individuals see discrimination strictly in terms that do not imply social responsibility for blacks' conditions — for example, as the result of individual whites acting out personal prejudice alone. In general, however, we believe it reasonably may be assumed that the large majority of persons endorsing discrimination see social responsibility of some kind for blacks' conditions.

Jim Crow Racism

We use three items — support for a ban on racial intermarriage, support for racial segregation in housing, and attribution of black-white differences in socioeconomic status to lesser innate ability — commonly used in previous analyses of racial prejudice (Schuman, Steeh, & Bobo 1985; Kluegel 1990).

DISTRIBUTIONS OF RACIAL BELIEFS AND ATTITUDES

Table 5.1 gives the distributions of whites' trait ratings for themselves and for blacks. These ratings clearly show that the perception of black inferiority to whites on important political, social, and economic characteristics is prevalent among white Americans. This perceived inferiority is highlighted in two summary measures.

TABLE 5.1
Whites' Trait Ratings of Whites and Blacks — 1990 General Social Survey

	Whites	Blacks
Patriotic		
1. Patriotic	24.9	8.5
2.	31.1	15.8
3.	20.1	19.3
4.	21.0	38.4
5.	1.8	11.2
6.	0.9	4.7
7. Unpatriotic	0.2	2.2
N	1,082.0	1,052.0
Balance	73.2	25.5
Mean	2.47	3.51
Mean Difference (s.d.)	−1.03*	(1.41)
Welfare		
1. Prefer to be self-supporting	16.1	1.9
2.	31.7	3.1
3.	25.9	8.3
4.	22.4	27.8
5.	2.5	24.5
6.	1.3	24.6
7. Prefer to live off welfare	0.2	9.8
N	1,101.0	1,096.0
Balance	69.7	−45.6
Mean	2.69	4.83
Mean Difference (s.d.)	−2.15*	(1.73)
Violent		
1. Violence prone	0.6	8.5
2.	3.6	17.7
3.	12.4	27.5
4.	44.7	30.1
5.	17.4	9.3
6.	16.6	5.1
7. Not violence prone	4.8	1.8
N	1,087.0	1,082.0
Balance	22.2	−38.5
Mean	4.44	3.36
Mean Difference (s.d.)	−1.07*	(1.79)
Work Hard		
1. Hardworking	8.3	2.0
2.	18.5	3.8
3.	30.0	11.8
4.	38.0	35.7

	Whites	Blacks
5.	3.9	25.5
6.	0.9	15.1
7. Lazy	0.3	6.0
N	1,102.0	1,094.0
Balance	51.7	−29.0
Mean	3.14	4.48
Mean difference (s.d.)	−1.34*	(1.56)
Intelligent		
1. Unintelligent	0.8	2.0
2.	1.8	7.5
3.	3.8	21.1
4.	35.1	48.8
5.	27.6	13.8
6.	21.4	5.2
7. Intelligent	9.4	2.3
N	1,090.0	1,079.0
Balance	52.0	−9.3
Mean	4.89	3.89
Mean Difference (s.d.)	−1.00*	(1.48)

*Mean difference is statistically significant at $p < .01$ (paired sample t-test); s.d. = standard deviation

The first is the difference in means between whites and blacks, computed such that a negative value indicates that blacks are perceived to possess less of a positive trait on average (mean trait ratings difference) than whites. Values of this measure are given in the row labeled "Mean Difference" for each trait. The second is a measure of the balance of positive to negative trait ratings, subtracting the total percent of ratings below the midpoint of the scale from the total percent above. A positive score indicates that a greater percentage of a group is seen to fall on the favorable side of a trait than on the negative side, and a negative score indicates the opposite. Values of this measure are given in the rows labeled "Balance" in Table 5.1.

The mean differences in Table 5.1 show a marked tendency for whites to give blacks negative trait ratings in comparison to whites' ratings of their own group. These negative ratings are most evident in the cases of traits related to work and socioeconomic success. The mean differences are greatest for the ratings of hard working or lazy and prefer to be self-supporting or prefer to live off welfare — in the latter case, it is greater than two for the perceived black-white difference.

The balance scores in Table 5.1 show that with the exception of patriotism (where whites and blacks are rated patriotic on balance), whites see blacks as much disproportionately occupying the negative side of trait distributions. For example, roughly 57 percent and 73 percent of whites are rated above the midpoint on hard work and self-support, respectively. In stark contrast, 47 percent of blacks are rated below the midpoint on hard work, and 59 percent below the midpoint on self-support.

As seen in the "Mean Differences" row of Table 5.1, the average trait difference for four of the five ratings is near 1.00. In addition, averaged across the five traits, roughly 35 percent of whites rate blacks and whites as equal (a score of 0) and another 20 percent rate blacks as only one unit inferior (a score of –1). Accordingly, one might conclude that the majority of whites see little or no difference between groups and that contemporary stereotypes are of little consequence; however, as can be seen from Figures 5.1 and 5.2, even a perceived one-unit negative difference between whites and blacks is highly consequential.

The 1990 GSS includes a question concerning government assistance to improve the living standards of blacks. The specific wording for this question is, "Some people think that blacks have been discriminated against for so long that the government has a special obligation to help

FIGURE 5.1

Mean "Government Help Blacks," by Black Ratings Relative to Whites

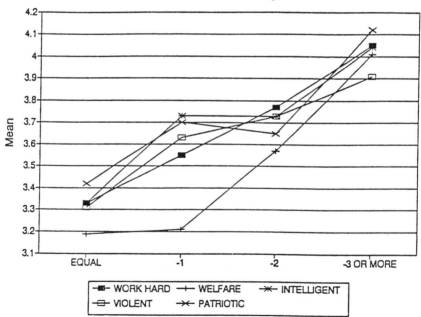

FIGURE 5.2
Oppose Marry Black by Trait Differences
(Percent "Oppose" or "Strongly Oppose")

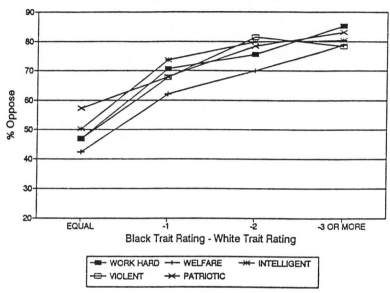

improve their living standards. Others believe that the government should not be giving special treatment to blacks." Respondents were asked to place themselves on a five-point scale, where "1" indicates strong agreement with the statement that government is obligated to help blacks, "5" indicates strong agreement with the statement that the government should not give special treatment to blacks, and "3" indicates agreement with both statements. Figure 5.1 gives the mean score for this question by categories of the trait difference scores (whites-blacks) — from whites who see blacks and whites as equal to those who see whites as three or more units superior to blacks. It quite clearly shows that opposition to government policy to equalize black-white economic standing increases with an increase in the perceived trait superiority of whites and that about one-half of the change over the entire range of negative trait ratings occurs with a shift from an equal rating to "–1."

Figure 5.2 graphs the percents who oppose having a close relative marry a black by the perceived trait differences between blacks and whites — again in categories from equality to pronounced white superiority. (This question is worded, "How about having a close relative or family member marry a black person? Would you be very in favor of it happening, somewhat in favor, neither in favor nor opposed to it happening, somewhat opposed, or very opposed to it happening?") There also is a clear, substantial increase in opposition to a close relative marrying a black as one moves from an "equal" rating to pronounced perceived trait superiority among whites, with a 30- to 40-percentage point difference between the end points. Relatedly, Farley and others (1994) show that black stereotypes — measured using the same approach and some of the same trait evaluations that we employ — strongly shape whites' preferences for living in integrated neighborhoods and their propensity for "white flight" in the face of racial integration. Overall, negative stereotypes of blacks strongly motivate white sentiment for maintaining social distance from blacks. As for the relationship of trait rating differences to support for government assistance, about one-half of the change over the entire range of negative trait ratings occurs with a shift from an equal rating to "–1." Findings concerning the prevalence of perceived trait inferiority of blacks cannot be dismissed simply because many whites see blacks as only "a little inferior." Our data confirm Jackman and Senter's (1983) claim that even the perception of small group differences amounts to saying "different, therefore unequal."

Table 5.2 gives the frequency distributions for Jim Crow items and perceived discrimination. Consistent with the progressive decline in Jim Crow racism found in other such measures, we see in Table 5.2 that roughly one-fifth of whites give prejudiced responses. Concerning the first two measures of perceived discrimination ("BLKJOBS" and "BLKHOUSE" in Table 5.2), whites in roughly equal percents see "a lot" of discrimination against blacks or dismiss its importance (that is, give responses of "a little" or "none"). The modal category of response for both measures is "some." This category is somewhat vague in meaning and may indeed mean that people see discrimination as a moderately important factor in influencing blacks' conditions or may choose it to indicate that they see slightly more than "a little" discrimination. The third measure of perceived discrimination ("DISCRIM") shows that about 63 percent deny that the black-white socioeconomic gap is "mainly" the result of discrimination. This suggests that the majority of people choosing "some" in response to the first two perceived discrimination measures are more likely indicating that they see slightly more than "a little" discrimination than that they see a moderate amount. Indeed, a cross-tabulation of "BLKJOB" and "DISCRIM" shows that among those choosing "some," roughly two-thirds deny that the black-white socioeconomic gap is "mainly due to discrimination." The combined message given by these three items is that the majority of whites perceive little social responsibility for blacks' conditions.

TABLE 5.2

Frequency Distributions for Jim Crow Items and Perceived Discrimination against Blacks — 1990 General Social Survey, Whites Only

		Percent	N
Jim Crow Items			
Do you think there should be laws against marriages between blacks and whites (RACMAR)	Yes	21.1	159
	No	78.9	595
White people have the right to keep blacks out of their neighborhood if they want to and blacks should respect the right. (RACSEG)	Agree Strongly	8.8	66
	Agree Slightly	14.9	112
	Disagree Slightly	27.1	203
	Disagree Strongly	49.2	369
On the average blacks have worse jobs, income, and housing than white people. Do you think these differences are because most blacks have less in-born ability to learn? (ABILITY)	Yes	19.0	210
	No	81.0	897
Perceived Discrimination			
How much discrimination would you say there is that hurts the chances of blacks to get good-paying jobs? (BLKJOBS)	A Lot	26.0	286
	Some	46.1	508
	A Little	17.0	187
	None At All	11.0	121
How much discrimination would you say there is that makes it hard for blacks to buy or rent housing wherever they want? (BLKHOUSE)	A Lot	32.4	354
	Some	41.2	450
	A Little	15.3	167
	None At All	11.0	120
On the average blacks have worse jobs, income, and housing than white people. Do you think these differences are mainly due to discrimination? (DISCRIM)	Yes	36.7	399
	No	63.3	688

FACTOR STRUCTURE

To test hypothesis 1, we conducted a confirmatory factor analysis, with the results given in Table 5.3. We first constructed a matrix of polychoric correlations (Joreskog & Sorbom 1989) and then tested the fit of three factor models relevant to hypothesis 1.

The models in the "MODEL FITTING RESULTS" panel of Table 5.3 are specified as follows. The "One Factor" model assumes that all of the 11 racial beliefs and attitudes items load on a single dimension that one may

TABLE 5.3

Confirmatory Factor Analysis Results for Racial Beliefs and Attitudes — 1990 General Social Survey, Whites Only

MODEL FITTING RESULTS

Model	Chi-Square	D.F.	p	GFI	AGFI	RMSR
				Model Fitting Statistics		
One Factor	966.390	44	0.000	0.780	0.670	0.124
Two Factor	751.840	43	0.000	0.880	0.730	0.118
Three Factor	210.520	41	0.000	0.950	0.920	0.060

THREE FACTOR MODEL PARAMTERS
Loadings

Variables	Jim Crow	Stereotype	Discrimination
		Factor	
RACMAR	0.78	0.00	0.00
RACSEG	0.79	0.00	0.00
ABILITY	0.62	0.00	0.00
WELFARE	0.00	0.78	0.00
INTELLIGENT	0.00	0.62	0.00
PATRIOTIC	0.00	0.57	0.00
VIOLENT	0.00	0.43	0.00
WORKHARD	0.00	0.75	0.00
BLKHOUSE	0.00	0.00	0.72
BLKJOBS	0.00	0.00	0.90
DISCRIM	0.00	0.00	0.57

Factor Correlations			
Jim Crow	1.00		
Stereotype	0.61	1.00	
Discrimination	−0.33	−0.17	1.00

Note:
   D.F. = degrees of freedom
   p = probability value
   GFI = Goodness of fit Index
   AGFI = Adjusted Goodness of Fit Index;
   RMSR = Root Mean Square Residual

call "generalized prejudice." This is, in effect, a counter-hypothesis to hypothesis 2, and it serves as a baseline for testing hypothesis 2. As seen from the "MODEL FITTING STATISTICS" in Table 5.3, this model fits very poorly. The "Two Factor" model corresponds to a simple division of items into those measuring Jim Crow racism and those proposed to measure laissez-faire racism; specifically, "RACMAR," "RACSEG," and "ABILITY" are assumed to load on the first factor only, and the remaining eight items on the second factor only. The "Two Factor" model fits better than the "One Factor" model, but nevertheless its overall fit is poor. (We estimated an additional two-factor model that groups the three Jim Crow items with the five trait ratings to define a prejudice factor, and the three discrimination items to define a separate perceived discrimination factor. This model also fits poorly: chi-square with 43 degrees of freedom = 466.72, goodness of fit index = 0.88, adjusted goodness of fit index = 0.81.) The "Three Factor Model" assumes that "RACMAR," "RACSEG," and "ABILITY" define the first — Jim Crow — racism factor; that the five trait ratings define the second — stereotype — factor; and that "BLK-HOUSE," "BLKJOBS," and "DISCRIM" define the third — discrimination — factor. Again, we assume a simple structure such that each item loads on only one factor, and there are no correlated errors.

The three-factor model fits markedly better than the two-factor model. Although we technically cannot reject the null hypothesis that the three-factor model does not fit, the adjusted goodness of fit index for this model is 0.92, greater than the minimum value for judging the fit of a model to be adequate (Byrne 1989; Joreskog & Sorbom 1989). In assessing how well models fit in our tests, we should keep in mind that goodness of fit measures are sensitive to sample size, especially sample sizes of 1,000 or more cases — which we have here. We estimated numerous additional models, adding correlated errors and allowing items to load on more than one factor. In all cases these additional parameters have trivial values, and the values for factor loadings and correlations differ very little to not at all from those reported in the "THREE FACTOR MODEL PARAMETERS" panel of Table 5.3. Consequently, we accept the three-factor model as the best representation of the correlations among the 11 racial beliefs and attitudes measured, and we conclude that hypothesis 1 is supported.

Two general observations may be made from the three-factor model parameters. First, the item loadings are strong overall. The "VIOLENT" trait item is the only one with a marginal loading (0.43), perhaps indicating that it may have a substantial behavioral component — that is, people reporting on perceived factual involvement with violence — as well as an evaluative component. Second, we see in Table 5.3 a substantial correlation (0.61) between the Jim Crow and stereotype factors. This is consistent with the notion of a cumulative dimension to racism (see Kleinpenning & Hagendoorn 1993), such that we expect those espousing the biological racism that is part of Jim Crow ideology to also embrace black stereotypes and reject social responsibility for blacks' conditions. The negative correlation (–0.33) between the Jim Crow and discrimination factors also supports the idea of cumulation. At the same time, the moderate size of these correlations shows that rejecting Jim Crow racism alone is by no means sufficient to lead people to eschew contemporary stereotypes or to assign social responsibility for blacks' conditions.

SOCIODEMOGRAPHIC CHARACTERISTICS

Education and Age Group Differences

To test hypothesis 2, we begin by plotting in Figures 5.3, 5.4, and 5.5 the distributions of Jim Crow and laissez-faire racism by education level and age groups. As noted above, research has underscored that Jim Crow racism decreases with years of formal education and increases with age. Although it is not possible to rule out an effect of aging per se, evidence regarding cohort change (see Firebaugh & Davis 1988) suggests that younger age groups led the way in the decline of Jim Crow ideology.

The education level and age group differences found in prior research are replicated in the 1990 GSS (Figure 5.3). It is noteworthy that among the youngest and most highly educated whites, Jim Crow racism is expressed by a very small minority. Indeed, among whites with 17 or more years of formal education, one might characterize the expression of Jim Crow racism as virtually absent.

Figure 5.4 arrays the percent of whites who give blacks an "inferior" rating for the three trait ratings that load most strongly on the stereotype factor (patterns for the remaining two are the same) — that is, have trait difference ratings for blacks that are one unit or more lower than the relevant white ratings — by education and age. Because we have seen that even a one-unit lower rating is highly consequential, whites who have trait difference scores of "–1" or lower may be validly characterized as having negative evaluations of blacks. We thus may compare whites who express Jim Crow racism to those who express a negative relative evaluation of blacks.

The overall pattern for Jim Crow racism is replicated in Figure 5.4. As level of education increases, the percent rating blacks inferior to whites with regard to hard work, self-support, and intelligence declines. Likewise paralleling findings on Jim Crow racism, the same ratings increase with increasing age. There is one marked difference, however, between patterns for Jim Crow racism and stereotyping. Here we call attention to the much higher level of willingness on the part of whites to rate blacks as inferior to whites on important traits than to endorse Jim Crow ideology. The markedly higher willingness to rate blacks as inferior holds even among the most highly educated (17+ years) and youngest (18–29 years) age groups, where prejudiced responses are nearly absent. For example, whereas only about 3 percent and 8 percent of whites with 17 or more

FIGURE 5.3
Jim Crow Racism by Education Level and Age Group

Percent "Prejudiced" by Education Level

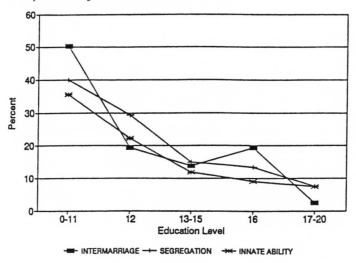

Percent "Prejudiced" by Age Group

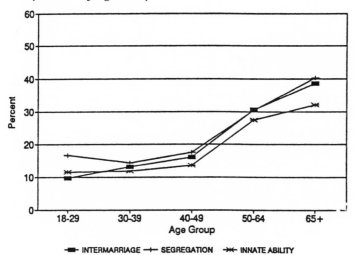

FIGURE 5.4
Ratings of Blacks as "Inferior" to Whites by Education Level and Age Group

Percent "Inferior" by Education Level

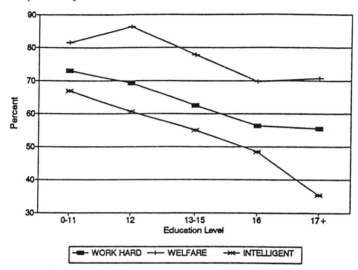

Percent "Inferior" by Age Group

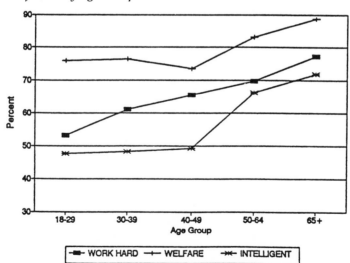

FIGURE 5.5
Perceived Discrimination by Education Level and Age Group

Percent "Mainly Due to . . ." or "A Lot" by Education Level

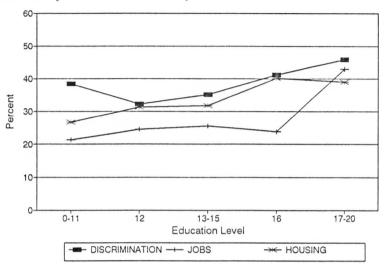

Percent "Mainly Due to . . ." or "A Lot" by Age Group

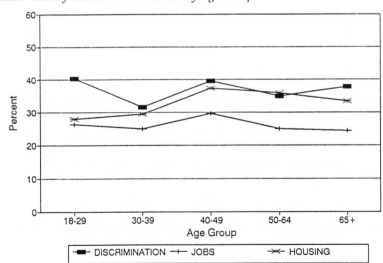

years of education would ban racial intermarriage or support the right to residential segregation by race, approximately 55 percent of such whites rate blacks as less hard working, and fully 71 percent as more prone to live off welfare. The same contrast holds for the relative ratings of intelligence versus endorsement of the Jim Crow racism item attributing black-white socioeconomic differences to innate ability. Approximately one-half of white respondents with 16 years of formal education rate blacks as less intelligent than whites, but fewer than 10 percent of these whites endorse "lesser innate ability" on the part of blacks as the cause of the black-white socioeconomic status gap.

Comparing Figures 5.3 and 5.4 supports hypothesis 2. There is roughly a 30- to 40-percent difference across the range of education levels and a 20- to 30-percent difference across the range of age groups in the endorsement of Jim Crow ideology. Consistent with hypothesis 2, the corresponding differences for trait ratings among education and age groups are smaller: 10 to 30 percent across education level and 10 to 20 percent across age groups.

The distribution of perceived discrimination by education level and age group given in Figure 5.5 provides even stronger support for hypothesis 2. With one exception — the greater tendency of the most highly educated (17–20 years) to see "a lot" of job discrimination — the perception of "a lot" of discrimination in getting jobs or housing or that the black-white socioeconomic gap is "mainly due to discrimination" varies little to not at all by education level or age group.

Regressions

To complete our test of hypothesis 2, we present the regression results in Table 5.4. These are regressions of indices of Jim Crow racism, black stereotypes, and perceived discrimination (formed according to previously discussed factor analysis results on several sociodemographic variables in addition to age and education [Table 5.3]). Unweighted averages of the items defining the respective factors in Table 5.3 were formed. Scores for three items were modified to place all items in each index in the same range of scores. "ABILITY," "DISCRIM," and "RACMAR" were recoded such that "No" equals "1.5" and "Yes" equals "3.5." For "JIM CROW RACISM" and "PERCEIVED DISCRIMINATION," an average was formed if a respondent had complete data for two or more of the three items defining these indices — otherwise, a respondent was assigned a missing data code. For "BLACK STEREOTYPES," an average was formed if a respondent had complete data for three or more of the five items forming this index — otherwise, a missing data code was assigned. Income is family income in categories from under $1,000 to $60,000 or more. Education is measured in years of schooling completed from 0 to 20 or more years. Age is measured in years. Gender is a categorical (0,1) variable, with female = 1. Region is coded in four categories and represented by four categorical (0,1) variables

South — Alabama, Arkansas, Delaware, District of Columbia, Florida, Georgia, Kentucky, Louisiana, Maryland, Mississippi, North Carolina, Oklahoma, South Carolina, Tennessee, Texas, Virginia, West Virginia;

Northeast — Connecticut, Maine, Massachusetts, New Hampshire, New Jersey, New York, Pennsylvania, Rhode Island, Vermont;

Midwest — Illinois, Indiana, Iowa, Kansas, Michigan, Minnesota, Missouri, Nebraska, North Dakota, Ohio, South Dakota, Wisconsin; and

West — Alaska, Arizona, California, Colorado, Hawaii, Idaho, New Mexico, Nevada, Oregon, Washington, Wyoming.

TABLE 5.4

Standardized Partial Regression Coefficients for the Effects of Sociodemographic Characteristics on Jim Crow Racism, Stereotypes, and Perceived Discrimination against Blacks — 1990 General Social Survey, Whites Only

	Jim Crow Racism	Black Stereotypes	Perceived Discrimination
Age	0.31*	0.20*	0.00
Education	−0.23*	−0.12*	0.15*
Gender (1 = female)	−0.01	−0.01*	0.05
Income	−0.10*	0.06	0.02
Prestige	−0.10*	−0.11	−0.01
Northeast	−0.03	0.05	0.01
South	0.09*	0.07*	−0.13*
West	−0.11*	−0.06	0.02
R-square	0.29	0.10	0.05

Note: See text for definitions of variables and indices; midwest is the reference (excluded) category for region of the country.
*$p < .05$

The results shown in Table 5.4 confirm and extend support for hypothesis 2. This support is evidenced overall by the R-squares for the respective equations, indicating the combined influence of all sociodemographic factors on Jim Crow and laissez-faire racism. As seen in Table 5.4, the R-square for Jim Crow racism is three to four times that for black stereotypes and perceived discrimination, respectively. The larger sized R-square for Jim Crow racism is not the result of the differential reliability of these indices. Cronbach's alpha reliability for each scale is, respectively: Jim Crow racism = 0.63, black stereotypes = 0.75, and perceived discrimination = 0.67. Adjusting results for attenuation due to unreliability of measurement would increase the differential in R-squares between regressions for Jim Crow racism and for the other two indices. Support also is evidenced in the larger size of the standardized coefficients for the effects of age and education on Jim Crow racism than on black stereotypes and perceived discrimination, confirming what we previously observed in Figures 5.3, 5.4, and 5.5.

We also note that more sociodemographic characteristics have statistically significant effects on Jim Crow racism than on our indices of laissez-faire racism. This is especially so for perceived discrimination, where only education and Southern residence have statistically significant effects. In general, our three indices may be placed on a continuum: from Jim Crow racism that is characterized by very substantial age and socioeconomic status differentiation; through black stereotypes that are only moderately so differentiated; to perceived discrimination that, in age and status terms, seems best characterized as largely undifferentiated.

SOCIOECONOMIC IDEOLOGY

Included in the 1990 GSS were five questions that allowed us to construct measures of socioeconomic ideology. Two questions each concerned structuralist and individualist causes of poverty, and the fifth question concerned equality of opportunity. Following results of our previous analysis using these questions (Bobo & Kluegel 1993), we formed two separate indices of structuralism and individualism. Respondents were asked, "Now I will give a list of reasons why there are poor people in this country. Please tell me whether you feel each of these is very important, somewhat important, or not important in explaining why there are poor people in this country." "Failure of society to provide good schools for many Americans" and "failure of industry to provide enough jobs" are structuralism items. "Loose morals and drunkenness" and "lack of effort by the poor themselves" are individualism items. Agreement or disagreement on a four-point scale with the item, "One of the big problems in this country is that we don't give everyone an equal chance" also is used as an indicator of structuralism. Indices of structuralism and individualism were formed by calculating unweighted averages of the respective three and two items. We thus have measures of a person's tendency to see inequality as the result of social forces, individual weakness or failure, or, of course, both.

Table 5.5 gives coefficients for the effects of structuralism and individualism on Jim Crow and laissez-faire racism. These effects are from

TABLE 5.5

Standardized Partial Regression Coefficients for the Effects of Individualism and Structuralism on Jim Crow Racism, Stereotypes, and Perceived Discrimination against Blacks (Net of Sociodemographic Characteristics) — 1990 General Social Survey, Whites Only

	Jim Crow Racism	Black Stereotypes	Perceived Discrimination
Individualism	0.11*	0.24*	–0.14*
Structuralism	–0.03	–0.05	0.24*
R-square	0.31	0.15	0.12
R-square increment	0.02	0.05	0.07

Note: See text for definitions of variables and indices. The sociodemographic characteristics of Table 5.4 also are included in the regression equations from which the effects of individualism and structuralism reported in this table are estimated.
$*p < .05$

regression models including all the sociodemographic characteristics shown in Table 5.3 as well as the structuralism and individualism indices.

The results presented in Table 5.5 clearly support hypothesis 3. The R-square increment row in Table 5.5 gives the increase in R-square over the parallel equation in Table 5.4 due to the combined effect of structuralism and individualism — that is, of socioeconomic ideology. The values in this row clearly show that overall socioeconomic ideology more strongly affects aspects of laissez-faire racism than it does Jim Crow ideology. Looking at individual coefficients, we see that structuralism has no statistically significant effect on Jim Crow racism, and individualism has a statistically significant but small effect. Although structuralism does not significantly affect black stereotypes, there is a statistically significant effect of individualism — and it is substantially larger than for the effect of individualism on Jim Crow racism. Perceived discrimination is significantly influenced by both individualism and structuralism.

RACIAL POLICY

To test hypothesis 4, we again make use of an item employed in Figure 5.1 concerning government obligation to help improve the standard of living for blacks ("GOVERNMENT HELP BLACKS"). (The 1990 GSS includes several other measures of support for racial policy. We focus on this particular item because it taps general support for government assistance for blacks and because it provides the most relevant test of hypothesis 4.) In its reference to improving the standard of living for blacks, this item invokes the economic redistributive focus central to current social policy debates (see Bobo & Kluegel 1993).

Table 5.6 gives a set of regressions from a model of the determinants of attitudes toward government help to improve the standard of living for blacks that includes the indices of Jim Crow racism, black stereotypes, and perceived discrimination. In this model we assume the direction of causation primarily to be from socioeconomic ideology and racial beliefs to racial policy attitudes — consistent with findings showing that general beliefs and affect are acquired in early childhood (Simmons & Rosenberg 1971; Sears 1975; Leahy 1983), whereas attitudes toward specific policy are formed in late adolescence or the early adult years (Torney-Purta 1983). Our assumed ordering of beliefs also is consistent with the hierarchical model of attitude constraint elaborated by M. Peffley and J. Hurwitz (1985). As they have shown (Peffley & Hurwitz 1985; Hurwitz & Peffley 1987), the public's attitudes toward specific policies are in effect "deduced" from general or abstract beliefs. We view Jim Crow and laissez-faire racism as ideologies that arise in the general defense of white privilege, and over time come to have an autonomous influence (see Wilson 1973). As J. M. Yinger explains, "Persistent discrimination against minority groups becomes 'justified' by a tradition of prejudice. Stereotypes 'explain' why certain groups are in disadvantaged positions. Even those persons who in no way stand to gain economically or politically absorb the culture of prejudice and this helps to perpetuate discriminatory ethnic patterns for others" (1983, pp. 399–400). Accordingly, we view Jim Crow and laissez-faire racism as general dispositions that respondents apply to the task of evaluating the policy proposed to them in the specific questions asked on surveys. As we have assumed in earlier analyses, individualism and structuralism are taken to be causally prior to Jim Crow and laissez-faire racism. Following our earlier discussion of their cumulative relationship, we assume that Jim Crow racism is causally prior to black stereotypes and perceived discrimination.

Column A of Table 5.6 gives the total effects of sociodemographic characteristics, both direct and indirect, through socioeconomic ideology and racial beliefs. Overall, sociodemographic characteristics little affect support of or opposition to government help for improving the standard of living of blacks. Although there is a significant tendency for support to increase with years of education, age has no statistically significant effect. The lack of an age effect is consistent with the general picture of stagnation in whites' racial policy attitudes discussed at the beginning of this chapter. From column B we see that the total effects of socioeconomic ideology (structuralism and individualism) are statistically significant and

TABLE 5.6
Standardized Partial Regression Coefficients for the Effects of Sociodemographic Characteristics, Socioeconomic Ideology, and Racial Beliefs and Attitudes on Support for Government Help to Improve the Standard of Living for Blacks — 1990 General Social Survey, Whites Only

	Government Help Blacks			
	A	B	C	D
Age	−0.01	0.02	0.11*	0.11*
Education	0.20*	0.19*	0.13	0.12*
Gender (1 = female)	0.03	0.01	−0.01	−0.01
Income	0.00	0.02	−0.02	−0.01
Prestige	−0.01	0.02	−0.01	−0.03
Northeast	−0.01	0.00	−0.03	−0.02
South	−0.08	−0.06	−0.04	0.01
West	0.00	0.00	−0.05	−0.04
Individualism	—	−0.14*	−0.13*	−0.05
Structuralism	—	0.27*	0.28*	0.20*
Jim Crow racism	—	—	−0.18*	−0.06
Black stereotypes	—	—	—	−0.21*
Perceived discrimination	—	—	—	0.26*
R-square	0.05	0.15	0.16	0.24

Note: See text for definitions of variables and indices; midwest is the reference (excluded) category for region of the country.
*$p < .05$
— = variable not included in relevant regression equation

substantially larger than the effects of sociodemographic characteristics. As we (Bobo & Kluegel 1993) and others (see Kuklinski & Parent 1981; Tuch & Hughes 1996a) have shown, attitudes toward racial policies are a function of more than racial ideology alone.

Results shown in columns C and D speak directly to the merits of hypothesis 4. As expected, we see in column C a statistically significant total effect of Jim Crow racism on support for government help to improve the standard of living of blacks. As we see in column D, black stereotypes and perceived discrimination also have statistically significant and substantial effects on "GOVERNMENT HELP BLACKS." These results strongly support hypothesis 4. We have run parallel analyses to those in Table 5.6 for a range of other measures of support for racial policy in the 1990 GSS. Results for a measure of support for government spending in general to help blacks are nearly identical to those in Table

5.6. Results for measures of support for specific kinds of programs to help blacks — for example, special college scholarships for black students who maintain good grades — differ somewhat. Perceived discrimination has substantially stronger effects on support for these kind of programs than does Jim Crow racism or black stereotypes. All of these results also clearly support hypothesis 4.

CONCLUSIONS

In this chapter we tested four hypotheses about the influence of sociodemographic characteristics and socioeconomic ideology on Jim Crow and laissez-faire racism, and the relationship of these forms of racism to support for government help to improve the standard of living for blacks. We found clear and strong evidence in support of each of the four hypotheses. Items drawn from the respective domains of Jim Crow and laissez-faire racism define separate factors in confirmatory factor analyses. Jim Crow racism is more strongly affected by sociodemographic characteristics — and especially by age and education — than is laissez-faire racism. Socioeconomic ideology has substantially stronger effects on contemporary black stereotypes and perceived discrimination against blacks than on Jim Crow racism. Jim Crow racism, black stereotypes, and perceived discrimination against blacks all significantly shape support for government help to improve blacks' standard of living.

The results of these analyses provide "micro" evidence that buttresses Bobo's explanation of progress and stagnation in racial beliefs and attitudes for which he primarily employs "macro" evidence. We have seen in our analyses that progress in racial beliefs and attitudes is largely limited to the decline of Jim Crow racism. Among young and highly educated white Americans, endorsement of Jim Crow ideology might well be characterized as simply absent. The picture for contemporary stereotypes and acknowledgment of social responsibility for blacks' conditions is quite different.

We focused in our analysis on contemporary or more subtle stereotypes, defined in relative terms rather than as categorical judgments. Negative stereotypes of blacks prevail among whites. Blacks are rated as less intelligent, more violence prone, lazier, less patriotic, and more likely to prefer living off welfare than whites. Not only are whites rated more favorably than blacks, but on four of the five traits examined (except patriotism), many whites rated the majority of blacks as possessing negative qualities and the majority of whites as possessing positive qualities.

We have no over-time national level data that permits us to analyze the trend in contemporary black stereotypes as we have measured them here; however, we may take certain implications for change from our cross-sectional analysis of stereotypes. This analysis suggests that we may expect some relative decline in stereotyping over the coming years, as younger cohorts replace older ones and if the trend of increasing enrollment in higher education continues. Projections from age group differences are always speculative, but such projections concerning Jim Crow racism have been borne out by analysis of historical trend data (Firebaugh & Davis 1988). Less optimistically, our findings suggest that the absolute level of black stereotyping will remain high. In contrast to Jim Crow racism, stereotypes are far from absent among the youngest and most highly educated whites. Indeed, as we have seen, the majorities of college-educated whites and whites aged 18 to 29 rate blacks as "inferior" to whites on important traits. Furthermore, our analyses have shown that negative stereotypes matter. Even the perception of only small group differences increased whites' expressed desire for social distance from blacks and reduced support for government intervention to help blacks get ahead in life.

The outlook for an increase in recognition of social responsibility for blacks' conditions is even less optimistic. Analyses of perceived discrimination presented in this chapter show that whites' endorsement of social responsibility is at best characterized as weak or halting, with the majority seeing little to no influence of discrimination against blacks. We have found that there are no significant age group differences in perceived discrimination and only a limited effect of education. These findings — combined with others showing that, from 1977 to 1989, a constant minority percent of white Americans have attributed the black-white socioeconomic gap to discrimination (Kluegel 1990) — argue for a stable denial of social responsibility in the future.

Our findings concerning the effects of Jim Crow and laissez-faire racism on support for government help to improve the standard of living for blacks lend further support to the laissez-faire racism explanation of the "paradox" of contemporary racial attitudes. Viewed in the light of the macro-level findings discussed in Chapter 2 and the micro-level findings of this chapter, the gap between increasingly egalitarian racial principles (the decline of Jim Crow racism) and resistance to policies such as affirmative action presents no paradox at all. Both are products of changes in U.S. social structure and politics that successfully deposed Jim Crow institutions but left large numbers of African Americans in economically disadvantaged and segregated communities. The high level of negative stereotyping and prevalent denial of social responsibility we find suggest that for many white Americans, blacks are viewed as undeserving of special treatment from government. To the extent that pressure from civil rights groups and white liberals have put such policies into effect, they would, perforce, breed resentment and resistance. Absent a change in the underlying social conditions that breathe life into stereotypes or a substantial increase in the perception by whites that discrimination pre-vents minorities from getting ahead economically, the political stalemate over policy interventions to help minorities is likely to continue.

6

Advance and Retreat: Racially Based Attitudes and Public Policy

Cedric Herring and Charles Amissah

As recently as the 1960s, Jim Crow segregation existed in parts of the United States. This system required black and white people to be segregated in public accommodations, housing, transportation, schools, cemeteries, and so forth solely on the basis of race. African Americans were subjected to personal humiliation and stripped of their human dignity on a daily basis. Moreover, they were set off from the rest of humanity and labeled as an inferior race. Needless to say, social distance — that is, the level of unwillingness among members of one (racial) group to accept or approve of interactions with members of another (racial) outgroup — was extremely high between blacks and whites, as public policy mandated that these groups should be separate.

Over the last three decades, however, race relations and racial attitudes in the United States have changed dramatically, or so we are told (for example, Smith, 1981; Pettigrew, 1985; Schuman, Steeh, & Bobo, 1985; Tuch, 1987; Herring, 1989; Bobo & Kluegel, 1993). Through its several important victories, the civil rights movement affected this situation in some fundamental ways, forcing the nation and its leaders to decide whether they were going to grant African Americans full citizenship rights or continue to side with racists who upheld white superiority and the subjugation of blacks. With pressure from the civil rights movement and the international community, several laws mandating segregation were changed. Clearly, the legal status of African Americans changed with legislation, such as the Voting Rights Act and the Civil Rights Act of 1965.

By the late 1970s, however, several societal forces were in place to question the very logic of the civil rights movement and to initiate measures aimed at reversing the gains. By the 1980s, the Reagan administration promoted a major reversal in race-relevant public policies (Hudson & Broadnax, 1982; Herring & Collins, 1995). Anti–equal opportunity policies were pursued even more vigorously during the Bush administration. President Bush, for example, promptly vetoed a new version of the Civil Rights Act on the grounds that it would require employers to establish quotas — despite the fact that the legislation broke no new ground, imposed no new burdens on employers, but simply restored the legal framework of the workplace to what it had been prior to a series of Supreme Court decisions in the late 1980s (Wilson, Lewis, & Herring, 1991). Also during the Bush era, confrontations over affirmative action and other measures designed to achieve racial equality triggered bitter disputes about the status of African Americans (Herring & Collins, 1995). Under the Clinton administration, many of these disputes continue but are being fought under the banner of such issues as welfare reform and labor force policy.

These are just a few of the historical conditions that have led to the circumstances African Americans find themselves in. In this chapter we examine levels of social distance between blacks and whites in the 1990s. Rather than examine specific policies that have facilitated or hindered reductions in social distance, we examine the degree to which various U.S. ethnic groups are willing to interact with black Americans in various social contexts and compare these groups' willingness to be integrated with blacks versus their willingness to be integrated with other racial and ethnic groups. The questions we are trying to answer include: Do nonblack Americans in the 1990s fully accept African Americans? Is there greater social distance between black Americans and various ethnic groups than there is between these ethnic groups and others? We use data from the 1990 General Social Survey to present some answers to these questions.

THEORIES OF INTERGROUP
RELATIONS AND PREJUDICE

As mentioned earlier, social distance refers to the level of unwillingness among members of a group to accept or approve of interactions with members of an outgroup (Bogardus, 1959). In racial and ethnic relations, it reflects the degree to which members of racial and ethnic groups are disinclined to accept members of other racial and ethnic outgroups in varying social contexts. This notion of social distance has become closely associated with theories of interethnic relations and prejudice.

In the United States, the dominant explanation of interethnic relations has been the "assimilation" perspective. This perspective, associated with

Robert E. Park, one of the first major American theorists of ethnic relations, suggests that intergroup contacts and relations regularly go through stages of a race relations cycle. This progressive and irreversible cycle consists of contacts, competition, accommodation, and eventual assimilation. Migration and exploration bring peoples from different cultures into contact with each other. Contact in turn leads to new forms of social organization for both the natives and the newcomers. With the new interactions also come economic competition and subsequent conflict between the indigenous population and the foreigners. In the accommodation stage, both groups are compelled to make adjustments to their new social situations so that relations might be stabilized. Finally, in the assimilation stage, there will be an inevitable disappearance of cultural and ethnic differences that distinguish these once-rivaling ethnic groups.

The assimilation perspective argues that cultural differences between national origin groups are passed on to later generations in progressively diluted forms and ultimately disappear in modern society. This belief rests on the assumption that the importance of ascriptively oriented relations wane with increasing emphasis on universalism. As time passes, therefore, ethnic antagonisms subside, and ethnic groups become increasingly similar in their worldviews.

The "Anglo-conformity" variant of the assimilation perspective (for example, Gordon, 1981) takes the position that to the degree that there is an identifiable "American culture," it is Anglo-Saxon (English). Furthermore, it suggests that most ethnic groups have adapted to the core Anglo-Saxon culture. This perspective suggests that U.S. ethnic groups will have some degree of consensus about which racial and ethnic groups are to be favored and which are to be disfavored: Virtually all assimilated U.S. ethnic groups will favor those nations that most closely resemble Anglo-Saxon cultural forms.

Milton Gordon (1964), in particular, explains assimilation as a series of stages through which various ethnic groups pass. He identified seven stages that correspond to ethnic groups' adaptation to the host society:

cultural assimilation or acculturation in which ethnic groups change their cultural patterns to more closely fit the patterns of the dominant culture in the host society;

structural assimilation in which members of the ethnic group are granted extensive access into the social organizations and institutions of the host society;

marital assimilation or amalgamation in which members of the ethnic group begin to date and intermarry with members of the dominant culture;

identificational assimilation in which members of the ethnic group develop a sense of peoplehood based virtually exclusively on the tendencies of the dominant culture;

attitude receptional assimilation in which members of the ethnic group are no longer the targets of any prejudicial feelings from members of the dominant culture;

behavior receptional assimilation in which members of the ethnic group are no longer the targets of any discriminatory practices from members of the dominant culture; and

civic assimilation in which there are no real signs of value or power conflict between members of the ethnic group and members of the dominant culture.

Assimilation, in this view, is invariably unidirectional and progressive.

In contrast, the "cultural pluralism" variant emphasizes the persistence of cultural heritage as the basis of the continued importance of ascriptive groups (Abramson, 1973; Greeley, 1974). It argues that immigrant groups often remain culturally distinct from the dominant Anglo culture beyond the timeframe predicted by the Anglo-conformity perspective (for example, Glazer & Moynihan, 1970; Greeley, 1974). As a result of multicultural interactions in the schools and the homogenizing influence of the media and other institutions, ethnic groups do become more similar to each other (that is, more "Americanized," not "Anglicized") over several generations. These analysts, however, point to pluralism in the United States and argue that a number of distinctive ethnic groups never assimilate to the Anglo-Saxon way of life. Instead, they argue, some immigrant groups migrated to the United States with cultural backgrounds that were already similar to that of English settlers. Thus, their apparent assimilation to Anglo ways is really nothing more than a continuation of patterns that existed prior to their coming to the United States. Other groups will retain certain distinctive cultural traits; bona fide aspects of the heritage from their native lands will continue to thrive in the United States. Thus, according to this perspective, U.S. ethnic groups share a number of cultural traits with the general society, but also they retain major nationality characteristics from their homelands.

The cultural pluralism perspective suggests that U.S. ethnic groups will have varied opinions about which groups are to be favored and which are to be disfavored. If, for example, there is an ethnic group that is a historical enemy of France but an ally of Mexico, Franco-Americans will be more likely to feel unfavorable toward these people, whereas Mexican Americans will be more likely to feel favorable toward them. By the same token, contemporary hostilities between different ethnic groups within the United States can emerge, as different groups with no prior histories of antagonism can also develop dislike for each other within the U.S. context. Still, to the degree that there are people from nations that closely resemble the United States socially, politically, and culturally, there should be relatively more support for the people from those nations among all U.S. ethnic groups. Conversely, if there are people from nations that are viewed as being very dissimilar from the United States, there should be relatively less support for the people from such countries among virtually all U.S. ethnic groups.

A third group of theories that attempts to account for interethnic relations are "group conflict" theories. Group conflict theories start with the premise that economic forces are at the root of ethnic antagonisms. Subordination, exploitation, and resource inequalities play major roles in ethnic stratification and interethnic relations. Variants of this paradigm include internal colonialism perspectives (for example, Hechter, 1975; Blauner, 1972), segmentation theories (for example, Bonacich, 1972), and middleman theories (for example, Bonacich & Modell, 1980). The focus of these explanations is on the special roles of "racial" ethnic groups who, unlike their "white" ethnic counterparts, have been excluded from aspects of U.S. society.

According to these perspectives, U.S. culture contains an arrangement of racial and ethnic images that supports the subordination of Asians, Africans, Latinos, and Native Americans. As a nation founded on the basis of Eurocentric images, the ethnocentric ideologies in force are those that purport the superiority of European cultural forms and promote the domination of nonwhites or non-Westerners. Because non-European, nonwhite ethnic groups do not share such worldviews, they are not likely to hold the same preferences as European ethnics. To the degree that racial ethnic groups empathize with Third World peoples, group conflict perspectives suggest that U.S. ethnic groups will have varied opinions about which nations' citizens are to be favored and which are to be disfavored. According to these formulations, the primary distinction will occur between those peoples favored by racial ethnics versus those favored by white ethnics. Of course, other (nonracial) conflicts can exist, but non-Western ethnic groups will be more likely to favor non-Western (Third World) nations than will European ancestry groups. Also, to the degree that there are nations that closely resemble the homelands of racial ethnic groups socially, politically, and culturally, there should be relatively more support for the peoples of those nations among those ethnic groups. Conversely, if there are nations that are viewed as antagonistic toward or very dissimilar from those racial ethnic groups' homelands, there should be relatively less support for the peoples from such countries among those racial ethnic groups.

Because these theories are ordinarily thought of as theories of ethnic relations or stratification, they should be instructive for understanding ethnic biases and sentiments. Accordingly, competing hypotheses can be derived from these three views:

the "Anglo-conformity" variant of the assimilation perspective predicts that virtually all U.S. ethnic groups will agree on which ethnic groups are to be favored and that those will be groups which are most socially, politically, and culturally similar to the dominant, Anglo group;

the "cultural pluralism" variant of the assimilation perspective predicts that generally there will be more favorable sentiments for those groups that are culturally similar to Anglos, but some ethnic groups will favor or disfavor others for historically contingent reasons; and

"group conflict" perspectives predict that nonwhite, non-Western ethnic groups will favor Third World peoples more (and Western peoples less) than their Western, white ethnic counterparts. These predictions are tested below. The data and operationalizations of variables are presented first, however.

METHODS

Samples

The data source for this chapter is the 1990 General Social Survey, an "independently drawn sample of English-speaking persons 18 years of age or over, living in non-institutional arrangements within the United States" (Davis & Smith, 1990). Data from respondents who reported their ancestry and responded to questions about sentiments toward various racial and ethnic groups were used to operationalize variables used in the analysis. These operationalizations and the variable labels (in all uppercase letters) are presented below.

Operationalizations

In order to operationalize ethnicity, respondents were asked, "From what countries or part of the world did your ancestors come?" Self-reported ethnic identifications include the following groups: AFRICAN (and West Indian), ASIAN (Chinese, Japanese, Filipino, Indian, and Arabic), WESTERN EUROPEAN (English, Welsh, Scottish, Irish, Italian, French, German, Austrian, Danish, Finnish, Norwegian, and Swedish), LATINO (Mexican, Puerto Rican, Spanish, and other Spanish), NATIVE AMERICAN INDIAN, EASTERN EUROPEAN (Polish, Czechoslovakian, Hungarian, Lithuanian, Russian, Yugoslavian, and Rumanian), OTHER ETHNIC GROUPS (that is, those who reported an ethnicity not among those groups listed above), and NON-ETHNICS (that is, those who reported their ethnic identification as "American" or reported no ethnic identity). In addition, respondents who reported that they were JEWISH or were raised as Jewish were coded for this ethnicity.

Several items were used to measure levels of assimilation and social distance. To measure resistance to integration in schools with black children, respondents were asked whether they would be willing to send their children to SCHOOLS where up to half the students were African

Americans. To tap sentiments about MARITAL assimilation with blacks, respondents were asked, "Do you think there should be laws against marriages between blacks and whites?" To measure attitude or behavior receptional assimilation, respondents were asked about their willingness to vote for a black PRESIDENT: "If your party nominated a Black for President, would you vote for him if he were qualified for the job?"

As an indicator of relative social distance from various racial and ethnic groups, respondents were asked about how favorably they viewed living in a neighborhood where about half their NEIGHBORS would be Jews, blacks, Asians, Hispanics, or northern whites. Similarly, they were asked how they would respond to a close relative MARRYING a Jewish, black, Asian, Hispanic, or northern white person. The relative preferences provide a sense of which racial and ethnic groups have the greatest social distance between them. In each case, responses were dichotomized into those who did not object and those who did object to such intermingling.

Other variables in the analysis include correlates of racial and ethnic tolerance. EDUCATION was measured by response categories that ranged from 0 to 20. AGE was measured in years (from 18 through 89). FAMILY INCOME was coded in thousands of dollars to correspond to the midpoints of the income categories. Political CONSERVATISM was coded from 1 for extremely liberal to 7 for extremely conservative. Gender was dummy coded 0 for male and 1 for FEMALE. Region of residence was dichotomized between the SOUTH (coded 1) and non-South (coded 0). Religion was dummy coded into PROTESTANT, CATHOLIC, and OTHER (the omitted category). URBANICITY, the size of the community in which the respondent lives, was coded from 1 (for open country within a township) to 10 (for a large central city over 250,000 in population). Class identification was coded 1 for those who thought of themselves as being MIDDLE (or upper) CLASS and 0 otherwise. IMMIGRANT status was coded 1 if the respondent was not born in the United States and 0 if he or she was native to the United States.

ANALYSIS AND RESULTS

Are some ethnic groups more likely to interact with African Americans than others? If differences on the magnitude of 20 percent are considered significant, and those of 10 percent are considered nontrivial, then Figures 6.1–6.5 show that there are nontrivial and significant differences in how likely various ethnic groups are to interact with African Americans in several contexts. Figure 6.1 presents the relationship between ethnicity and unwillingness to send one's children to schools where up to half the students are African Americans. This graph shows that although only one out of ten (10 percent) African Americans are unwilling to send their children to such schools, nearly four out of ten (37 percent) Asian Americans report that they would be unwilling to send their children to schools where half the students are black. Other ethnic groups fall between these extremes, as 16 percent of Latinos, 25 percent of Western European Americans, 30 percent of Eastern European Americans, 24 percent of Native Americans, and 27 percent of Jewish Americans report that they are unwilling to send their children to such schools. These patterns produce a chi-square statistic of 104.9, with 8 degrees of freedom ($p < .01$).

Figure 6.2 presents the relationship between ethnicity and support for laws banning interracial marriages. Support for such laws varies widely by ethnicity, ranging from a low of 6 percent of African Americans to a high of 35 percent of those who claim no ethnicity. Generally, support for such laws is much higher among European Americans and Native Americans, as 25 percent of those with Eastern European ancestry, 28 percent of those with Western European ancestry, and 33 percent of Native Americans report support for such laws. In contrast, 6 percent of Asian Americans, 11 percent of Jewish Americans, and 12 percent of Latinos support such thinking. The patterns produce a chi-square statistic of 532.8, with 8 degrees of freedom ($p < .01$). These results serve to undermine some of the basic claims of the Anglo-conformity perspective. Inasmuch as differences in sentiments appear to fall along racial lines, the results provide substantial support for group conflict formulations and less support for the cultural pluralism perspective.

Figure 6.3 presents the unwillingness to vote for a black presidential candidate by ethnicity. Again, there are nontrivial differences by ethnicity, with only 1 percent of African Americans saying they would be unwilling to vote for a black presidential candidate, but 20 percent of Asian Americans reporting that they would be unwilling to vote for a black presidential candidate. These ethnic variations do not, however, appear to occur along racial lines. Still, the relationships produce a chi-square statistic of 123.0, with 8 degrees of freedom ($p < .01$). These findings provide little support for the Anglo-conformity view, at best mixed verification of group conflict theories, but more support for the cultural pluralism perspective.

Overall, the results shown in Figures 6.1–6.3 provide little endorsement of Anglo-conformity views. The results give some support for the cultural pluralism view, but they furnish the greatest amount of support for the group conflict theories, as there were substantial ethnic differences in willingness to interact with African Americans in several contexts that occurred along racial lines. These results do not, however, provide much information about whether the social distance between African Americans and other ethnic groups is as great as it is between nonblacks and other ethnic groups. Figures 6.4 and 6.5 provide information about the relative social distance between African Americans and other ethnic

FIGURE 6.1
Percentage Objecting to Having Their Children Attend Integrated Schools, by Race and Ethnicity

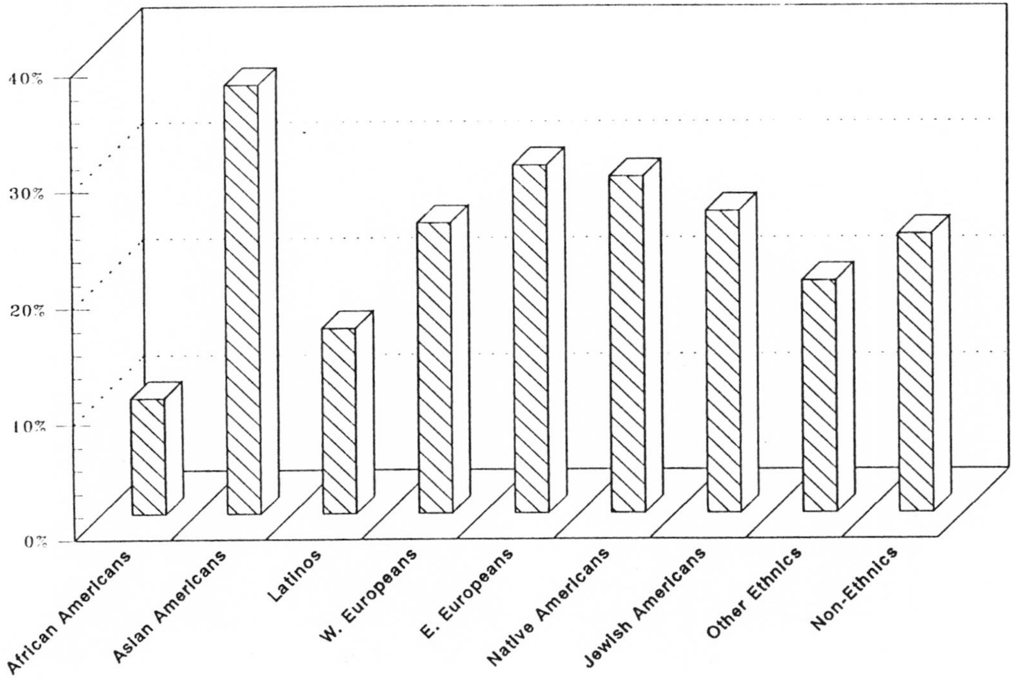

FIGURE 6.2
Percentage Favoring Laws Banning Interracial Marriages, by Race and Ethnicity

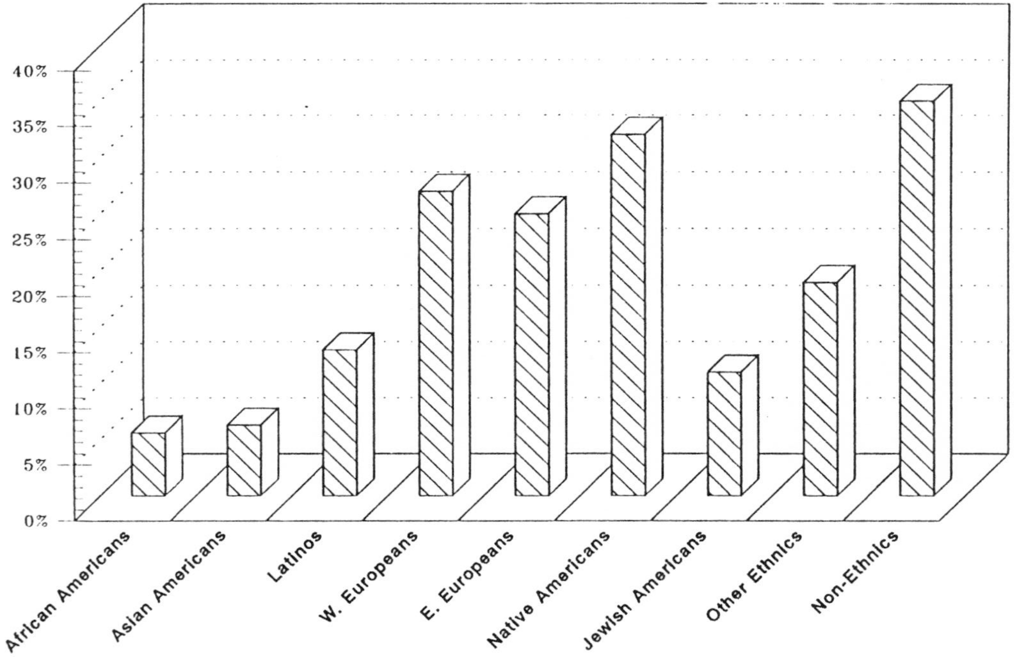

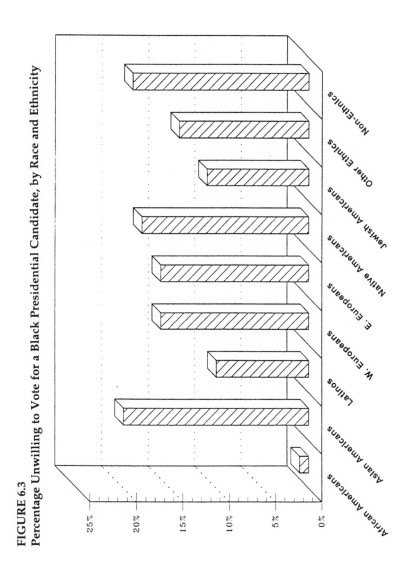

FIGURE 6.3
Percentage Unwilling to Vote for a Black Presidential Candidate, by Race and Ethnicity

131

groups versus the social distance between nonblacks and other ethnic groups.

Figure 6.4 shows the percentage of people from various racial and ethnic groups who are opposed to living in neighborhoods in which half the residents are white, black, Jewish, Asian, or Hispanic. With only a couple of exceptions, this chart shows that higher proportions of the ethnic groups report opposition to living among blacks than among any other racial or ethnic group. The only exceptions are African Americans and Jewish Americans. It is also interesting to note that, although there are some rank-order differences among the racial and ethnic groups, none of them are as likely to oppose living among whites as they are to disagree with living among other racial and ethnic groups. Also, European Americans show a great deal of opposition to living in neighborhoods with all racial ethnic groups. These results conform most closely to the expectations of the group conflict perspective, as there are cleavages that separate the various ethnic groups along racial lines.

Figure 6.5 presents the percentage of people from various racial and ethnic groups who are opposed to a close relative marrying a person who is white, black, Jewish, Asian, or Hispanic. This chart shows results that are very similar to those presented in Figure 6.4: With only one exception, Figure 6.5 shows that higher proportions of the ethnic groups report opposition to marriage with blacks than with any other racial or ethnic group. The only exception is African Americans. Although there are again some rank-order differences among the racial and ethnic groups, none of them are as likely to oppose marriage with whites as they are to oppose marriage with other racial and ethnic groups. Also, European Americans again show a great deal of opposition to marriage with all racial ethnic groups. These results conform most closely to the expectations of the group conflict perspective, as there are cleavages that separate the various ethnic groups along racial lines.

Thus far, the results suggest that there are racial and ethnic variations in how willing people are to interact with African Americans in various settings and conditions. Although the graphs provide basic information about which ethnic groups are most likely to endorse interracial interactions with blacks, they do not consider other factors that potentially influence the relationship between ethnicity and willingness to integrate.

Table 6.1 presents more rigorous multivariate evidence about the linkage between ethnicity and social distance from blacks using logit (logistic regression) analysis. The logit (logistic probability unit) model — a special case of the general log-linear model — is appropriate when the dependent variable can take on only limited values and thus violates the ordinary least squares regression model assumptions that the variables will be continuous and measured on an interval scale. In contrast to ordinary least squares regression analysis in which one is interested in predicting

FIGURE 6.4
Percentage Opposed to Living in a Neighborhood with Various Ethnic Groups,
by Race and Ethnicity

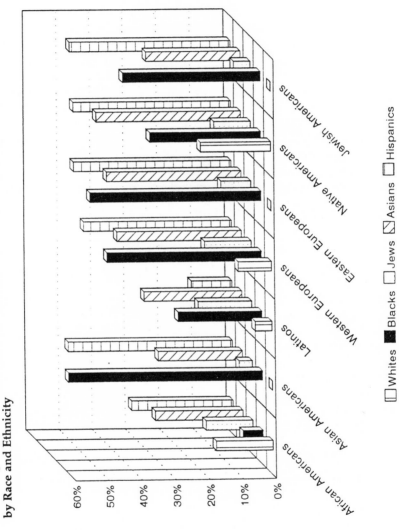

FIGURE 6.5
Percentage Opposed to Marriage with Various Ethnic Groups, by Race and Ethnicity

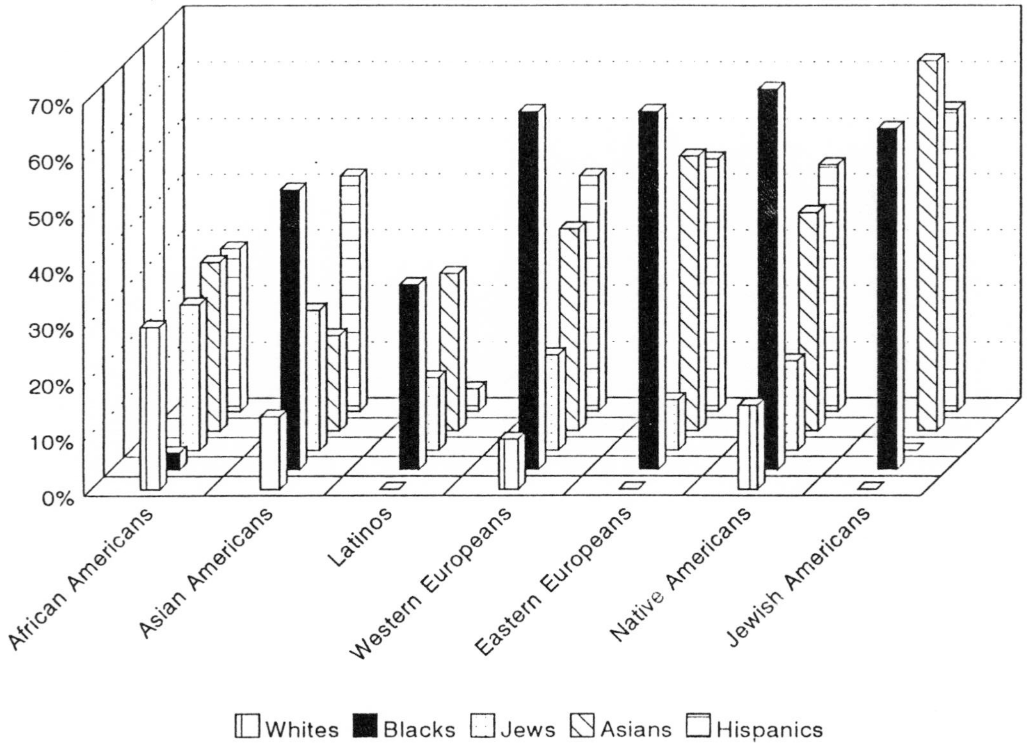

TABLE 6.1
Logistic Regression Models Predicting Social Distance by
Race or Ethnicity, Net of Other Factors

Independent Variable	I Objecting to Integrated Schools	II Favoring Bans on Intermarriages	III Unwilling to Vote for a Black President
Constant	−2.077**	−3.024**	−4.039**
Race or ethnicity			
Asian	1.421*	3.008**	3.354†
Latino	0.375	0.460	3.423**
Western European	1.087**	1.508**	3.114**
Eastern European	1.661**	0.893	2.677**
Native American	1.143**	1.218†	2.601**
Jewish	2.374**	1.155	5.022**
Other ethnicity	0.470	0.522	1.030
No ethnicity	1.118**	2.113**	3.436**
Education	−0.126†	−0.263**	−0.191**
Income	0.009**	−0.005	0.003
Age	0.005	0.039**	0.011†
Middle class	0.386†	−0.142	−0.164
Female	0.118	0.390**	−0.166
Protestant	0.127	0.426	0.217
Catholic	0.109	0.111	0.220
Immigrant	0.513*	−0.747	0.486
Southern	0.090	0.957**	0.340*
Urbanicity	−0.029	0.106**	0.054*
Conservatism	0.070	0.065	0.169†
R^2 analog	0.055**	0.263**	0.127**
−2 log likelihood	521.006	293.867	294.339
N	1,143	794	793

Notes:
Coefficients are unstandardized. For the dummy (binary) variable coefficients, significance
    levels refer to the difference between the omitted dummy variable category and the
    coefficient for the given category.
The R^2 analog statistic is the proportion of reduction in a baseline model X^2 (a model fitting
    only the constant term) attributed to the model shown. It is calculated as follows:

    R^2 = (Baseline model X^2 − Selected model X^2) / Baseline model X^2

*p < .1
†p < .05
**p < .01

values for the dependent variable for each case in the sample, logit models predict probabilities of being in one category of the dependent variable versus others, given some set of independent variables. The logit model assumes that the underlying probabilities are logistic — that is, in the form:

$$F(p) = 1 / (1 + e^{-P}) = \ln (P / 1 - P)$$

where p is the probability of the occurrence of an event, and e, an irrational number, is the base of natural logarithms such that $\ln(e^x) = X$ and the antilog of X is e^x.

The logit is the logarithm of the odds of success, that is, the ratio of the probability of the occurrence of an event to the probability of nonoccurrence of that event. The function confines the value of (p) between 0 and 1. When the odds of success are even (0.5), the logit (coefficient) is zero; when they are greater than even, the logit has a positive value; and when they are less than even, its value is negative.

Table 6.1 presents the results from logit analysis for the relationship between race/ethnicity and resistance to integration in schools with black children (model I), support for laws banning interracial marriages (model II), and unwillingness to vote for a black president (model III). Model I of Table 6.1 discloses the log-odds of being opposed to integrating schools. This model shows that, net of the other factors, Asian Americans are marginally more likely than are African Americans to oppose having their children attend integrated schools. Those of Western European ancestry, Eastern European ancestry, Native American Indian ancestry, and Jewish ancestry and those claiming no ethnicity are significantly more likely than are African Americans to oppose having their children attend integrated schools. In addition, those with middle-class identifications and higher incomes are also more likely to oppose having their children attend schools with black children. The log-odds of opposition to having one's children attend schools with black children decreases with education, however. Overall, this model explains little about opposition to sending one's children to schools with black students because it accounts for only about 5 percent of the variance.

Model II shows the correlates of support for laws banning interracial marriage. This model shows that Asian Americans, those of Western European ancestry, Native Americans, and those claiming no ethnicity are significantly more likely than are African Americans to support such laws. Support for such laws is also significantly greater among older people, women, those in the South, and those in larger cities. Education decreases the likelihood of support for such measures. This model explains more than 25 percent of the variance in support for laws banning interracial marriages.

Model III presents the log-odds of being unwilling to vote for a black president. This model suggests that virtually all other racial and ethnic groups are significantly less willing to vote for a black presidential candidate than are African Americans. This unwillingness to support a black for president is also positively correlated with age, being from the South, living in a larger city, and holding more conservative political views. Education significantly reduces one's unwillingness to support a black person for president. This model explains 12 percent of the variance in unwillingness to support a black person for president.

Table 6.2 presents the results from logit analysis for the relationship between race/ethnicity and opposition to living in a neighborhood with various ethnic groups. Model I of Table 6.2 discloses the log-odds of opposition to living in a neighborhood with predominantly whites from outside the South. This model shows that, net of the other factors, no racial or ethnic groups differ significantly from African Americans in their level of willingness to live in such neighborhoods. Only those of Native American ancestry are marginally more likely than are African Americans to oppose living in such neighborhoods.

Model II of Table 6.2 discloses the log-odds of opposition to living in a predominantly black neighborhood. This model shows some substantially different patterns. Net of the other correlates, all racial and ethnic groups are significantly more likely than are African Americans to oppose living in predominantly black neighborhoods.

Model III shows that, net of other factors, those of Jewish ancestry are less likely than are African Americans to oppose living in predominantly Jewish neighborhoods. Those of Western European ancestry, those of Eastern European ancestry, and those claiming no ethnicity, however, are significantly more likely than are African Americans to oppose living in predominantly Jewish neighborhoods.

Model IV indicates that no groups are less likely than are African Americans to oppose living in predominantly Asian neighborhoods. Net of other variables, however, Latinos, those of Western European ancestry, those of Eastern European ancestry, Native Americans, those claiming no ethnicity, and those of other ethnicities are significantly more likely than are African Americans to oppose living in predominantly Asian neighborhoods.

Model V presents the log-odds of opposition to living in a neighborhood that is predominantly Hispanic. It shows that net of the other correlates, only Latinos are significantly less likely to oppose living in such neighborhoods than are African Americans. Those of Western and Eastern European ancestry, Native Americans, those claiming no ethnicity, and those of some other ethnicity are significantly more likely than are African Americans to oppose living in predominantly Hispanic neighborhoods.

TABLE 6.2
Logistic Regression Models Predicting Objections to Neighborhood Integration with Various Ethnic Groups by Race or Ethnicity, Net of Other Factors

Independent Variable	I Objecting to Integration with Whites	II Objecting to Integration with Blacks	III Objecting to Integration with Jews	IV Objecting to Integration with Asians	V Objecting to Integration with Hispanics
Constant	0.048	-0.594	1.299**	1.859**	1.366†
Race or ethnicity					
Asian	0.210	2.653**	0.370	0.051	1.194
Latino	0.749	2.187**	-0.094	1.289**	-0.939†
Western European	0.075	3.067**	0.666**	1.515**	1.338**
Eastern European	0.717	3.465**	0.784**	2.011**	2.381**
Native American	0.861*	2.983**	0.319	1.002†	1.057†
Jewish	-0.445	2.573**	-1.906**	0.695	1.113*
Other ethnicity	0.400	2.954**	0.801*	1.347†	1.933**
No ethnicity	0.257	3.266**	0.559†	1.911**	1.291**
Education	0.012	-0.026	-0.028	-0.081†	-0.049*
Income	0.017**	0.003	0.005*	0.006*	0.008†
Age	-0.0003	0.004	-0.002	-0.0004	-0.004

Middle class	-0.086	-0.175	-0.007	-0.204	0.074
Female	0.366*	-0.289*	-0.236†	-0.132	-0.167
Protestant	-0.359	0.373	-0.299	0.125	0.099
Catholic	-0.609	0.060	-0.247	-0.033	-0.191
Immigrant	-0.494	0.095	-0.087	-0.024	-0.182
Southern		0.619**	0.446**	0.235	0.401†
Urbanicity	0.034	-0.073†	-0.013	-0.048*	-0.029
Conservatism	-0.002	-0.018	-0.012	-0.047	0.008
R^2 analog	0.036**	0.173**	0.038**	0.059**	0.084
-2 log likelihood	224.515	419.186	625.445	438.610	422.287
N	380	1,166	1,161	1,153	1,155

Notes:

Coefficients are unstandardized. For the dummy (binary) variable coefficients, significance levels refer to the difference between the omitted dummy variable category and the coefficient for the given category.

The R^2 analog statistic is the proportion of reduction in a baseline model X^2 (a model fitting only the constant term) attributed to the model shown. It is calculated as follows:

$$R^2 = (\text{Baseline model } X^2 - \text{Selected model } X^2) \, / \, \text{Baseline model } X^2$$

*p < .1
†p < .05
**p < .01

TABLE 6.3
Logistic Regression Models Predicting Objections to Integration by Intermarriage with Various Ethnic Groups by Race or Ethnicity, Net of Other Factors

Independent Variable	I Objecting to Intermarriage with Whites	II Objecting to Intermarriage with Blacks	III Objecting to Intermarriage with Jews	IV Objecting to Intermarriage with Asians	V Objecting to Intermarriage with Hispanics
Constant	0.191	-1.592†	0.881*	1.486†	1.358†
Race or ethnicity					
Asian	0.129	2.760**	0.833	-0.630	0.949
Latino	-1.629†	2.196**	-0.433	0.264	-1.654**
Western European	-0.829†	3.824**	0.386*	1.364**	0.963**
Eastern European	0.487	4.995**	1.249**	1.778**	1.787**
Native American	0.581	4.736**	0.238	1.203†	1.005†
Jewish	-0.427	2.533**	-2.496**	0.453	0.321
Other ethnicity	-1.217	2.596**	0.040	-0.185	0.136
No ethnicity	-0.661†	4.433**	0.490†	1.589**	1.157**
Education	0.004	-0.030	0.015	-0.070†	-0.061†
Income	0.010*	-0.001	0.004	0.006	0.007*
Age	-0.002	0.017†	-0.006*	0.002	-0.003

Middle class	0.083	-0.130	-0.180	-0.179	0.159
Female	0.650**	-0.098	-0.064	-0.028	0.071
Protestant	0.228	0.438	0.199	-0.023	0.020
Catholic	0.588	0.126	-0.250	0.121	-0.139
Immigrant	-0.198	0.339	0.010	0.228	-0.394
Southern		0.251	0.100	0.184	0.154
Urbanicity	-0.026	-0.086†	-0.004	-0.040	-0.010
Conservatism	0.136*	0.156†	0.047	0.138†	0.166**
R^2 analog	0.061**	0.321**	0.127**	0.067**	0.105
-2 log likelihood	216.447	272.602	560.136	339.476	373.685
N	383	1,164	793	1,161	1,163

Notes:

Coefficients are unstandardized. For the dummy (binary) variable coefficients, significance levels refer to the difference between the omitted dummy variable category and the coefficient for the given category.

The R^2 analog statistic is the proportion of reduction in a baseline model X^2 (a model fitting only the constant term) attributed to the model shown. It is calculated as follows:

R^2 = (Baseline model X^2 – Selected model X^2) / Baseline model X^2

*p < .1
†p < .05
**p < .01

Table 6.3 presents the results from logit analysis for the relationship between race/ethnicity and opposition to a relative marrying members of various ethnic groups. Model I of Table 6.3 discloses the log-odds of being opposed to a relative marrying a white person from the North. This model shows that, net of the other factors, Latinos, those of Western European ancestry, and those claiming no ethnicity are less likely to oppose such unions than are African Americans.

Model II shows parallel results with respect to marriage with blacks. It shows that all racial and ethnic groups are significantly more likely than are African Americans to oppose a relative's marriage to a black person. Model III suggests that only those of Jewish ancestry are less likely than are African Americans to oppose a relative's marriage to a Jewish person; however, those of Western European ancestry, those of Eastern European ancestry, and those claiming no ethnicity are more likely than are African Americans to oppose such marriages. Model IV shows that Western European Americans, Eastern European Americans, Native Americans, and those claiming no ethnicity are significantly more likely than are African Americans to oppose a relative's marriage to an Asian. Model V shows that although Latinos are significantly less likely than are African Americans to oppose a relative's marriage to a Hispanic person, Western European Americans, Eastern European Americans, Native Americans, and nonethnic Americans are significantly more likely than are African Americans to oppose a relative's marriage to such a person.

SUMMARY AND CONCLUSIONS

What, if anything, do these results tell us about racial attitudes and public policy? First, they tell us that despite the supposed declines in racial intolerance and prejudice and years of legislation and regulation, there are still sizeable segments of the U.S. population who do not want their children to go to school with black children, who do not want to live in the same neighborhoods with black people, who do not want to be led by black leaders, and who definitely do not want their relatives to be married to a black person. Although African Americans tend to be more tolerant of and open to interaction with other groups than all other racial and ethnic groups, the desire for social distance from African Americans is generally greater than the desire for social distance from virtually all other groups on virtually all fronts.

To the degree that public opinion has a bearing on the kinds of public policies government pursues, these results suggest that policies based on African Americans being socially accepted by whites and others in order for us to make material gains may not be very viable. If public leaders are sincere in their concerns about assisting blacks realize equal access, then perhaps they will again need to ruffle some feathers, as was the case in dismantling Jim Crow.

7

White Ethnic Identification and Racial Attitudes

James E. Coverdill

The past decade has seen a number of outstanding contributions to our understanding of racial attitudes and white ethnicity. H. Schuman, C. Steeh, and L. Bobo (1985) published *Racial Attitudes in America: Trends and Interpretations,* an example of the former; R. D. Alba's *Ethnic Identity: The Transformation of White America* (1990) exemplifies the latter. What is common to these streams of research is a relative neglect of the other. Alba's otherwise sensitive and probing analysis of the meaning and content of white ethnicity in the contemporary United States presents no data and few hints as to how ethnicity may be linked to racial attitudes. Likewise, one can search through the insightful treatment of racial attitudes by Schuman and colleagues without encountering an argument or evidence linking racial attitudes to contemporary manifestations of white ethnicity. The relative isolation of the two areas of scholarship is particularly striking in light of provocative interpretations of the white ethnic revival of the 1970s that link white ethnicity and racial attitudes. For example, S. Steinberg's *The Ethnic Myth: Race, Ethnicity and Class in America* (1981) suggested that the revival of white ethnicity could be seen at least in part as a racist response to celebrations of racial and ethnic identities by nonwhites and the civil rights movement.

The goal of this chapter is to take a small step toward bringing the literatures on racial attitudes and white ethnicity into a dialogue. I do this by elaborating and then bringing evidence to bear on an intriguing argument advanced by Mary Waters in *Ethnic Options: Choosing Identities in America* (1990). Waters argues that there might be close and important links between white ethnic identification and racial attitudes. More specifically, she claims that white ethnic identification produces highly individualistic accounts of racial inequality and little support for government programs aimed at boosting minority achievement. Unfortunately, her evidence, drawn from 60 in-depth interviews with third- and fourth-generation suburban ethnics, is not well designed to address this aspect of her argument. Without doubt, a sample of white ethnics is exactly what we need if the task is to understand how whites go about constructing ethnic identities; that was, after all, Waters's main goal. If we seek to examine empirically how white ethnic identification influences racial attitudes, however, then we need to be able to compare white ethnics with those who lack an ethnic identification. In short, we need variation in the intensity or existence of white ethnic identification in order to examine its association with racial attitudes. The empirical status of Mary Waters's argument thus remains uncertain. I explore her hypotheses in more detail here with evidence drawn from the 1990 General Social Survey (GSS).

The balance of the chapter unfolds in four sections. I first describe in more detail Waters's argument that links white ethnic identification and racial attitudes. In the second and third sections I describe the variables, statistical approaches, and results of my empirical analyses. The final section presents a broader discussion of the results and some conclusions.

LINKS BETWEEN SYMBOLIC ETHNICITY, RACE-SPECIFIC STRATIFICATION BELIEFS, AND SUPPORT FOR RACE-TARGETED SOCIAL POLICIES

Recent scholarship on white (non-Hispanic) ethnicity in the United States emphasizes two basic themes. The first points to what might be called the objective decline of white ethnicity. In the past, ethnicity was often a powerful determinant of life chances. Recent research (for example, Alba, 1990; Neidert & Farley, 1985; Lieberson & Waters, 1988), however, suggests that a profound leveling process has dramatically decreased the consequences of social distinctions deriving from European origins. The objective decline of white ethnicity is documented in the general convergence of life chances in education and employment and the ease and extent of intermarriage. Trajectories of change, moreover, point to continued convergence and hence smaller objective ethnic differences in life chances and behavior.

A second theme in recent research involves the exploration of the subjective salience and meaning of ethnicity among whites. Whether it is called symbolic, voluntary, public, imagined, or any number of other terms, white ethnicity nowadays is portrayed as akin to a jacket that can be put on or taken off at will (for example, Yinger, 1985; Gans, 1979; Kellogg, 1990; Alba, 1990). An ethnic identification is assumed or shed easily over time and in different situations. It is a source of warm gratification, adding what Alba aptly calls "spice" to social events and relationships. The "wearing o' the green" on St. Patrick's Day, the consumption of fish on Christmas Eve (an Italian custom), and indulgence at Oktoberfest are examples of the kinds of activities that might serve as markers of contemporary white ethnicity. Ethnic identification provides benefits while having few, if any, costs. It is an achieved rather than an ascribed status.

Waters's *Ethnic Options* (1990) largely confirms that portrait of symbolic ethnicity. Her data consist primarily of two sets of in-depth interviews, one conducted in San Jose, California, the other in Philadelphia, during 1986 and 1987. A secondary source of evidence stems from fieldwork conducted at family gatherings, christenings, and holiday celebrations. All of her respondents are middle class, suburban, of European extraction, and Roman Catholic. All expressed some form of ethnic identification; no data, however, are presented regarding the strength or degree of commitment to a given ethnic identification. Overall, these respondents underscore the general conclusion that white ethnic identification nowadays lacks social costs, provides enjoyment, and is chosen voluntarily.

The voluntary nature of white ethnicity, its diluted content, and the leveling of objective differences across ethnic groups might lead one to conclude that contemporary manifestations of ethnicity are largely uninteresting and sociologically inconsequential. In her concluding chapter, however, Waters suggests that the costless and voluntary character of ethnicity influences how whites account for the social and economic situations of blacks and other minorities in the United States. The flexible, symbolic, and voluntary character of white ethnicity clashes rather dramatically with the experience of race and ethnicity for U.S. minority groups. Waters's respondents, however, "did not make a distinction between their own experience of ethnicity as a personal choice and the experience of being a member of a racial minority" (p. 158). Moreover, people "equated their European ancestral background with the backgrounds of people from minority groups and saw them as interchangeable. Thus respondents told me that they just did not see why blacks and Mexican-Americans were always blaming things on their race or their ethnicity" (p. 160). The mechanism behind this hypothesized link between symbolic ethnicity and individualistic explanations of minority disadvantage thus involves the reduction of all racial and ethnic statuses to the symbolic, costless variety experienced by Waters's respondents.

Waters supports this argument with a series of extracts from her interviews (see pp. 160–161). The extracts are rife with individualistic accounts of the social and economic situations of minorities. One theme is equality of opportunity regardless of one's race or ethnicity. For example, one respondent claimed that "I think everybody has the same opportunities";

he went on to say that "I think a black kid has the same opportunity as one of my own" (p. 160). Another theme involves the idea that anyone who works hard will succeed. For example, respondents talked about the importance of "industrious energy" and the "gumption" to aggressively pursue opportunities to better oneself. In general, Waters argues that white ethnics tend to believe a person's fortune or misfortune stems from attributes like hard work and perseverance in the face of difficulties — not from opportunities or constraints based on the color of one's skin.

A second prong of Waters's argument centers on a connection between symbolic ethnicity and a lack of support for government programs designed to boost the status of minorities. It is easy to imagine that a pattern of this sort might come about in part through the purportedly individualistic orientation of the symbolic ethnics. Previous studies provide some indirect support for Waters's hypotheses in that they show that those who hold individualistic accounts of social inequality are less likely than others to support public policies aimed at redressing minority disadvantages (Kluegel, 1990; Bobo & Kluegel, 1993; Tuch & Hughes, 1996a; see also Chapter 2 of this volume). Individualism, however, is not at the heart of Waters's explanation of the social policy preferences of white ethnics. Rather, Waters emphasizes the role of stories about the past: "In fact, a large part of what people want to pass on to their children is the history of discrimination and struggle that ancestors faced when first arriving in the United States" (p. 161). Waters goes on to argue that her respondents "often pointed to the similarities between the experience of their ancestors and the discrimination experienced by non-whites now" (p. 162). That perspective makes affirmative action and other programs designed to ameliorate the deleterious effects of minority status seem like so much unnecessary special treatment and reverse discrimination. After all, if white ethnics believe that their ancestors heroically overcame whatever obstacles were placed in their path, then they might well conclude that blacks and other minorities ought to stop playing the victim and get on with the business of pulling themselves up into the mainstream.

As in her analysis of the link between white ethnicity and individualism, Waters draws upon excerpts from her interviews to suggest a link between family stories about past discrimination and current-day policy preferences. The evidence is suggestive and consistent with her interpretations. A problem with her evidence on these issues, however, is that individualistic accounts of social inequality and a lack of support for race-targeted policies tend to be very common among all white Americans — not just those who embrace some form of symbolic ethnicity. It is thus impossible to tell from the evidence that Waters presents whether it is white ethnic identification per se that lies behind the rampant individualism and policy preferences of those in her sample. In short, we need to assess variation in the degree or extent of white ethnic identification before we can conclude that the experience of symbolic ethnicity is even associated with — let alone causes — how whites interpret and act upon the social and economic circumstances of blacks and other minorities in the United States.

Waters's own characterization of white ethnicity as "voluntary" surely suggests that we ought to be able, at least in principle, to first distinguish those who have an ethnic identification and those who do not and, secondarily, those for whom an ethnic identification serves as an important influence on thought and behavior and those for whom it does not. Previous studies using data from the GSS and the Census show that 10–15 percent of American whites cannot name the countries or parts of the world from which their ancestors came (Alba & Chamlin, 1983; Lieberson, 1985). Alba (1990) makes a strong case for the idea that knowledge of — or at least beliefs about — ancestries is a necessary but not sufficient condition for the development of what he calls an ethnic identity. An ethnic identity presumes an ethnic identification, an ethnic label based on beliefs about one's ancestry, but goes beyond that labeling process to include the salience of that ethnic identification as a personally meaningful aspect of one's ways of thinking and acting. Alba's (1990, p. 51) evidence, a 1985 sample of 524 whites from the Albany, New York, area, suggests that about half of his respondents can state an ethnic identification and think of themselves in that way at least occasionally (thus giving them a modest-to-strong ethnic identity); the other half either do not state an ethnic identification or qualified or disavowed the significance of one they stated (thus leading to, at most, a very weak ethnic identity). Alba's findings underscore the conclusion that there are important variations in the existence and strength of white ethnic identifications and identities.

Unfortunately, it is very uncommon for surveys to include questions that probe ethnic identities. The few that do fail to include questions that measure beliefs about race differences in socioeconomic achievement and support for race-targeted policies. In the analyses that follow, I explore aspects of Waters's arguments about white ethnicity and racial attitudes with evidence drawn from the 1990 GSS (Davis & Smith, 1991), which contains unusually rich information regarding beliefs about social stratification and race-targeted social policies. The GSS, however, offers only a simple measure of ethnic identification that fails to capture Alba's notion of ethnic identity. The bulk of the analyses that follow thus center on exploring the strength and direction of associations between ethnic identification (not ethnic identity), beliefs about social stratification, and support for race-targeted social policies.

It is important to recognize at the outset some empirical implications of the use of a measure of ethnic identification rather than one of ethnic identity for an assessment of Waters's hypotheses. Because ethnic identification is necessary for the development of an ethnic identity, it is clear that those who lack an ethnic identification — the "unhyphenated whites" in Lieberson's (1985) terminology — are almost certainly not engaged in the kinds of ethnic-oriented behavior described by Waters. It is inconceivable that any of her respondents would state that they do not have an ethnic ancestry. Those who state an ethnic identification are less clearly linked to Waters's characterization of symbolic ethnicity, as there is a definite difference between knowing about one's ethnic past and weaving it into one's identity, action, and thought. Consequently, it is certain to be the case that only a portion of those having an ethnic identification are akin to the symbolic ethnics described by Waters. Because the "ethnic" category used here is heterogeneous (containing a mix of those like Waters's respondents and those who probably lack an ethnic identity), observed associations should be weaker than those we would observe if we were able to create a more homogeneous category of "symbolic ethnics." The evidence presented here is thus likely to indicate the correct direction of associations while underreporting the true magnitude of those associations. This chapter thus offers a conservative and admittedly tentative assessment of Waters's hypotheses.

DATA AND VARIABLES

The data are drawn from the 1990 GSS, a full-probability sample of English-speaking adults living in households in the continental United States (Davis & Smith, 1991). The survey included 1,372 respondents and had a response rate of 73 percent. The analyses here are restricted to whites; those of "other" races (nonblack) were not included because of their heterogeneous racial and ethnic characteristics. These restrictions leave the maximum sample size at 1,150. Split-ballots on several key questions reduce the sample size in some analyses to as few as 518 respondents. While Ns of that size are not large by contemporary standards, they still permit a fairly high degree of confidence in making generalizations on the basis of the sample data.

The measure of ethnic identification is derived from responses to the following question: "From what countries or part of the world did your ancestors come?" This question falls into the category of "subjective" rather than "behavioral" or "natal" approaches to ethnicity (Smith, 1980, 1985). The first category of ethnic identification actually represents non-identification with an ethnicity. Of the 1,150 white respondents, 9.7 percent (111 cases) could not name any country from which their ancestors came. Three respondents claimed that they were "American" and refused to identify any other country from which their ancestors had come. I group these three respondents with the "no ethnic identification" group because it does not seem sensible to think of the generic category "American" as an ethnic identification for whites in the United States.

The category called "no ethnicity" thus coincides with the unhyphenated whites described by Lieberson (1985). The second category of ethnic identification includes respondents who named one or more countries from which their ancestors came. These two categories form the dummy variable called "ethnic"; those with an ethnic identification are scored 1 (0 otherwise). Table 7.1 presents a summary description of this variable and others used in the analyses.

TABLE 7.1
Variable Descriptions

Variable	Description
Ethnic	A dummy variable scored 1 (0 otherwise) if the respondent reported an ethnic identification (GSS variables ETHNIC and ETHNUM).
Race-specific structuralism	A dummy variable coded 1 (0 otherwise) if the respondent stated that socioeconomic differences (in jobs, income, and housing) between blacks and whites are because most blacks do not have the chance for education that it takes to rise out of poverty (GSS variable RACDIF3).
Race-specific individualism	A dummy variable coded 1 (0 otherwise) if the respondent stated that socioeconomic differences (in jobs, income, and housing) between blacks and whites are because most blacks just do not have the motivation or willpower to pull themselves up out of poverty (GSS variable RACDIF4).
Opportunity enhancement index	The average of responses to three items that entail race-targeted, opportunity-enhancing policies. The policies involve "things that the government in Washington might do to deal with the problems of poverty and unemployment among black Americans" including giving business and industry special tax breaks for locating in largely black areas; spending more money on the schools in black neighborhoods, especially for preschool and early education programs; and providing special college scholarships for black children who maintain good grades. The index is coded so that higher values indicate greater support for these policies (GSS variables BLKZONE, BLKSCHS, and BLKCOL).
Special treatment	A 5-point scale based on the following question: "Some people think that blacks have been discriminated against for so long that the government has a special obligation to help improve their living

Variable	Description
	standards. Others believe that the government should not be giving special treatment to blacks." Responses range from 1 = "I strongly agree that government should not give special treatment" to 5 = "I strongly agree the government is obligated to help blacks" (GSS variable HELPBLK).
Government assistance	A 3-point scale based on the following question: "We are faced with many problems in this country, none of which can be solved easily or inexpensively. I'm going to name some of these problems, and for each one I'd like you to tell me whether you think we're spending too much money on it, too little money, or about the right amount." Coded so that 1 = too much, 2 = about right, 3 = too little (GSS variable NATRACEY).
South	A dummy variable coded 1 if the respondent lived in the South (0 otherwise). Three Census regions form the South: South Atlantic (Delaware, Maryland, West Virginia, Virginia, North Carolina, South Carolina, Georgia, Florida, and the District of Columbia); East South Central (Tennessee, Alabama, and Mississippi); and West South Central (Arkansas, Oklahoma, Louisiana, and Texas) (GSS variable REGION).
Urban	A dummy variable coded 1 (0 otherwise) if the respondent lived in an SMSA (GSS variable XNORCSIZ where codes 1–6 = 1 and 7–10 = 0).
LnIncome	The natural logarithm of family income adjusted to constant 1986 dollars before the logarithmic transformation (GSS variable REALINC).
Age	Respondent's age (GSS variable AGE).
Education	Years of school completed (GSS variable EDUC).

The bulk of the analyses presented later in this chapter explores the association between the measure of ethnic identification and five dependent variables that fall into two groups: accounts of black-white differences in socioeconomic attainment, and support for race-targeted social policies. One of Waters's two main arguments suggests that white ethnics fail to see a difference between the voluntary and costless nature of their ethnic identifications and the involuntary and often very costly nature of being black in the United States. This projection of the characteristics of symbolic ethnicity onto minority groups leaves ethnics unable to understand the various ways in which being a minority constrains opportunities and achievements. Reasoning of this type involves what have been called stratification beliefs, a set of ideas that represent an explanation for why individuals end up in higher or lower positions in society. Kluegel and Smith (1986) argue that observers of U.S. culture have long noted the prominence of individualistic accounts of social stratification. Individualistic accounts "locate the causes of achievement within the individual person, in ability, efforts, or other characteristics such as personality traits and educational achievement" (Kluegel & Smith, 1986, p. 75). An alternative to an individualistic account of social inequality shifts attention to one or more aspects of an individual's social environment, which may enhance or impede the individual's efforts to succeed. A structuralistic account of social stratification thus emphasizes "such factors as the lack or abundance of available jobs, society's provision of adequate or inadequate schools, racial or sexual discrimination, and inherited wealth or its lack" (Kluegel & Smith, 1986, p. 75).

I examine the first prong of Waters's argument with two measures of race-specific stratification beliefs. Race-specific measures of structuralism and individualism assess how respondents account for differences in the social positions held by blacks and whites in the United States. The variable called race-specific structuralism assesses whether respondents believe that socioeconomic differences between blacks and whites in jobs, income, and housing stem from racial differences in educational opportunities; agreement represents a structuralistic account of racial inequality. The variable called race-specific individualism is a measure that locates socioeconomic differences between blacks and whites in the failure of blacks to muster the motivation and will to pull themselves out of poverty. Both of these variables are single items that are dummy coded; scores of 1 (0 otherwise) indicate agreement with individualism or structuralism.

The rationale behind my consideration of measures of both race-specific individualism and structuralism is based on the fact that Waters makes reference to both types of stratification beliefs. I have described the first prong of Waters's argument as one that makes a link between white ethnicity and individualistic accounts of racial differences in socioeconomic attainment. Her argument suggests that individualistic accounts of inequality are on a continuum where the polar opposite of an individualistic account is a structuralistic one. Although that conceptualization makes intuitive sense and represents a stylistically reasonable way to describe stratification beliefs, recent research on stratification beliefs (for example, Kluegel, 1990; Kluegel & Smith, 1986) shows that, empirically, structuralism and individualism are not two components of a single, unidimensional construct. In short, many individuals appear to meld aspects of both individualism and structuralism in their overall account of social stratification. I interpret Waters's argument to imply that those with an ethnic identification should be more individualistic and less structuralistic than those who lack an ethnic identification when they account for race differences in socioeconomic achievement.

The second prong of Waters's argument involves a link between ethnic identification and support for government programs designed to increase opportunities for blacks. I consider three measures of support for race-targeted policies that fall into two main groups. As Bobo and Kluegel (1993) argue, it is sensible to distinguish race-targeted policies that aim to enhance opportunities for blacks from those designed to promote equal outcomes for blacks and whites. In general, whites are much more supportive of opportunity-enhancing policies than of policies that attempt to intervene directly in the distribution of outcomes (Bobo & Kluegel, 1993; Kluegel & Smith, 1986). Attitudes toward opportunity-enhancing policies are measured by the opportunity enhancement index, which represents the average response to three questions about policies the federal government might enact to help alleviate problems of poverty and unemployment among blacks. The items include tax breaks for businesses locating in black areas, increased spending on schools in black neighborhoods, and special college scholarships for academically talented black students.

Attitudes about equal-outcome policies are measured indirectly by two variables. The first variable, called special treatment, is based on a single question that probes opinions about the government's obligation to provide "special treatment" to blacks to help improve their standard of living. Responses ranged from "I strongly agree the government is obligated to help blacks" (coded 5) to "I strongly agree that government shouldn't give special treatment" (coded 1). The second variable is called government assistance and is also based on a single item that assesses beliefs about whether the government is spending an appropriate amount of money on assistance to blacks. Responses range from "too little" (coded 3) money is being spent to "too much" (coded 1). Although neither variable directly refers to a specific equal-outcome policy, Bobo and Kluegel (1993, pp. 450–451) make a strong case that respondents who do not support equal-outcome policies are unlikely to support increased government spending or special treatment for blacks. Because the opportunity enhancement index and the two measures of support for equal-outcome policies are identical to those used by Bobo and Kluegel (1993), their defense and interpretations of the measures are thus equally valid in the analyses conducted here.

Waters's argument implies that those with an ethnic identification should be less supportive of both opportunity-enhancing and equal-outcome policies than those who lack an ethnic identification. Importantly, however, Waters's argument suggests that stratification beliefs should not be the sole driving force behind that pattern. Stories about immigrant experiences and the ability of ethnic ancestors to overcome early discrimination are hypothesized to play an important role in shaping the policy views of symbolic ethnics. Waters's argument would be supported if those with an ethnic identification are less supportive of race-targeted policies than those without an ethnic identification, net of the effects of stratification beliefs on such policy preferences.

A final block of variables includes controls found to be important predictors of stratification beliefs and policy preferences (Kluegel & Smith, 1986; Kluegel, 1990; Bobo & Kluegel, 1993). These variables include region of residence, urbanism, family income, age, and education and are described in some detail in Table 7.1.

RESULTS

Columns 1 and 2 in Table 7.2 present means on key study variables for nonethnics and ethnics. The third column contains the t statistics for the mean differences across the two categories of ethnic identification. The fourth and final column reports the number of cases available for these bivariate analyses. Three overall patterns stand out. First, means for race-specific measures of structuralism and individualism differ substantially and significantly for ethnics and nonethnics. Those mean differences, however, are inconsistent with Waters's hypothesis because they show that ethnics are, on the average, more structuralistic and less individualistic

TABLE 7.2
Variable Means for Ethnics and Unhyphenated Whites

| Variable | Ethnic Identification | | t-value | N of cases |
	No	Yes		
Race-specific structuralism	0.333	0.539	−4.16*	1,107
Race-specific individualism	0.773	0.631	3.13*	1,075
Opportunity enhancement index	3.260	3.503	−2.03*	553
Special treatment	2.327	2.403	−0.57	1,108
Government assistance	1.741	1.983	−2.80*	518
Southern	0.649	0.254	8.31*	1,150
Urban	0.496	0.731	−4.74*	1,150
LnIncome	9.750	10.106	−3.61*	1,041
Age	43.090	46.991	−2.15*	1,150
Education	11.000	13.202	−6.97*	1,149

*Means are significantly different at $p < .05$ (two-tailed test). Variables are defined in Table 7.1.

than those who lack an ethnic identification. Waters's argument implies the opposite pattern.

A second pattern involves the means of the three measures of support for race-targeted social policies. The results show that ethnics are more supportive of opportunity-enhancing policies (the opportunity enhancement index) than are nonethnics. Moreover, both measures of support for equal-outcome policies show that ethnics are more supportive of them than nonethnics, although only the measure "Government Assistance" indicates a statistically significant mean difference for ethnics and nonethnics. As with the results for the two measures of stratification beliefs, these means are at odds with Waters's argument that ethnics are less supportive than nonethnics of race-targeted social policies. Thus far, the results flatly contradict Waters's hypotheses.

A third pattern shown in the table suggests the need for some caution in making strong statements about Waters's hypotheses on the basis of the simple mean-difference analysis. A cursory glance at the distribution of the control variables across categories of ethnic identification reveals several very strong associations. Respondents who express an ethnic identification tend to live outside the South and in urban areas; they are also somewhat older and have higher levels of family income and education than the nonethnics. Some of these associations are simply huge. For example, only 25 percent of ethnics live in the South, whereas nearly 65 percent of those who lack an ethnic identification live in the South, a difference of 40 percentage points. Education levels are also very different for ethnics and nonethnics. Past research has documented the important role played by region and education in shaping both stratification beliefs and support for race-targeted social policies (Kluegel & Smith, 1986; Kluegel, 1990; Bobo & Kluegel, 1993; see also Chapter 8 of this volume). Given the strong association between those two variables, in particular, and the measure of ethnic identification, some caution needs to be exercised in drawing strong conclusions about Waters's hypotheses from the bivariate mean differences presented thus far.

Table 7.3 presents the results of logistic regression models in which the two race-specific stratification beliefs serve as dependent variables. The table contains four models. For each dependent variable, the first model indicates the bivariate effect of ethnic identification on the stratification belief. That model establishes a baseline that is compared to the net effect of ethnic identification in the second model. Models 1 and 3 thus replicate the mean-difference analysis in Table 7.2, with the exception that data missing on the control variables has now been deleted in a listwise fashion. Those two models mirror the earlier results, showing that ethnics are more structuralistic and less individualistic than nonethnics in their accounts of racial inequality. Models 2 and 4 show that the net effect of ethnic identification on stratification beliefs is substantially smaller in

magnitude than the zero-order effect. The analysis of race-specific structuralism in model 2 shows that the net effect of ethnic identification is
about half the magnitude of the zero-order effect; moreover, the net effect
is significant only at the $p < .10$ level, not the conventional threshold of
0.05. A similar though more dramatic change occurs in model 4, the multivariate analysis of race-specific individualism. After the control variables are taken into account, the effect of ethnic identification on individualism drops by about 50 percent and becomes statistically insignificant.
Overall, the results show only slight differences in stratification beliefs for
ethnics and nonethnics. If there is a difference between the two groups
that is not simply a product of their different levels of education, region
of residence, and so on, then that difference is contrary to Waters's
hypothesis.

TABLE 7.3
**Results of the Logistic Regressions of Race-Specific Stratification Beliefs on
Ethnic Identification and Control Variables**

Independent Variable	Dependent Variable			
	Race-specific Structuralism		Race-specific Individualism	
	1.	2.	3.	4.
Ethnic	0.974*	0.469†	−0.720*	−0.379
South		−0.363*		0.376*
Urban		−0.126		−0.165
LnIncome		0.103		0.021
Age		0.008*		0.010*
Education		0.203*		−0.118*
Constant	−0.807*	−4.197*	1.253*	1.861*
−2(LL)	1,377	1,291	1,271	1,229
N of cases	1,008		982	

Notes:
   Variables are defined in Table 7.1
   *$p < .05$
   †$p < .10$ (two-tailed tests)

Table 7.4 presents the results of ordinary least squares regressions that
take as dependent variables the three measures of support for race-targeted social policies. I report three models for each of the three dependent
variables. The first model (models 1, 4, and 7) mirrors the bivariate mean
difference analysis presented in Table 7.2; it differs only in that missing
data on the two measures of stratification beliefs and the control variables

TABLE 7.4
Results of Ordinary Least Squares Regressions of Support for Race-Targeted Policies on Ethnic Identification, Race-Specific Stratification Beliefs, and Control Variables

	Dependent Variable								
	Opportunity Enhancement Index			Special Treatment			Government Assistance		
Independent Variable	1.	2.	3.	4.	5.	6.	7.	8.	9.
Ethnic	0.291*	0.117	-0.090	0.151	-0.059	-0.216	0.295*	0.159†	0.098
Race-specific individualism		-0.384*	-0.350*		-0.450*	-0.404*		-0.227*	-0.201*
Race-specific structuralism		0.444*	0.368*		0.641*	0.583*		0.391*	0.377*
Southern			-0.230*			-0.211*			-0.169*
Urban			0.217*			0.138†			0.075
LnIncome			-0.032			-0.054			-0.052
Age			0.002			-0.002			-0.003
Education			0.048*			0.044*			0.005
Constant	3.215*	3.386*	3.088*	2.250*	2.405*	2.588*	1.688*	1.756*	2.361*
R-square	0.009	0.141	0.184	0.001	0.136	0.157	0.018	0.147	0.168
N of cases	474	474	474	935	935	935	443	443	443

Notes:
Variables are defined in Table 7.1

*p < .05

†p < .10 (two-tailed tests)

are deleted listwise. In accord with the results from Table 7.2, models 1 and 7 show that ethnics are more supportive of race-targeted policies than is the case for nonethnics. The dependent variable "special treatment," once again, shows that ethnic identification does not appear to influence support for social policies designed to boost the living standards of black Americans.

Models 2, 5, and 8 control for the two measures of race-specific stratification beliefs. The point of these models is to determine whether ethnic identification, net of its association with stratification beliefs, influences support for race-targeted social policies. Waters's argument about the link between ethnicity and policy preferences suggested that stories about immigrant experiences, not heightened individualism (or lowered structuralism) per se, predisposed ethnics to reject social policies that give preferential treatment to blacks. The mechanism in her argument would be made more plausible by the evidence if, in fact, ethnics were less supportive than nonethnics of race-targeted policies, net of the influence of stratification beliefs. The results are not supportive of Waters's line of reasoning. The first and most formidable problem for her argument remains the fact that ethnics tend to be more supportive than nonethnics of race-targeted social policies.

A second problem is that the introduction of the two measures of stratification beliefs in model 2 dramatically cuts the size of the slope on ethnic identification and renders it statistically insignificant. A similar, though less dramatic, pattern holds for the results of model 8. After control variables are added in models 3, 6, and 9, the effects of ethnic identification on support for race-targeted social policies become uniformly small in magnitude and statistically insignificant.

Overall, the results suggest that ethnic identification has only a slight effect on how whites account for socioeconomic differences between blacks and whites in the United States. That difference, however, indicates that ethnics are more "liberal" than nonethnics in that they tend to be somewhat more likely to espouse a structuralistic explanation and less likely to offer an individualistic account of racial differences in socioeconomic attainment. Those patterns are opposite those expected by Waters. Support for race-targeted social policies differs for ethnics and nonethnics only because those two groups differ somewhat in their stratification beliefs. After stratification beliefs are controlled, ethnics and nonethnics are largely indistinguishable in terms of their support for race-targeted social policies.

DISCUSSION

I explored several factors that might account for the differences between my results and those suggested by Waters. Because her sample was exclusively suburban and Catholic, I estimated models that included a dummy variable scored 1 (0 otherwise) when the respondent was Roman Catholic. I also considered the possibility that urbanism and religious preference might condition the effects of other variables; I thus estimated sets of interaction models based on religion and urban residence. I do not present the results here because they showed nothing of interest. Some caution, however, is in order because the relatively small sample sizes and the skewed distributions on some of the variables (for example, the measure of ethnic identification) can make the results of complicated interaction models rather unstable. Even so, I was unable to identify any plausible factors that might account for the discrepancy between the results reported here and those expected by Waters.

Another potential line of argument is tethered to measurement error in the ethnic identification variable. To be sure, the symbolic ethnicity embraced by Waters's respondents is not well measured by the GSS question about ethnic origins. It is tempting to dismiss the results by saying that my measure of ethnic identification is too crude to get at the kind of behavior and thought so well described in Waters's *Ethnic Options* (1990). Despite the limitations of the GSS questions about ethnic identification, I believe that such a conclusion is unwarranted.

Consider the top panel of Figure 7.1, a graph showing the percentage of respondents who expressed an individualistic response to the race-specific measure of individualism. The first two groups on the x-axis represent the observed categories of the ethnic identification variable, nonethnics and ethnics. The y-axis is scaled as the percentage of respondents who indicated an individualistic response. Per the results in Table 7.2, the graph indicates that 77 percent of nonethnics and 63 percent of ethnics expressed an individualistic response. So far, the graph just shows what we know from the simple mean-difference analysis.

The point here is to use the figure to help puzzle through what we would have to argue to end up with the results predicted by Waters's argument. The category of nonethnics seems relatively straightforward in its connection to symbolic ethnicity: These people are almost certainly not engaged in the kinds of ethnic-oriented behavior described by Waters. As I stated earlier, it is inconceivable that any of her respondents would claim that they do not have an ethnic ancestry when confronted with the GSS question on ethnicity. The ethnics — those who expressed an ethnic identification — are less clearly linked to the kind of symbolic ethnicity described by Waters. After all, Alba's (1990) study underscored important differences between ethnic identifications and ethnic identities. In short, many who know about an ethnic past fail to weave it into their sense of self, thought, and behavior. Consequently, it is almost certain to be the case that only a portion of those having an ethnic identification are akin to the symbolic ethnics described by Waters.

FIGURE 7.1

Illustrations of the Likely Substantive Implications of Unmeasured Heterogeneity in the Measure of Ethnic Identification

Panel A: Equal Groups (Proportion Symbolic = 0.5; Proportion Uncommitted = 0.5)

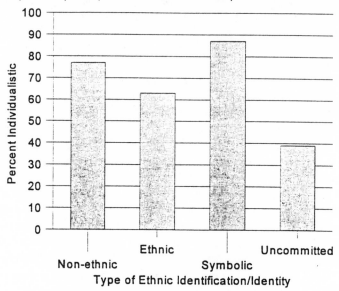

Panel B: Unequal Groups (Proportion Symbolic = 0.1; Proportion Uncommitted -= 0.9)

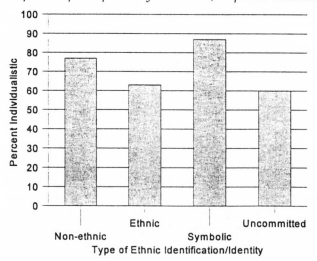

Imagine, then, that the category of ethnics fails to distinguish "symbolic" ethnics from what might be called "uncommitted" ethnics — those who state an ethnic identification while lacking an ethnic identity. It is possible that the symbolic ethnics are more individualistic in perspective than the uncommitted ethnics and, importantly, those without an ethnic identification. My inability to distinguish empirically these two groups of ethnics leaves me with only the weighted average of the responses of the symbolic and uncommitted ethnics. Consider my hypothetical differentiation of symbolic and uncommitted ethnics on the right-hand side of Figure 7.1. I have assumed that of the 978 ethnics, about half are symbolic and half are uncommitted. (The "equal groups" scenario is fairly close to that suggested by Alba [1990, especially page 64].) In this case, the uncommitted and symbolic groups are assumed to be the same size; each group thus has 489 cases.

Waters's hypothesis would expect the symbolic ethnics to be more individualistic than the uncommitted ethnics and, especially, those who lack an ethnic identification. In accord with that prediction, I assume that about 87 percent of the symbolic ethnics would express an individualistic response. A 10-percentage-point difference between nonethnics and symbolic ethnics would, in my opinion, be both statistically significant and sufficiently large to support Waters's hypothesis. Recall, though, that the weighted average of the responses for the symbolic and uncommitted ethnics needs to be 67 percent (what we observe for the overall ethnic group). In order to boost the percentage of individualistic responses among the symbolic ethnics to 87 percent, we need to lower the percentage for the uncommitted ethnics to a mere 39.2 percent. This value is derived from a simple weighted-average calculation where $63.1 = 87(0.5) + X(0.5)$. In words, the overall percentage of ethnics indicating an individualistic response (63.1 percent) is decomposed into the percentage of symbolic ethnics expressing an individualistic response (assumed to be 87 percent) and the percentage of uncommitted ethnics expressing an individualistic response (noted as an x in the expression given above and calculated as 39.2 percent). Note that the two groups of ethnics (symbolic and uncommitted) are assumed to be equal in size (thus the use of the multiplier 0.5 with each percentage).

In order to get a mean individualism for the symbolics that is about 10 percentage points above the percentage for the nonethnic group, we would have to be willing to argue that it is reasonable to expect the uncommitted ethnics to largely disavow the individualistic perspective. That seems extremely unlikely. In the bottom panel of Figure 7.1, labeled "unequal groups," I imagine the symbolic ethnics to be vastly outnumbered by the uncommitted ethnics. In this figure, I assume that 90 percent of ethnics are uncommitted ethnics, leaving only 10 percent symbolic. Because the weighted average of the two groups will look much like the mean individualism for the uncommitted ethnics, there is no need to argue that the uncommitteds will disavow individualism to the extent that was required in the equal groups example at the top of Figure 7.1. This scenario seems more plausible, although it requires one to assume that symbolic ethnics are vastly outnumbered by uncommitted ethnics, an assumption that is not consistent with Alba's (1990) findings.

One rather nagging problem with that line of thought remains. Uncommitted ethnics and people who do not express an ethnic identification would seem, conceptually, more similar to each other than to those who embrace symbolic ethnicity. In order to boost the mean individualism for symbolic ethnics above that for those lacking an ethnic identification, we need to push the mean individualism for uncommitted ethnics down and farther away from the mean for those without an ethnic identification. This seems patently unreasonable: We are required to assume that the two most conceptually similar groups (uncommitted ethnics and those who lack an ethnic identification) are quite distinct in their accounts of the status of black Americans.

The argument and the two figures are built on the simple logic of weighted means and various assumptions about group sizes and levels of individualism. What we observe directly is that those with an ethnic identification are less individualistic (and more structuralistic) than nonethnics in their understanding of socioeconomic differences between whites and blacks in the United States. The figures suggest what we might observe if we were able to pull apart the broad category of "ethnic" and distinguish symbolic ethnics from those I have called uncommitted ethnics. In my view, the only plausible conclusion is that my inability to differentiate symbolic ethnics from uncommitted ethnics weakens the patterns we observe. I thus doubt that the somewhat crude measure of ethnic identification used in this chapter lies behind my inability to find support for Waters's hypothesis.

CONCLUSIONS

For many whites, ethnic identification is voluntary, gratifying, and largely costless. In the concluding chapter to *Ethnic Options* (1990, p. 158), Mary Waters argues that ethnicity has a sinister consequence: "This approach to their own ethnicity leads to a situation where whites with a symbolic ethnicity are unable to understand the everyday influence and importance of skin color and racial minority status for members of minority groups in the United States." That mindset should prompt white ethnics to maintain that racial inequality stems from individual failings on the part of black Americans. It should also leave white ethnics unsupportive of government programs designed to overcome some portion of the cost of race for blacks. The press of social structure and individual acts of discrimination against blacks would be discounted; blacks themselves would be held responsible for racial stratification.

I investigated these ideas with reasonable, though obviously imperfect, evidence from the 1990 GSS. The first prong of the analysis probed accounts of inequality between blacks and whites in the United States; the second prong explored support for race-targeted government policies. The empirical results provide absolutely no support for Waters's speculations. The zero-order results are either null (one policy measure) or radically different from the patterns she anticipated (the measures of stratification beliefs and two of the three policy measures). The results provide some support for the idea that an ethnic identification leaves people slightly less individualistic in their accounts of racial inequality and more supportive of race-targeted policies than is the case for those who lack an ethnic identification. When statistical controls are added, the results still fail to support Waters's hypothesis.

My effort to bring Waters's hypothesis into a dialogue with imperfect yet reasonable evidence thus produces unsupportive and somewhat perplexing findings. It is not clear why people with an ethnic identification would be less individualistic and more structuralistic than others in their accounts of racial inequality. One possibility is that those who lack an ethnic identification are insensitive to (or unaware of) their place in the waves of immigration that mark the history of the United States. That insensitivity might be part of a larger outlook that discounts historical patterns and, more generally, the influence of social structure. In many ways, such an outlook seems strikingly "American" in its likely emphasis on individualism, achievement over ascription, and the image of the United States as a melting pot where ethnic differentiation gives way to cultural homogeneity. This is, of course, speculation, and I am left only with confidence in a negative conclusion: Ethnic identification does not lead to individualistic and nonstructuralistic explanations of racial inequality in the United States, nor does it increase white opposition to government programs designed to boost the social and economic status of black Americans.

Future analyses of the issues explored in this chapter would be greatly facilitated by more direct measures of the kind of symbolic ethnicity described by Waters, Gans, and others. Such data could be either quantitative or qualitative. My use of quantitative data to evaluate Waters's argument is not meant to imply that quantitative data are more appropriate for the substantive problems at hand. What is essential is that we be able to measure whether — and to what degree — a person's ethnic identification enters into his or her thought and action. Variation in the intensity or existence of white ethnic identifications and identities is, of course, logically necessary if we want to argue that ethnic identifications or identities bring about certain racial attitudes. The GSS allows for variation in ethnic identification; the simplicity of the GSS questions on ethnicity, however, leave the analyses presented here suggestive but less than completely satisfying.

NOTE

This research was supported by a grant from the University of Georgia Research Foundation. An early version of this chapter was presented at the 1993 annual meeting of the American Sociological Association in Miami Beach, Florida. I thank Woody Beck, William Finlay, Pat Horan, Joan Marie Kraft, Mary Ann Mauney, and Steven Tuch for helpful comments.

8

Regional Differences in Whites' Racial Policy Attitudes

Steven A. Tuch and Jack K. Martin

In *An American Dilemma: The Negro Problem and Modern Democracy* (1944), Gunnar Myrdal highlighted the paradox posed by pervasive white racism toward blacks in the face of dominant U.S. cultural and political values emphasizing freedom and equality. As documented by five subsequent decades of social science research, Myrdal's work ushered in a period of unprecedented liberalization of white Americans' attitudes regarding race (for reviews of this literature see Jaynes & Williams, 1989; Schuman, Steeh, & Bobo, 1985; Sigelman & Welch, 1991). Since the 1940s, whites' support for principles of racial equality in such areas as voting rights, the workplace, housing, and school integration has increased dramatically. This period is also marked by declines in many of the race-based social, economic, and political inequalities Myrdal highlighted in his seminal work.

By most measures, however, racial inequalities and intergroup conflicts have persisted into the 1990s. One indication of continuing racial animus is whites' strong support for principles of racial equality, on the one hand, coupled with their failure to endorse specific policies designed to implement the principles, on the other (Bobo & Kluegel, 1993; Tuch & Hughes, 1996a) — a discrepancy that has led some analysts to question whites' commitment to meaningful racial change (Jackman, 1981; Tuch & Hughes, 1996b). Racial policies are initiatives, usually but not exclusively by the federal government, designed to fight current racial discrimination and ameliorate the effects of past discrimination. Such policies cover a broad political spectrum, ranging from relatively benign programs such as compensatory education to more controversial programs based on racial preferences and quotas in hiring, promotions, and college admissions (see Steeh and Krysan [1996] for a review of survey-based racial policy questions). We use the term "racial policy" broadly to refer to all types of programs that are intended to promote racial equality, whether or not they incorporate quotas or preferences.

There is little consensus in the racial attitudes literature over what factors account for the principle-policy divide. Some analysts point to a combination of antiblack affect and a view of blacks as violating "mainstream" values — so-called "modern" or "symbolic" racism — as the underlying cause of whites' opposition to ameliorative racial policy. Others focus on whites' stratification beliefs, especially their tendency to explain black disadvantage by reference to alleged personal failings of blacks themselves, a viewpoint that implicitly legitimizes inequality. A third account centers on the role of group interest or self-interest in shaping policy preferences. Still others argue that opposition to an intrusive federal government, not to race targeting per se, underlies whites' intransigence on policy issues (for a recent review of this literature that evaluates the competing explanations, see the exchange between Tuch and Hughes [1996b] and Davis [1996], Jackman [1996], Sears and Jessor [1996], and Stoker [1996]).

Our purpose in this chapter is primarily descriptive. Our goal is to describe regional differences in whites' racial policy attitudes, with a particular focus on regions whose residents have traditionally exhibited the greatest levels of racial antipathy, that is, the South and so-called Deep South.

REGIONAL DISTINCTIVENESS IN RACIAL ATTITUDES

Popular and journalistic accounts of the emergence of the "New South" can be traced back at least a century (Reed, 1991), although most social science research dates the onset of the transition from the "Old South" to the 1940s. According to some commentators (see Reed, 1991, 1986; Reed & Black, 1985), regional differences in racial prejudice "are so much smaller now than twenty years ago that they can almost be ignored" (Reed, 1991, p. 229). Arguably, this change reflects the emergence of a New South where large-scale demographic, economic, residential, and educational changes of the past 50 years have combined to transform the traditional South into a place that is increasingly similar to the rest of the country. The thesis that sectional cultural differences have diminished over time is not new. Two-and-a-half decades ago, for instance, J. C. McKinney and L. B. Bourque (1971) predicted that to the extent that the "daily occupational and educational environment of the southerner becomes similar to that of the non-southerner, the attitudes and the values of the two will also become indistinguishable" (p. 408; see also Mayo, 1964).

Such optimistic accounts of the emergence of the New South, while common, have not been uniformly supported by the empirical evidence (see Glenn & Simmons [1967] for early conflicting evidence and Glaser [1994] for recent evidence). This is particularly so when the focus is on the transformation of racial attitudes. Although the regional gap in racial prejudice has gradually narrowed over time (see Firebaugh & Davis [1988] and Wilson [1996]), South–non-South differences in endorsement of racial principles have tended to disappear only when a ceiling on these attitudes is reached in the non-South (Schuman, Steeh, & Bobo, 1985).

Considerably less is known about regional differences in whites' racial policy preferences. We know less about regional variations in policy views in part because analysts of regional patterns have tended to treat the New South as a demographically, economically, and politically homogeneous place, ignoring differences between peripheral and Deep South (Alabama, Georgia, Louisiana, Mississippi, and South Carolina) states. Such intra-South comparisons are particularly important for the study of racial attitudes. For instance, there is evidence that within the Deep South, regional identification is stronger now than 15 years ago (Reed, Kohls, & Hanchette, 1990). Deep South states are also distinctive in that they include within their borders fewer non–Southern-born migrants, fewer metropolitan areas, more African-American residents, and more racially conservative whites than the peripheral South (Glaser, 1994).

In sum, we examine whether white residents of the South, particularly Southerners in the regional core, are more resistant than non-Southern residents to policies designed to change the racial status quo, despite marked demographic and economic changes in their region's social structure over the last half century. We first examine evidence of regional distinctiveness in racial policy attitudes, using data from two recent national surveys. Next, we supplement the national survey data with a Deep South sample in order to assess whether attitudinal patterns typical of the South are mirrored in the regional core.

DATA

We use data from three sources: the 1990 General Social Survey (GSS) administered by the National Opinion Research Center; the 1990 American National Election Study (ANES) conducted by the Institute for Social Research at the University of Michigan; and the 1994 and 1995 Georgia polls administered by the Survey Research Center at the University of Georgia. Both the GSS and the ANES are national surveys based on full-probability sampling designs and are representative of the noninstitutionalized adult population of the continental United States. For a complete discussion of GSS sampling methodology, see Davis and Smith (1990); see Miller (1990) for a discussion of ANES sampling procedures. The data we report for the Deep South are a combination of two separate single-stage random-digit dialing telephone surveys of current Georgia residents collected in the springs of 1994 and 1995 and stratified by area code to provide proportional representation of adult respondents (18 years of age and older) residing in north Georgia, south Georgia, and the Atlanta metropolitan area. The 1994 data are based on completed interviews with 414 of the 527 households contacted, a response rate of 78.6 percent. The 1995 data are based on the responses of 401 of the 607 households contacted, a 66.1 percent response rate. The sampling error is no more than ±4.8 percent in 1994 and ±4.9 percent in 1995. The combined overall response rate for the two years is 72 percent. Georgia poll interviewees were asked whether they were natives of the state or whether they had migrated to Georgia from another state. Those who had migrated were asked to identify the state in which they were raised. The Deep South category consists of Georgia natives plus those raised in Alabama, Louisiana, Mississippi, or South Carolina. Georgia residents are similar demographically to residents of other Deep South states, but because our Deep South sample is composed only of current Georgia residents, the South–Deep South comparisons we make below should be considered suggestive.

FINDINGS

Table 8.1 presents data on responses to nine questions on racial policy issues that have recently generated heated debate among the U.S. public. Questions 1–7 are GSS items that address white respondents' views toward various kinds and degrees of government intervention to improve the life chances of African Americans; questions 8 and 9 are ANES items that deal with the most controversial aspects of racial policies — quotas and preferences. In our item-by-item summary of responses to the questions, we first describe distributions for the national sample of whites; we then compare the policy preferences of whites residing outside the South with those residing in the South; and finally, we examine the preferences of Southerners relative to those who grew up in the Deep South.

Questions 1 and 2 refer to government spending and economic aid, respectively. The first question asks respondents about government spending on programs to assist blacks. Nationally, half of all respondents consider current spending levels to be adequate, with the other half roughly divided between those who think too little (27.7 percent) or too much (22.4 percent) is being spent. Large regional differences characterize these views. Only 18.2 percent of non-Southern whites view current spending levels as too high, compared to 32.8 percent of white Southerners and fully 67.4 percent of Deep South whites. Responses to question 2

TABLE 8.1
**Whites' Racial Policy Attitudes: National,
Regional, and Deep South Samples**
(in percent)

	National Sample	Non-South	South	Deep South

1. We are faced with many problems in this country, none of which can be solved easily or inexpensively. I'm going to name some of these problems, and for each one I'd like you to tell me whether you think we're spending too much money on it, too little money, or about the right amount. Are we spending too much, too little, or about the right amount on assistance to blacks?

	National Sample	Non-South	South	Deep South
Too little	27.7	30.6	20.7	4.2
About right	49.9	51.2	46.5	28.4
Too much	22.4	18.2	32.8	67.4
N	1,035	736	299	359

2. Some people think that blacks have been discriminated against for so long that the government has a special obligation to improve their living standard. Others believe that the government should not be giving special treatment to blacks. Where would you place yourself on this scale?

	National Sample	Non-South	South	Deep South
Government help	6.3	7.3	4.0	4.5
	9.3	9.7	8.4	7.2
	33.9	35.9	29.2	24.7
	18.6	18.7	18.3	15.0
No special treatment	31.9	28.5	40.1	48.6
N	1,108	786	322	401

Here are several things that the government in Washington might do to deal with the problems of poverty and unemployment among black Americans. I would like you to tell me if you favor or oppose them.

3. Provide special college scholarships for black children who maintain good grades.

	National Sample	Non-South	South	Deep South
Strongly favor	16.6	18.8	11.2	7.6
Favor	53.1	53.5	52.1	41.3
Neither	14.1	14.3	13.6	6.1
Oppose	11.5	9.0	17.2	35.0
Strongly oppose	4.8	4.3	5.9	9.9
N	567	398	169	394

4. Give business and industry special tax breaks for locating in largely black areas.

	National Sample	Non-South	South	Deep South
Strongly favor	7.3	8.4	6.1	1.8
Favor	35.5	39.4	26.2	20.6

	National Sample	Non-South	South	Deep South
Neither	25.0	23.4	28.7	12.2
Oppose	24.6	21.6	31.7	50.0
Strongly oppose	7.2	7.1	7.3	15.4
N	557	393	164	384

5. Spend more money on the schools in black neighborhoods, especially for preschool and early education programs.

	National Sample	Non-South	South	Deep South
Strongly favor	17.4	20.3	10.7	11.8
Favor	50.8	53.2	45.2	40.8
Neither	15.3	14.4	17.3	7.8
Oppose	12.3	8.6	20.8	31.1
Strongly oppose	4.3	3.5	6.0	8.5
N	563	395	168	399

6. Suppose there is a communitywide vote on the general housing issue. There are two possible laws to vote on. One law says that a homeowner can decide for himself whom to sell his house to, even if he prefers not to sell to blacks. The second law says that a homeowner cannot refuse to sell to someone because of their race or color. Which law would you vote for?

	National Sample	Non-South	South	Deep South
Owner decide	45.8	42.3	54.5	58.5
Cannot refuse	54.2	57.7	45.6	41.5
N	1,095	775	320	398

7. In general, do you favor or oppose the busing of black and white school children from one school district to another?

	National Sample	Non-South	South	Deep South
Favor	30.8	33.4	24.3	12.0
Oppose	69.2	66.6	75.7	83.0
N	1,078	769	309	376

8. Some people say that because of past discrimination it is sometimes necessary for colleges and universities to reserve openings for black students. Others oppose quotas because they say quotas give blacks advantages they haven't earned. What is your opinion — are you for or against quotas to admit black students?

	National Sample	Non-South	South	Deep South
Strongly favor	13.2	13.8	11.8	1.4
Favor	17.7	17.4	18.4	11.7
Oppose	24.3	25.0	22.8	59.3
Strongly oppose	44.8	43.9	46.9	27.6
N	773	545	228	366

	National Sample	Non-South	South	Deep South

9. Some people say that because of past discrimination blacks should be given preference in hiring and promotion. Others say that such preference in hiring and promotion of blacks is wrong because it gives blacks advantages they haven't earned. What about your opinion — are you for or against preferential hiring for blacks?

	National Sample	Non-South	South	Deep South
Strongly favor	8.3	7.3	10.7	1.6
Favor	9.2	9.5	8.6	4.5
Oppose	21.1	21.9	19.3	58.0
Strongly oppose	61.4	61.4	61.4	35.9
N	782	549	233	376

Sources: Data for the national samples and for the non-South and South subsamples for items 1–7 are from the National Opinion Research Center's 1990 General Social Survey. For items 8 and 9, data for the national samples and for the non-South and South subsamples are from the Institute for Social Research's 1990 American National Election Study. For all items, data for the Deep South subsamples are from the combined 1994 and 1995 Georgia polls.

indicate that three in ten whites nationally, but four in ten in the South and nearly one in two of those raised in the Deep South, believe that the government does not have any special obligation to help improve blacks' living standards.

The next three questions refer to specific policies that the federal government might pursue to address black poverty and unemployment. Question 3 addresses college scholarship set-asides for academically deserving black students. Only 16.3 percent of whites nationwide oppose or strongly oppose such set-asides, although distinct regional differences exist, with 13.3 percent of non-Southerners, 23.1 percent of Southerners, and 44.9 percent of Deep Southerners voicing opposition. Next is a question that asks about the establishment of enterprise zones in black neighborhoods. Nationally, 31.8 percent of whites either oppose or strongly oppose such incentives, with 28.7 percent of non-Southerners, 39.0 percent of Southerners, and more than half (65.3 percent) of Deep Southerners registering opposition. Question 5 speaks to the issue of spending on schools in black neighborhoods. Nationally, only 16.6 percent of white Americans oppose or strongly oppose increased spending on black schools, but 26.8 percent of Southerners and 39.6 percent of Deep Southerners are opposed.

Questions 6 and 7 are about fair housing practices and busing. By a 12-point margin, 54.4 percent to 42.3 percent, Southerners express more acceptance than non-Southerners of discriminatory sales practices that violate federal antidiscrimination laws. Deep Southerners do not stand out from other Southerners on this issue, with both groups more in favor than residents of the country as a whole of allowing racial bias in home sales. Not surprisingly, on the basis of previous research (see Jaynes & Williams, 1989), about seven whites in ten oppose cross-district busing to achieve racial integration in schools, including two-thirds of non-Southerners, three-fourths of Southerners, and more than eight in ten Deep Southerners.

Questions 8 and 9 address the most controversial aspects of racial policies: quotas and preferences. Question 8 solicits respondents' views about reserving openings for black students in colleges and universities; question 9 addresses the use of preferences in the workplace. The most noteworthy finding is that very substantial majorities of whites in all regions oppose these programs. Collapsing the oppose and strongly oppose categories, opposition to racial quotas in education varies little across the national (69.1 percent), non-South (68.9 percent), and South (69.7 percent) samples, with a somewhat larger percentage of Deep Southerners (86.9 percent) opposed to such quotas. Attitudes toward the use of racial preferences in hiring display an identical pattern, but with even higher absolute levels of opposition. Nationally, 82.5 percent of whites oppose or strongly oppose preferences in hiring and promotion; 83.3 percent of non-Southerners, 80.7 percent of Southerners, and 93.9 percent of Deep Southerners also oppose such policies.

So far we have presented evidence of regional distinctiveness in whites' racial policy attitudes without addressing the possibility that the differences may not be the result of region per se but of the varying compositional attributes of non-South, South, and Deep South places. For example, support for more liberal racial policies is greater among political liberals than conservatives, and the density of liberals is lower in the South than in the rest of the nation. Do such compositional differences explain the associations described above, or is there something distinctive about the South beyond these compositional differences? If the latter is the case, then regional differences in racial policy views should persist when compositional differences are controlled.

To assess these possibilities we fitted regression models for each of the nine attitude items considered above, including as predictors measures of educational attainment (in years of schooling completed), household income (in pretax dollars), urban versus rural residence, age (in years), and political ideology (measured on a seven-point continuum from "extremely liberal" to "extremely conservative"), along with region (South versus non-South). Although we do not present the statistical results, for six of the seven GSS items (busing is the exception), the effect of region on policy attitudes persisted even with the other predictors taken into account. (Full regression results are available from the authors.

We could not, of course, include the Deep South subsample in this analysis because, for these respondents, region does not vary.) All effects were in the expected direction, with Southerners more negatively disposed than non-Southerners to the various policy initiatives. No regional differences were uncovered on the two ANES items, a finding we attribute to the fact that, like the busing item, large majorities of whites of all regions are opposed to these particular policies. This latter pattern notwithstanding, controlling for compositional influences does little to alter our original findings. Net of controls, residents of Southern places emerge as less tolerant than others of policies aimed at alleviating racial disadvantage.

SUMMARY AND DISCUSSION

For more than three decades, mass society theorists have argued that increased urbanization coupled with economic growth will create a kind of cultural uniformity in U.S. society (Kasarda, Hughes, & Irwin, 1991; Mayo, 1964; Reed, 1983; Reissman, 1965). According to this thesis, exposure to standard socialization agents, such as schools, mass communication, and media, as well as successive waves of in-migration, will cause regional cultural differences to gradually diminish. Although our use of cross-sectional data gathered at one time does not allow us to assess over-time trends, we have found considerable evidence of Southern distinctiveness in racial policy attitudes. By examining data on whites' racial policy attitudes for the nation as a whole as well as for non-South, South, and Deep South residents separately, we find that Southerners in general — and Deep Southerners in particular — are the least likely to endorse policies intended to ameliorate racial inequality. Moreover, it is not just that Southerners tend to be more politically conservative, poorer, and less educated than non-Southerners that accounts for their more negative policy attitudes; the legacy of Southern racism is one of old, deeply ingrained attitudes dying slowly. It is also notable that because our samples of Southerners in the GSS and ANES include residents of the Deep South, our estimates of South–Deep South differences are likely to be conservatively biased.

In sum, the data reported here yield evidence of considerable regional differences in whites' racial policy attitudes. This pattern of greater resistance to racial change among South and Deep South residents is noteworthy, not only because it casts doubt on the utility of the mass society framework, but also because opposition to ameliorative policies is interpreted by many analysts as a new and more sophisticated language of racial antipathy that views blacks as violating "such traditional American values as individualism and self-reliance, the work ethic, obedience, and discipline" (Kinder & Sears, 1981, p. 416; see also Sears, 1988; See & Wilson, 1988; Chapter 3 of this volume). If, as some commentators argue, old-fashioned prejudice has been replaced by a kind of negative racial affect, there is little reason to be sanguine about the regional variations in policy attitudes that we have documented.

IV

THE RACIAL ATTITUDES OF AFRICAN AMERICANS

9

Blacks, Whites, and the Changing of the Guard in Black Political Leadership

Lee Sigelman

During the 1960s, Martin Luther King, Jr., towered over all others as the African-American leader most visible to and most esteemed by members of his race. Many other prominent black leaders were widely admired, including those revered for breaking the color line, including Jackie Robinson and James Meredith; activist entertainers, such as Dick Gregory and Harry Belafonte; members of the civil rights establishment, such as Roy Wilkins and Thurgood Marshall; and an occasional elected official, such as Adam Clayton Powell, Jr., and Charles Evers. Following King's assassination in 1968, Ralph Abernathy briefly came to the fore, and "Black Power" advocates, such as H. Rap Brown, Stokely Carmichael, Eldridge Cleaver, Huey Newton, and Bobby Seale, gained notoriety, but no one ever inherited King's mantle as the preeminent black American leader (see Table 9.1).

Capitalizing on the gains achieved by the civil rights movement during the 1950s, 1960s, and early 1970s, by the mid-1970s many African Americans came to believe that the attainment of public office constituted the most promising avenue toward further advancement. Their strategic focus therefore shifted away from demonstrations, confrontations, and boycotts and toward greater use of the ballot (White, 1990). African Americans began to be elected to public office in increasing numbers, almost always in jurisdictions where they constituted a majority or near-majority (Darden, 1984). In a few cases, though, black candidates were elected in constituencies where most voters were whites. The most notable of these breakthroughs were the elections of Edward Brooke as U.S. Senator from

TABLE 9.1
Blacks' Evaluations of Black Leaders, 1960s

	1963			1966			1968		
	Positive	Unsure	Negative	Positive	Unsure	Negative	Positive	Unsure	Negative
Martin Luther King, Jr.	88	8	4	88	9	3			
Jackie Robinson	80	12	8	66	23	11			
James Meredith	79	15	6	71	19	10			
Medgar Evers	78	19	3						
Roy Wilkins	69	24	7	64	30	6			
Thurgood Marshall	65	30	5	48	47	5			
Dick Gregory	62	30	8	56	33	11			
Ralph Bunche	62	28	10	53	37	10			
Lena Horne	55	27	18						
Harry Belafonte	54	36	10						
Floyd Patterson	53	27	20						
Adam Clayton Powell, Jr.	51	26	23	44	42	14			
James Baldwin	42	50	8						
Elijah Muhammad	15	50	35	12	45	43	3	43	54
Charles Evers				54	38	8			
James Farmer				47	45	8			
A. Phillip Randolph				35	60	5			
Whitney Young				33	59	8	10	54	36
Julian Bond				31	57	12			
Bayard Rustin				22	68	10	1	89	10
Stokely Carmichael				19	68	13	4	24	72
Floyd McKissick				19	71	10	3	66	31

Ralph Abernathy	49	17	34
Carl Stokes	11	52	37
Edward Brooke	6	65	29
H. Rap Brown	2	28	70
Ron Karenga	1	96	3
Perry Wolff	0	96	4

Sources: 1963 — Brink and Harris (1964, pp. 120–122), based on a 1963 national Harris survey with 1,257 black respondents. 1966 — Brink and Harris (1966, pp. 244–257), based on a 1966 national Harris survey with 1,059 black respondents. 1968 — Chandler (1972, p. 26), based on a national CBS News-Opinion Research corporation survey with 487 black respondents; this survey was conducted a month after the King assassination and the ensuing rioting. Question wording: 1963 and 1966 — "Now I want to read off to you a list of groups and people who have been prominent in the fight for Negro rights. For each I wish you would tell me how you would rate the job that person or group has done — excellent, pretty good, only fair, or poor." "Positive" refers to the percentage responding either "excellent" or "pretty good." "Unsure" to the percentage unable to answer the question, "Negative" to the percentage responding "only fair" or "poor." 1968 — "Please read over this list of people and tell me which of them you have heard about or read about. Which, if any of these, is a leader to whom you would give active support?" "Positive" refers to the percentage expressing active support for a leader, "Unsure" to the percentage indicating that they had not heard about a leader, "Negative" to the percentage withholding support from a leader.

Massachusetts and Tom Bradley as mayor of Los Angeles (see, for example, Becker & Heaton, 1967; Hahn, Klingman, & Pachon, 1976). Still, at the end of the 1960s, there were only 29 black mayors in the United States, and only two in large cities: Richard Hatcher in Gary, Indiana, and Carl Stokes in Cleveland, Ohio. That number, however, quadrupled within five years (Hahn, Klingman, & Pachon, 1976). These newly elected mayors owed their election to cohesive black support and high black voter turnout. Hatcher and Stokes carried only 15 and 19 percent, respectively, of the white vote, but in Gary, Cleveland, and several other cities, the sheer size of the African-American population permitted black candidates to overcome strong white opposition. Because of the racial bifurcation of the vote, some analysts feared that the nation might be witnessing "the emergence of a new breed of leadership, which could inflict deep-seated cleavages and divisions within both white and black segments of the electorate" (Hahn, Klingman, & Pachon, 1976, p. 520).

During the 1980s, African-American leadership on a national level remained fragmented. Although some second-echelon leaders from the 1960s and 1970s remained active, there was something of a national leadership vacuum. In 1980, *Black Enterprise* magazine reported after a poll of 5,000 readers that "over the last ten years, the absence of clear-cut leadership has been the single most noticeable handicap of the black struggle for equality" (White, 1990, p. 14). The only truly national leader visible to the incoming generation was Jesse Jackson (Wills, 1988, p. 4), who in the eyes of many was "the undisputed leader of black America" (Colton, 1983, p. 283) — if only by default. Others, however, would dispute that judgment. For example, Henry Louis Gates (1996, p. 128) considers Jackson "the leading spokesman of the American left rather than of black America" — although I would add that many white liberals seem to want no part of Jesse Jackson.

By the 1980s, the main thrust of African-American politics had changed. The initial goal of the electoral strategy had been to gain and maintain control of the governmental apparatus in black-majority locales; however, abetted by the civil rights revolution, the growth of the black middle class, and the demonstration effect of victories in places where African Americans were in the majority (Smith, 1981), blacks soon began to run for — and, in a remarkable number of cases, to be elected to — public office in places where they composed only a small fraction of the population. To be sure, even by the mid-1980s most black mayors of medium or large U.S. cities were found in cities with white majorities; the salient point, however, is that there were few such mayors.

Following the lead of Los Angeles, voters in many cities with large but minority African-American populations, including Chicago, New York, and Philadelphia, elected black mayors. Even more remarkably, black mayors were also elected in cities, such as Denver and Seattle, where there were scarcely any African Americans and in cities, such as Birmingham and Charlotte, where, even though African Americans were numerous, the election of a black mayor would have been unimaginable only a few years earlier. African Americans also gained a variety of other positions that had once seemed far beyond their grasp: Ron Brown was named chairman of the Democratic Party and then Secretary of Commerce; Douglas Wilder sat in the governor's chair in Richmond, Virginia, the erstwhile capital of the Confederacy; Colin Powell was appointed Chairman of the Joint Chiefs of Staff, and, after retiring from military service, emerged in 1995 as a presidential prospect before taking himself out of the race; and Clarence Thomas was named to the Supreme Court by a conservative Republican president.

The emerging black leaders owed much to, but differed markedly from, their predecessors. In white-majority cities and at the state and federal levels, it was not civil rights movement-nurtured, nor militant, nor dissident black leaders who achieved breakthrough political victories. Rather, just as in industry, where trained managers eventually supplant the founding entrepreneurs, a "new breed" of black political leader began to emerge — though this was not at all the new breed that analysts in the 1970s had feared would prove to be racially divisive. This new breed, eschewing the characteristic styles and appeals of black leaders of the 1960s and 1970s, emphasized pragmatism and skills, articulating means and ends that sounded racially and culturally inclusive rather than pitched specifically toward African Americans (Williams, 1990, p. 62). Mayors Kurt Schmoke of Baltimore and David Dinkins of New York were exemplars of this new black politician: mainstream moderates who shunned political labels and racial rhetoric (Chafets, 1990, p. 231). Dinkins, for example, came to power by convincing whites that he could be trusted, defusing "the potential dynamite of the racial factor" by conducting a nonthreatening campaign (Arian, Goldberg, Mollenkopf, & Rogowsky, 1991, p. 77).

Thus, whereas the most visible black leaders of the 1960s and 1970s were insurgents dedicated to the sweeping reform or, in some cases, even the overthrow, of "the system," the new breed of black leaders sought to advance within — or even to gain control of — the system. Signs of the arrival of the new breed became more and more abundant. A textbook example of the changing of the guard occurred in Cleveland, where during the 1960s, Mayor Carl Stokes mobilized the black community, using protests, voter registration drives, bloc voting, and other tested tactics of the civil rights movement to carry out a fundamental redistribution of political power (Nelson, 1987). During the post-Stokes era, the city's dominant black leader, George Forbes, a forceful spokesman for black interests, sparked bitter resentment among the city's white residents. In 1989 Forbes ran for mayor against another black, Michael White, who campaigned on "city-wide" issues and presented himself as a conciliator, running what has come to be known as a "deracialized" campaign (Perry, 1991). White won by 56 percent over Forbes's 44 percent, carrying 80 percent of the white vote and only 30 percent of the black vote (Ardrey & Nelson, 1990). A few years later, a similar succession occurred in Detroit, where the long, racially divisive reign of Coleman Young finally gave way to the new breed leadership of Dennis Archer.

In sum, the confrontational style of the 1960s and 1970s lost ground to the more modulated style of electoral politics in racially heterogeneous settings. To be elected in such settings, black candidates had to build outward from their core black support. Accordingly, as the focus changed from protest politics to electoral politics, a whole new set of strategic considerations came into play, and many traditional tactics of black influence became obsolete. This is not to portray deracialization as an irresistible force; however, it is worth noting that cases sometimes cited as evidence of the continuing vitality of an earlier style of black leadership, such as the 1986 victory of John Lewis and his "old warriors of the sixties" over Julian Bond and his "'buppies' of the eighties" (Yancey, 1988, p. 14), generally occurred in settings where white electoral strength was minimal. Elsewhere, black candidates whose appeal was largely confined to black voters fared poorly. The lesson for black candidates seeking office in racially diverse settings was not that they had to forsake their race and abandon their principles, but that they had to extend their appeal to other groups and project an image with which these groups felt comfortable.

Against this backdrop of changing leadership styles, the present study probes public evaluations in the early 1990s of four prominent black leaders of the 1980s and 1990s: Jesse Jackson, Douglas Wilder, Colin Powell, and Louis Farrakhan. These four individuals represent a wide range of backgrounds, styles, outlooks, and appeals. Wilder, who worked his way up through the chairs of state elective office in Virginia, was something of a prototype for the new breed. Running for governor against a white opponent, he won four white votes in ten and one conservative vote in four (Shexnider, 1990). His political agenda reflected what political scientist Robert Holsworth called an "unwavering commitment to establishing his credentials as a fiscal conservative," and his record was "devoid of social experimentation on either the left or the right" (quoted by Harris, 1991). To be sure, he lost considerable credibility with Virginia voters as a consequence of his short-lived run for the Democratic presidential nomination soon after being elected governor, and his 1994 challenge for a U.S. Senate seat never got off the ground. Still, his "evolution from the loud, militant Doug Wilder with the Afro into the low-key, mainstream Doug Wilder in the banker's gray suit" was an instructive example of the "larger evolution of black leadership in America" (Yancey, 1988, p. 13).

By contrast, Powell was a career military officer who had not been actively involved in either the civil rights movement or partisan politics. He emerged from the 1991 Persian Gulf conflict as a hero with a public image as an apolitical military leader, much like Omar Bradley, George Marshall, or even Dwight Eisenhower after World War II. A few years after the opinion data analyzed here were collected, he emerged as a popular choice for the presidency in 1996; numerous polls suggested that if he had chosen to run, he might have more than held his own when matched against the likes of Bill Clinton, Bob Dole, and Ross Perot.

Whereas neither the moderate Wilder nor the seemingly apolitical Powell could credibly be depicted as an antiestablishment insurgent, Farrakhan belonged to no establishment, black or white. The outspoken minister of the Nation of Islam outraged Jews in 1984 by praising Adolf Hitler as a great man, widening the gulf between Jesse Jackson (whom Farrakhan publicly backed for president) and the Jewish community, and he gained greater notoriety a decade later for his leadership in the Million-Man March in Washington.

Jackson, the only one of the four with deep roots in the civil rights movement, first came to national attention as one of Martin Luther King's lieutenants and gained national visibility for his oratorical prowess. Often criticized for his flamboyance and relentless self-promotion, he had rocky relations with many civil rights leaders. Jackson's bid to capture the 1984 Democratic presidential nomination bore witness to the evangelical zeal and confrontational tension of his years in the civil rights movement. He rolled up huge majorities among black voters but won few votes from whites, who considered him antiwhite, threatening, and out of control (Crotty, 1989; Morris & Williams, 1989; Page, 1990). Although much of the hostility Jackson engendered among whites carried over to 1988, many observers (for example, Smith, 1990a) saw his more subdued style in 1988 as the key to his somewhat improved showing among whites.

Public views of these four leaders as the 1980s shaded into the 1990s are of interest in and of themselves, given the leaders' prominence and diversity. I make no claim, however, that the patterns that existed in 1991 in opinions concerning these four particular black leaders continue to hold today. Indeed, in the concluding discussion I contend that in some important respects, these patterns have changed; some of the leaders (Powell and Farrakhan, in particular) have become much more prominent, and Wilder's star has fallen. However, analysis of public views of these leaders may yield new insights about public preferences for certain types of black leaders, as represented by the new breed politician Wilder, the apolitical Powell, the dissident Farrakhan, and the civil rights activist Jackson. Wilder and Jackson both sought to forge biracial coalitions, although Jackson in particular was unsuccessful in this respect; Farrakhan, on the other extreme, made no attempt to reach out to whites — if anything, the opposite; and Powell's appeal seemed to transcend normal political, class, or racial lines.

Among the key issues addressed here are how much members of the black rank and file differentiated among the four leaders. How clearly did African Americans perceive these leaders, and which leader or leaders did they prefer? Did support for a given black leader imply opposition to another? How closely were African Americans' views matched by those of whites? Did certain black leaders appeal primarily to certain types of people? Were Wilder and Powell, for example, especially popular in the black middle class, whereas less educated and less prosperous blacks were more drawn to Jackson and Farrakhan? How did the determinants of support for a given leader among African Americans compare with the determinants of support for the same leader among whites? Did Jackson, for example, appeal disproportionately to less educated blacks but to more educated whites?

I address these questions through analysis of data from a national telephone survey conducted by the Gallup Organization for *Newsweek* magazine between April 23 and 25, 1991.[1] For this survey, a sample of 619 whites and 56 blacks was supplemented by an oversample of 249 blacks, bringing the total sample size to 924, including 305 blacks. For present purposes, the key question in the survey consisted of four parts: "For each of the following men, tell me whether or not you feel black Americans would benefit if he took a larger leadership role. First . . . Jesse Jackson? Douglas Wilder? Colin Powell? Louis Farrakhan?"

Every survey question has its limitations, and this one is no exception. Although the question explicitly asked whether "black Americans would benefit" from the leadership of Jackson, Wilder, Powell, or Farrakhan, there is no way of knowing whether a given white respondent answered in terms of what he or she considered best for blacks or for whites, or whether this distinction even occurred to the respondent. Moreover, the question did not explicitly identify the four leaders as blacks; even though it seems clear in context, some respondents may not have known, for example, that Farrakhan and Wilder are black. These ambiguities are not serious enough to invalidate conclusions based on responses to this question, but they do need to be borne in mind in interpreting these responses.

The pollsters' decision to ask about four specific leaders rather than about preferences for various types of leaders cuts both ways in terms of our ability to understand public views of black leaders. Obviously, each leader is a complex individual, not an abstract type. When people evaluate a particular leader, their evaluations are shaped by the leader's unique personality as well as by their preference for a certain type of leadership. Considerable care must therefore be taken when drawing conclusions about evaluations of types of leaders on the basis of evaluations of specific leaders. On the other hand, in the real world of politics people respond to particular individuals, not to abstract types. Williams (1990, p. 53) notes in this regard that even though there has been a dramatic increase over time in the percentage of whites who say they would vote for a "well qualified" black candidate for president, such responses may be meaningless in practice. After all, whites can always rationalize opposition to a particular black candidate on the grounds that he or she is not well qualified. Indeed, in 1988 only 26 percent of white interviewees in a national survey said they considered any black who was then on the political scene to be well qualified to be president (Williams, 1990, p. 53). The lesson is simply that there can be considerable slippage between willingness to support a certain type of leader and actual support for a particular leader who seems to be of that type.

THE LEADERS' VISIBILITY AND POPULARITY

Relatively little is known about what people look for in political leaders, let alone what they look for in black political leaders. The scattered evidence that is currently available, however, makes it possible to piece together some general expectations about public views of Jackson, Wilder, Powell, and Farrakhan.

For one thing, Jackson's 1984 and 1988 bids for the presidential nomination greatly enhanced his national visibility, so he should almost certainly have been the best known of the four, even though the others had all been in the public eye — especially Powell, as a result of his involvement in the Persian Gulf conflict. More important, Wilder and Powell, as relatively nonthreatening, establishmentarian figures, might be expected to have found greater favor among whites than Jackson and surely greater than Farrakhan. Which of the four would be the favorite of blacks is impossible to predict with any confidence, although the likeliest choice would be Jackson, based on the enthusiasm his presidential campaigns generated among blacks.

As indicated in Table 9.2, the Gallup/*Newsweek* survey data revealed marked differences in both visibility and popularity among the four leaders. Jackson was by far the most visible, as can be seen in the low incidence of "don't know" responses he evoked: Only one interviewee in ten, black or white, failed to express an opinion about him. Lagging far behind Jackson in visibility were, in order for both blacks and whites, Powell, Farrakhan, and Wilder (who had not yet declared his brief presidential candidacy when the survey was conducted). Almost half of the black interviewees and two-thirds of the whites answered "don't know" when asked about Wilder, and almost as many whites expressed uncertainty about Farrakhan as about Wilder. Blacks were significantly more opinionated than whites about both Wilder ($Z = 5.95$, $p < .05$) and Farrakhan

($Z = 6.28$, $p < .05$) but not about Powell, toward whom "don't know" responses were actually more common than among whites ($Z = 2.35$, $p < .05$). Powell's higher profile among whites than blacks may have stemmed from a combination of his uninvolvement in civil rights issues and greater white attentiveness to the Persian Gulf conflict; but whatever the cause, Powell alone of the four leaders was better known among whites than he was among blacks.

TABLE 9.2
The Visibility and Popularity of Four Black Leaders, 1991
(in percent)

	Jesse Jackson	Douglas Wilder	Colin Powell	Louis Farrakhan

For each of the following men, tell me whether or not you feel black Americans would benefit if he took a larger leadership role.

	Jesse Jackson	Douglas Wilder	Colin Powell	Louis Farrakhan
Blacks				
Yes	68.5	33.8	45.6	29.5
No	22.0	19.3	20.3	32.5
Don't know	9.5	46.9	34.1	38.0
(Yes/No	3.1	1.8	2.2	0.9)
Whites				
Yes	46.1	18.3	55.3	8.4
No	44.7	14.5	18.1	31.6
Don't know	9.2	67.3	26.6	60.0
(Yes/No	1.0	1.3	3.1	0.3)

Source: Gallup/*Newsweek* May 1991 national survey of 608 whites and 305 blacks.

It is one thing to be known, and something else to be liked. The bottom row in each section of Table 9.2 shows the ratio of favorable to unfavorable assessments of each leader, with "don't know" responses omitted from consideration. Among blacks, the possibility of Jackson's assumption of a larger leadership role drew a three-to-one ratio of positive to negative reactions. The black positive-to-negative ratio was slightly above two-to-one for Powell and somewhat lower for Wilder. Only for Farrakhan did negative reactions surpass positive ones in blacks' responses. By contrast, what stood out in whites' responses was their overwhelmingly positive assessment of Powell as a black leader. The great majority of whites expressed an opinion about Powell, and the great majority of these opinions were favorable. By contrast, whites split almost evenly about whether an expansion of Jackson's leadership would help blacks, just as they were divided about Wilder's leadership (although, again, most whites had no opinion about Wilder, one way or the other). Like Wilder, Farrakhan was not widely known among whites; in contrast to Wilder, only a small minority of whites who expressed an opinion about Farrakhan viewed his leadership as a plus for blacks.

In sum, the leader about whom both blacks and whites were most opinionated was Jackson, followed by Powell, Farrakhan, and Wilder. Whereas Jackson was very well known among both blacks and whites, Farrakhan and Wilder were better known by blacks than whites, and Powell by whites than blacks. Farrakhan was easily the least popular of the four: Of those who stated an opinion, a narrow majority of blacks and a resounding majority of whites doubted that blacks would benefit if Farrakhan assumed a greater leadership role. Both blacks and whites were more positive than negative about Wilder's leadership potential, but the jury remained out on Wilder, about whom almost half of blacks and roughly two-thirds of whites had not formed an opinion. Powell was quite favorably regarded by whites, as expected, and also by blacks; indeed, only Jackson's standing among blacks approached Powell's three-to-one ratio of favorable-to-unfavorable responses among whites. As expected, Jackson was the clear-cut favorite of blacks, but white reactions to him were mixed. The issue of whether these differences endured or were subsequently disrupted by such visible events as Farrakhan's leadership of the Million-Man March and Powell's flirtation with a presidential bid is considered in the concluding discussion.

SUPPORT LINKAGES AMONG THE LEADERS

Notwithstanding obvious differences among Jackson, Wilder, Powell, and Farrakhan in background, personality, and outlook, the four leaders tended to appeal to the same people (see Table 9.3). The analyses reported in Table 9.3 (and in Table 9.4) were based solely on pro or con answers; "don't know" responses were excluded. Obviously, then, the number of cases in Tables 9.3 and 9.4 falls considerably below the number in Table 9.2. Of course, the black sample was not large in the first place (N = 305), and elimination of the 46.9 percent of blacks who expressed no opinion about Wilder left only about 150 blacks in that portion of the analysis. Conclusions based on such small subsamples must be treated with caution.

Among African Americans, endorsement of a greater leadership role for any one of the four was significantly associated with endorsement of a greater leadership role for every other one of the four; the correlations ranged from 0.270 (between support for Jackson and Powell) to 0.590 (between support for Wilder and Powell). It bears emphasis that all these correlations were positive. A positive linkage between support for

TABLE 9.3
Correlations between Endorsements of the Four Leaders, 1991

	Jesse Jackson	Douglas Wilder	Colin Powell	Louis Farrakhan
Blacks				
Jesse Jackson	1.000	0.514*	0.270*	0.396*
Douglas Wilder		1.000	0.590*	0.285*
Colin Powell			1.000	0.304*
Louis Farrakhan				1.000
Whites				
Jesse Jackson	1.000	0.222*	0.152*	0.383*
Douglas Wilder		1.000	0.569*	0.227*
Colin Powell			1.000	0.011
Louis Farrakhan				1.000

*$p < .05$

Source: Gallup/*Newsweek* May 1991 national survey of 608 whites and 305 blacks. The entries in the table are polychoric correlation coefficients.

Jackson and Farrakhan follows logically in light of Farrakhan's endorsement of Jackson's presidential candidacy and Jackson's refusal to disassociate himself from Farrakhan (although Jackson did put greater distance between himself and Farrakhan in 1988 than he had in 1984). The strong positive correlation between endorsements of the moderate Wilder and the apolitical Powell is also easy to understand, for it is Wilder and Powell who should appeal most to the least radical blacks. More surprising are the positive correlations between support for Jackson and Wilder. At the time the survey was conducted, not only were Jackson and Wilder considered potential rivals for the 1992 Democratic presidential nomination but also their political styles were so different that the positive correlation between support for the two of them poses something of a puzzle. Also somewhat puzzling are the positive correlations between endorsement of Farrakhan, on the one hand, and of both Wilder and Powell, on the other. All three, of course, were African Americans, and all three embodied strong leadership — albeit of very different styles and with vastly different political agendas. Why, then, did blacks who voiced support for Farrakhan's leadership tend to look favorably upon Wilder and Powell?

Because it is difficult to discern similarities between Jackson and Wilder, let alone between Farrakhan and Powell or Wilder, it seems logical to look elsewhere for an explanation of the positive correlations linking support for all four leaders. One possibility is that these positive correlations are methodological artifacts, products of response bias.

TABLE 9.4
Determinants of Endorsements of the Four Leaders, 1991

	Jesse Jackson	Douglas Wilder	Colin Powell	Louis Farrakhan
Blacks				
Constant	1.651*	0.648	1.262	1.741*
Education	−0.110*	−0.015	0.021	−0.141*
Middle-aged	−0.586	0.628	0.300	−0.063
Older	−1.124*	−0.038	−0.047	−0.506
Gender	0.018	−0.059	−0.303	−0.002
East	0.363	0.073`	−0.670	−0.008
Midwest	0.037	0.269	−0.110	−0.439
West	−0.598	−0.149	−1.219*	0.308
Democrat	1.101*	0.365	0.061	0.122
Independent	0.514	−0.549	−1.303*	−0.292
Societal fault for poverty	0.485*	−0.585	−0.830*	0.267
Chi-squared (10)	35.411*	13.467	21.704*	16.428
Pseudo R^2	0.165	0.113	0.143	0.115
Whites				
Constant	0.477	−1.459*	−1.383*	0.079
Education	−0.052	0.079	0.123*	−0.074
Middle-aged	−0.188	−0.197	0.214	0.028
Older	−0.244	0.497	0.369	−0.221
Gender	0.077	−0.091	−0.124	0.187
East	0.142	0.229	0.332	−0.317
Midwest	−0.106	0.192	0.212	−0.245
West	−0.138	−0.306	0.116	0.038
Democrat	0.177	0.161	−0.070	0.129
Independent	0.038	0.212	0.241	−0.162
Societal fault for poverty	0.527*	0.343	0.255	0.181
Chi-squared (10)	26.447*	14.717	21.373*	5.877
Pseudo R^2	0.066	0.089	0.067	0.032

*$p < .05$

Source: Gallup/*Newsweek* May 1991 national survey of 608 whites and 305 blacks. The entries in the table are maximum likelihood estimates from eight separate multivariate probit analyses.

Occurrences of positivity and negativity bias in evaluations of political figures are well documented, reflecting the general tendency of some people to look on the bright side while others habitually look on the dark side (Lau, 1982; Sears, 1983). When asked to evaluate a particular leader, a Gallup/*Newsweek* interviewee who held no strong opinion may nonetheless have responded favorably or unfavorably, depending on his or her general predisposition toward positivity or negativity. Every interviewee biased toward positivity and every interviewee biased toward negativity would contribute to a matrix full of positive correlation coefficients, and therein may lie the solution to the puzzle.

This methodological explanation is plausible, but it needs to be followed a step further rather than being taken at face value. Response biases are most common among less educated interviewees (Schuman & Presser, 1981). If predispositions toward positivity or negativity account for the consistent positive correlations in blacks' assessments of the four leaders, then these biases should have been especially pronounced — and the positive correlations should therefore be especially strong — among less educated blacks. Further analysis reveals that this was not the case. Not only were the correlations between evaluations of the four leaders uniformly positive for both less and more highly educated blacks; these positive correlations were even stronger for more educated blacks than they were for less educated blacks.[2]

This evidence casts doubt on the idea that the uniformly positive correlations linking blacks' support for the four leaders were artifacts of response bias. It therefore seems appropriate to consider a more substantive explanation. The starting point for this explanation is the observation that although the four leaders may appear to have had little in common, there is a lowest common denominator among them: For all their differences, each was a prominent black leader. To some extent, when an African American says that he or she would like a particular black leader to play a larger leadership role, he or she is expressing symbolic affirmation of a strong black presence in the nation's leadership. Especially in light of the black leadership vacuum of recent years as noted above, the key political distinction within the black public may be less between supporters of various leaders than between those who enthusiastically embrace the commandment to "Seek ye first the political kingdom" and those who are alienated from political life. Thus, interviewees' support for expanding the role played by a given leader may have reflected, in large measure, a more general commitment to a strong black political voice — a commitment that would presumably have carried over to endorsement of other black leaders. If endorsing a particular black leader was part of a broader endorsement of black political power, then positive correlations should link support for the various black leaders.

Whites' evaluations of the four leaders should also have been affected by their perception of the urgency of a stronger black role in the nation's political leadership. White racists would have opposed a larger role — indeed, any role — for any black leader, and such blanket rejection would have produced consistency in their responses to the questions about the four leaders. Most whites, however, would not have responded so dogmatically. Rather, it seems reasonable to assume that the average white would have fallen somewhere between the average black, on the one hand, and white racists, on the other, in terms of support for an expanded black role in national affairs. The average white's willingness to endorse a particular black leader would thus have depended on how positively or negatively he or she felt toward the leader in question. Accordingly, while we might expect some consistency in whites' responses, we should anticipate a more differentiated set of intercorrelations for whites than for blacks.

The correlation matrix for whites, given in the bottom half of Table 9.3, resembles that for blacks in that neither contains any negative coefficients. This means that for neither blacks nor whites was there any tendency for support for one of this diverse set of black leaders to be associated with opposition to another one of the four. Overall, though, the correlations for whites were weaker and more differentiated than the corresponding correlations for blacks, consistent with the idea that whites' evaluations would more likely be on a case-by-case basis, whereas blacks' evaluations would more likely follow from a general rule. For example, whites who welcomed a larger leadership role for Powell were neither more nor less likely to take the same posture toward Farrakhan, and at several other points the coefficients in the white correlation matrix fell below those in the black matrix. The only exceptions to this pattern were the two strongest linkages in the white matrix: those between support for Wilder and Powell and support for Jackson and Farrakhan — two clusters that provide a key to Jackson's poor showing among whites in the 1984 and 1988 presidential primaries. Among blacks, support for Jackson was most closely associated with support for the moderate, "deracialized" Wilder, but among whites support for Jackson was most closely associated with support for the dissident, menacing Farrakhan.

DETERMINANTS OF ENDORSEMENTS
OF THE LEADERS

Finally, to what degree and in what manner were endorsements of the four leaders structured along social or political lines? In the past, considerable attention has focused on sources of support for Jesse Jackson in the 1984 and 1988 Democratic primaries. The black middle class has often been depicted as the backbone of Jackson's electoral coalition (see Reed, 1986; and surveys cited by Gurin, Hatchett, & Jackson, 1989, pp. 147–148). P. Gurin and colleagues (1989), however, report that with age — which strongly affected support for Jackson — held constant, socioeconomic status exerted no independent impact on blacks' support for Jackson. The primary determinants of blacks' support for Jackson, according to Gurin and colleagues, were age, education, and place of residence, with pro-Jackson sentiment running highest among blacks who were young, well educated, and lived in nonurban areas (see also Preston, 1989).

Among whites, Jackson drew support in 1984 and 1988 disproportionately from liberal, well-educated, middle-class voters (Colasanto & Williams, 1987; Smith, 1990a; Williams & Morris, 1989) — an ironic outcome in view of Jackson's hope to include less affluent whites in his "rainbow coalition." "Apparently, Jackson's campaign appeal could not overcome the racism and conservatism of the white working class" (Smith, 1990a, p. 227). Nor did Jackson draw heavily from any portion of the white electorate, from which he received only fragmentary support in both 1984 and 1988.

These analyses of the 1984 and 1988 primaries suggest how those who endorsed Jackson's leadership might have differed from those who did not. Beyond this, analysis of the determinants of support for the three other leaders can be guided by nothing firmer than the suppositions, first, that Wilder and Powell, as paragons of stolid moderation, might have appealed especially to members of the middle class of both races; second, that endorsement of the often immoderate Farrakhan would have been most pronounced among members of the black underclass.

Table 9.4 summarizes a series of eight probit analyses in which blacks' and whites' endorsements of the four leaders were modeled as functions of a set of demographic and political determinants: gender, age, education, region of residence, party identification, and — to capture a sense of one's basic outlook on racial issues — attribution of responsibility for black poverty to society as a whole rather than to poor blacks themselves.

Gender was coded 0 for men, 1 for women. Age was treated as three categorical (0, 1) variables — younger (less than 30), middle-aged (30–49), and older (50 and above) — in order to allow for curvilinear effects. Level of education was defined as number of years of school completed. Region was treated as four categorical variables: East, including the New England and Middle Atlantic states; Midwest, including the East Central and West Central states; South, including the Southeast and Southwest; and West, including the Rocky Mountain and Pacific states. Party identification was coded into three categories, depending upon how a respondent answered when asked, "In politics today, do you consider yourself a Republican, Democrat, or Independent?" Fault attributions were based on answers to the following question: "Why do you think poor blacks have not been able to rise out of poverty? Is it mainly the fault of blacks themselves, or is it mainly the fault of society as a whole?" Responses were coded 0 if the respondent blamed poor blacks themselves, 1 if the respondent blamed society as a whole. For extensive discussions of the importance of fault attributions in blacks' and whites' thinking about racial issues, see Sigelman and Welch (1991) and Sniderman with Hagen (1985). In the probit analyses summarized in Table 9.4, the "younger" age

category, the "South" region category, and the "Republican" party identification category were treated as the omitted or reference variables.

A scan of the eight sets of results reveals that in every case, social and
political factors had modest predictive power at best, as evidenced by the
chi-square and pseudo–R^2 statistics. Indeed, for both blacks and whites,
the equations linking these predictors to endorsements of two of the leaders were statistically nonsignificant. Earlier I noted the low visibility of
both Wilder and Farrakhan, about whom 40 percent or more of black
interviewees and 60 percent or more of white interviewees took no position, either pro or con. In light of their low visibility, it seems only natural that it was Wilder and Farrakhan toward whom endorsements were
least structured by the social and political factors considered here. The
overall impressions these findings convey are that neither Wilder nor Farrakhan was a salient attitude object, that assessments of both as black
leaders were not highly crystallized, and that uncertainty prevailed about
what each stood for and about whose interests would be served if either
were to assume a greater leadership role.

On the other hand, the African Americans and whites who endorsed
the leadership of Jackson and Powell differed in several respects from
those who did not. The idea that blacks stood to benefit from an expansion of Jackson's leadership role was especially common among less educated blacks and those who considered themselves Democrats. Moreover,
consistent with findings reported in studies of the 1984 and 1988 presidential primaries, younger blacks were significantly more enthusiastic
about Jackson than older blacks were. Finally, blacks who blamed society
for racial socioeconomic differences were more favorably disposed
toward Jackson's leadership than were those who blamed black poverty
on poor blacks themselves.

For whites, the determinants of endorsements of Jackson's leadership
were less clear-cut. In contrast to the pattern of white support for Jackson
in the 1984 and 1988 primaries, education, age, and social class had no significant effect. What did matter, for whites as well as for blacks, was the
conviction that poor blacks are not responsible for their poverty. A basic
difference between the racial beliefs of black Americans and white Americans lies in their explanations for the persistence of race-based socioeconomic inequality: Blacks tend to perceive poor blacks as victims of society
at large, whereas whites tend to blame the poor for being poor (see, for
example, Sigelman & Welch, 1991). Besides separating the two races, disagreement about whether black poverty stems from "internal" or "exter-
nal" causes separated whites who endorsed Jackson's leadership (or, for
that matter, the leadership of any of the four) from those who did not.
This tendency of those who blamed society to regard Jackson favorably
while those who blamed the poor to view him negatively follows naturally from Jackson's longstanding role as an advocate for poor blacks. It

also goes far toward explaining why Jackson's bids for the presidential nomination won such widespread support among blacks but so little among whites. His message to blacks played strongly on the theme of black self-help, intertwined with a determination to overcome the legacy of a racist society and to ensure that government would do more than it had done in the past to redress the balance. This message won ready acceptance among blacks; however, what seemed to come through most powerfully to whites was Jackson's fault-finding, whether because of his selective targeting of his message, whites' selective perception, or the selective emphasis. In any event, both the message and the messenger tended to encounter steadfast resistance among whites.

As noted earlier, about one black in three did not express an opinion about Powell, but those who did viewed his leadership quite favorably. Positive responses were particularly widespread among Southern blacks and least common among those from the West. More importantly, the partisan bases of blacks' support for Powell's leadership differed from the pattern for Jackson. For Jackson, the split was along party lines; he was viewed very positively by black Democrats but significantly less so by black Republicans, with Independents about midway between the two. For Powell, however, the contrast was between widespread support among Democrats and Republicans alike, and significantly less widespread support among Independents. Perhaps because of his detachment from the partisan fray and his image as a victorious general, Powell's appeal to blacks transcended party. Any attempt to account for his relatively poor standing among black Independents quickly passes into the realm of speculation, but it is worth considering that those who reject party labels may be of two different types: "insiders," who want to work within the system but not under the banner of either major party; and "outsiders," who are alienated from, or perhaps even antagonistic to, established political institutions, including political parties. This is a more extreme contrast between insiders and outsiders than has sometimes been drawn. For example, Gurin and colleagues (1989) use the term "insiders" to refer to African Americans who advocate an independent black voice in electoral politics. Both of these would qualify as insiders, according to the usage employed here. It is pertinent to observe that Gurin and colleagues (1989, p. 255) ultimately reject their version of the contrast between insiders and outsiders on the grounds that it overdraws the distinction between two fairly similar groups and excludes true outsiders.

Insiders, thus defined, would have been strongly drawn to Jackson's messianic leadership, and even some outsiders might have seen a glimmer of hope in him. Powell, a high-ranking military officer and trusted adviser of a Republican president, was presumably not the type of leader who would normally be sought out by those who yearned for a different political approach — and is certainly not the type of leader to whom those

who were acutely dissatisfied with established institutions would logically turn.

Even more telling is the final difference in patterns of black endorsements of Jackson and Powell. Those who blamed society for the persistence of racial socioeconomic differences were significantly more likely to
endorse Jackson's leadership than were those who saw poor blacks as the
cause of their own problems. Whether blacks endorsed Powell as a leader
also depended on their understanding of the causes of black poverty, but
it was those who blamed the poor — not those who blamed society —
who were more likely to endorse Powell. Thus, notwithstanding the moderate positive correlation between blacks' support for Jackson and Powell,
the very same understanding of racial socioeconomic differences that
helped promote support for Jackson helped discourage support for Powell. Accordingly, African Americans, who as a group favor societal over
individual explanations of racial inequality (Sigelman & Welch, 1991),
were more likely to see Jackson than Powell as someone from whose leadership blacks would benefit. By the same token, whites, who as a group
reject societal explanations of racial inequality (Sigelman & Welch, 1991),
saw blacks as standing to benefit less from Jackson's leadership than from
Powell's.

DISCUSSION

These data have revealed widespread public unfamiliarity with prominent black leaders in the early 1990s. Sizeable proportions of both African
Americans and whites nationwide had no opinion about whether blacks
would benefit from greater leadership by Douglas Wilder, Colin Powell,
or Louis Farrakhan. The exception was Jesse Jackson, about whom nine
interviewees in ten, irrespective of race, expressed an opinion. To be sure,
just a few years later, surveys indicated much more widespread opinion-
ation about Powell as a consequence of his 1995 flirtation with a presidential bid and about Farrakhan as a consequence of his key role in the
Million-Man March; Wilder, for his part, dropped completely off the
radar screen of the pollsters, who no longer even mentioned him in the
polls.[3]

In the early 1990s, blacks' opinions of Jackson were extremely favorable, but whites' were decidedly less so. Most African Americans who
offered an opinion about either Wilder or Powell were favorably disposed
(though less so than to Jackson), but their appraisals of Farrakhan's leadership leaned slightly toward the negative. The relatively few whites who
expressed opinions about Wilder and Farrakhan were lukewarm toward
Wilder and hostile toward Farrakhan. Whites were extremely favorable
toward Powell, however — as favorable toward Powell, in fact, as blacks
were toward Jackson. These differences proved to be enduring. In an

October 1995 NBC News/*Wall Street Journal* poll, 64 percent of respondents nationwide named Powell as "the most important black political leader today," with only 21 percent choosing Jackson and 8 percent Farrakhan; 1 percent volunteered another name, and 6 percent were unsure. In a different survey conducted the same month, black respondents in a national Gallup Poll provided an entirely different perspective when asked to name "the most important national leader in the black community today": 28 percent named Jackson, 12 percent Farrakhan, and only 9 percent Powell, with 12 percent naming someone else, 5 percent asserting that no one really fit the bill, and 34 percent expressing no opinion.

Because these results are from separate national surveys conducted by different organizations, comparisons between them are subject to all the usual caveats. The former survey was conducted between October 27 and 31, 1995, by Hart and Teeter Research for the NBC News/*Wall Street Journal* poll; the question was, "Who do you think is the most important black political leader today — Jesse Jackson, Colin Powell, or Louis Farrakhan?" The latter survey was a Gallup Poll conducted between October 19 and 22, 1995; the question was, "Who do you feel is the most important national leader in the black community today?" These opinion distributions were obtained from the Roper Center's online POLL database.

No tendency emerged for those who held a favorable view of one leader to hold an unfavorable view of another. This could reflect a tendency for support of various leaders to key only in part on the leaders themselves, beyond which such expressions tap into more general convictions about the importance of a strong African-American role in the nation's political leadership. Only for Jackson and, to a lesser extent, Powell did public evaluations follow any recognizable social or political contours. Both African Americans and whites who viewed black-white socioeconomic differences as caused by society were strongly drawn to Jackson, whereas blacks who considered such differences as caused by poor blacks looked more favorably upon Powell.

To this point, I have touched on, but have not squarely confronted, an issue that seems destined to become more and more crucial in the future: Can black leaders who enjoy widespread black support reasonably hope to achieve wide acceptance among whites as well? One answer to this question is simply that no black leader is apt to gain much support from whites. After considering Jackson's 1984 campaign for the presidential nomination and a number of mayoral elections in the early 1980s, Lucius Barker (1987) concluded that "Black candidates, no matter how qualified or how they conduct their campaigns, simply are unable to attract strong white support." More recent experience, however — including Wilder's election as governor in a conservative Southern state, the election of black mayors in several cities where African Americans do not compose anything close to a majority of the voters, and strong white support for a

Powell presidential candidacy in 1996 — suggests a more equivocal answer. Indeed, opinion surveys conducted in 1995 suggested that, if anything, whites were more enthusiastic about the prospect of a Powell candidacy than blacks were, although this could well have changed had members of each race actually been confronted with an opportunity to vote for a black American for president. Thus, the qualms that many African Americans had about Clarence Thomas's political views were ultimately overridden by their desire to have an African-American member of the Supreme Court. Thus, too, many whites apparently find themselves unable to pull the lever for a black candidate even when they have stated a willingness to do so.

In *An American Dilemma: The Negro Problem and Modern Democracy*, Gunnar Myrdal (1944) counterposed accommodation and protest as the two main streams of black American leadership. Early in this century, this split was embodied by Booker T. Washington and W.E.B. Du Bois. Of the black leaders considered here, Douglas Wilder was no Booker T. Washington, and Jesse Jackson was no W.E.B. Du Bois. Any of a growing number of black conservatives had far more in common with Booker T. Washington than Wilder did. For his part, Du Bois was an intellectual and an elitist, two terms seldom used to describe Jesse Jackson. The contrast between Jackson and Wilder bears some marks of the historical clash between accommodation and protest, however:

Doug Wilder represents a new type of black leader — a professional, not a preacher, a career politician with close ties to the white power structure, not a civil rights leader who marched in the streets.

The black ministers who led the civil rights movement spoke for a black community with a common concern: dismantling segregation. But in the three decades since the *Brown* decision, and the two decades since the Civil Rights Act, the black community has become divided — into those who have been able to translate legal protections and educational opportunities into economic success and those who haven't. Jesse Jackson represents the latter. He speaks for the poor and downtrodden and emphasizes race by talk of building a "rainbow coalition." Wilder, though, won election in a conservative Southern state because he espoused solid middle-class values that were neither black nor white. (Yancey, 1988, p. 12–13)

Indeed, Wilder was offered as a textbook example of "how a black political candidate might seek to win over skeptical, if not just plain racist, whites": by employing the so-called PIES (pragmatism, independence, experience, and skills) strategy of emphasizing managerial competence and downplaying ideology (Williams, 1990, p. 62).

The point is certainly not that Wilder himself seems likely to emerge as the next major national black political leader; his abortive runs in 1992 for the Democratic presidential nomination and in 1994 for the U.S. Senate left no doubt about his failure to ignite a spark among either blacks or whites. The point is rather that whites seem to be attracted to — or they at least seem not to be repulsed by — practitioners of a particular black leadership style, a style that is more generically "American" than distinctively "black." Wilder exemplified this style, but so do an increasing number of others, including several political liberals and moderates, some political conservatives, and a few who may not be widely viewed as "political" at all. Of those currently on the scene, the black leader most likely to play that role is clearly Colin Powell.

All these leaders lack the charismatic appeal of a Jesse Jackson; Powell is widely respected as a person of character and integrity but is hardly charismatic in the usual sense. The rhetoric in which Powell and other new-breed black leaders couch their messages smacks more of the managerialism of the 1990s than of the crusading zeal and intense militancy of the 1960s and 1970s. And their followers, although committed, are subdued by comparison to the fervor previous generations of black leaders often inspired. For these reasons, the new breed of black leader has often been criticized for not speaking in an authentically "black voice" (Carter, 1991). They certainly do not speak in the voice of Black Power advocates, circa 1970. It must be understood, however, that the reorientation of black leadership from protest to electoral politics means that whites will inevitably exercise considerable — and often decisive — influence in determining which African-American would-be leaders succeed and which fail. In historical context, such white influence constitutes a difference of degree rather than one of kind, but it could prove to be a vital difference. Throughout American history, African Americans have rarely had a free hand in selecting their leaders. Citing the ideologically diverse cases of Frederick Douglass, Booker T. Washington, and W.E.B. Du Bois, White (1990, pp. 1–2) concludes that "black American leaders have historically depended on white as well as Negro recognition of their claims to speak for their race."

Just as today's new breed of black leaders would have been woefully out of place in the civil rights movement of the 1960s and 1970s, the leadership styles and strategies that advanced the cause of African Americans in earlier decades would not mesh with the realities of multiracial, electoral politics in the 1990s. It seems doubtful that on a national level, most African Americans view any current or emerging new-breed leader with anything approaching the enthusiasm they continue to feel for Jesse Jackson. Nonetheless, the survey data analyzed here suggest that although African Americans know less about other black leaders than they do about Jackson, they would welcome an expanded role for leaders who are not cut from the same cloth as Jackson. More concretely, election outcomes in various states and localities confirm that African Americans will rally behind new-breed black candidates. Just as concretely, the failed

Jackson candidacies of 1984 and 1988 establish that whites — even liberal Democratic whites — will not turn out in sufficient numbers to nominate, let alone elect, a Jesse Jackson. The survey data analyzed here, however, signify a greater white openness to a distinctive new type of black leader, and it is this openness — in combination with very strong support from black voters — that accounts for the recent electoral successes of new-breed black candidates and that betokens many such successes in the future.

Of course, not all politics, whether local, state, or national, is electoral. Different styles of political leadership — pragmatic or uncompromising, modulated or strident, low-key or charismatic, accommodating or confrontational — that stand one in good stead in one political arena may work to one's disadvantage in another. Thus, the very same qualities that have often seemed to work to Jesse Jackson's disadvantage at the ballot box have kept him in the forefront of black leaders. The same traits that seemed, in 1995, to make Colin Powell a more viable contender for the presidency than Jesse Jackson (or, for that matter, than Bill Clinton, Bob Dole, or Ross Perot) tend to mute blacks' enthusiasm for Powell. The same style that propelled Louis Farrakhan to the front tier of black leaders nationwide disqualifies him as a leader who could expect to receive white support or would make any serious effort to do so. The new breed of African-American political leader is oriented toward the electoral arena. To argue that other styles are increasingly ill suited to compete in that arena is not to argue that such styles are doomed to fail. It is simply to argue that they are unlikely to succeed electorally.

The remaining question is whether the incorporation of blacks into governing institutions will produce greater responsiveness to black demands (Browning, Marshall, & Tabb, 1984). Ever since Charles Hamilton (1977) introduced the concept of deracialization, debate has raged about whether the election of new-breed black candidates is a hollow victory from the standpoint of the traditional black political agenda (see, for example, Walters, 1981). Citing achievements by Mayors Sidney Barthelemy in New Orleans, David Dinkins in New York, and Harvey Gantt in Charlotte, Huey Perry (1991) has forcefully argued that the deracialized campaign strategy does not necessarily lead to a deracialized governance strategy. On the other hand, critics, such as Manning Marable (1990), portray the new "post-black" officeholders as providing no solution to the crises that confront urban blacks. From this perspective, the crucial question for black Americans is not whether Colin Powell or some other black with Powell's mainstream credentials and appeal to white Americans will ultimately become president, any more than it was whether a Clarence Thomas would ever become a member of the Supreme Court. Robert C. Smith (1990b, 1992) dismisses electoral politics as a sideshow that diverts blacks from more basic concerns. As Smith sees it, integration into "establishment" institutional structures and processes isolates black leaders and would-be leaders, physically and psychologically, from the mass base of the black community:

Talented people who today might constitute the organizing cadre instead seek niches in relatively insignificant electoral office or in corporate and public bureaucracies. Today, a young Stokely Carmichael might well end up with the equivalent of a GS–16 job in the Atlanta or the District of Columbia bureaucracies. Most black leaders act as if fundamental changes can come about as a result of playing the routine power games of Washington or city politics when clearly such changes, if possible, are *only* possible as a result of mass mobilization inside the black community. (Smith, 1992, p. 119)

What the changing of the guard in black politics portends and whether a hopeful or a cynical interpretation of its effects will ultimately prevail remain unclear at this point; however, that new-breed black politicians have the ability to forge winning interracial electoral coalitions looms as a core reality of the politics of the 1990s.

NOTES

1. These data were obtained from the Roper Center for Public Opinion Research. Neither the Roper Center nor the collectors of the data bear any responsibility for the analyses or interpretations presented here.

2. In this part of the analysis, the black sample was partitioned into those who had attended college (N = 101) and those who had not (N = 201). The polychoric correlations were as follows, with the entries in each cell representing first the less educated and then the more educated group.

	Jackson	Wilder	Powell	Farrakhan
Jackson	1.000	0.473	0.253	0.430
	1.000	0.642	0.312	0.377
Wilder		1.000	0.483	0.210
		1.000	0.731	0.395
Powell			1.000	0.327
			1.000	0.404
Farrakhan				1.000
				1.000

3. This characterization of opinion trends in the mid-1990s is based on survey responses available in the Roper Center's online POLL database.

10

African-American Employers' Attitudes toward African-American Workers

Joleen Kirschenman

The morning reading of any major city newspaper serves as a daily reminder of the racial divide that exists in this country. Sometimes implicitly, sometimes explicitly, race underlies struggles over public policy issues at every turn, whether these are over welfare reform at the federal level or land use at the local level. Is welfare reform about diminishing the deficit or penalizing African Americans for not conforming to conservative ideals about family structure? Is it happenstance that grand, new public parks are planned for neighborhoods where growing numbers of professional, white urban pioneers have purchased homes, while residents of largely black neighborhoods see their political leaders exit in disgrace under accusations of accepting bribes from toxic dumpers?

While racial divisions and racial antagonisms continue to whither the spirits of egalitarians and to provide substantive material for social scientists, the role of attitudes in racial inequality has not commanded much attention. Despite the centrality of race to a multitude of controversial issues facing this nation — and the plausible notion that attitudes toward parties in the conflicts must matter — with significant exceptions (many the fruits of labor of contributors to this volume), racial attitudes have often been scrutinized in a vacuum. The degree to which groups might have negative attitudes about other groups has been measured, trends and variations have been analyzed, and causes of these trends and variations have been addressed. These approaches to the study of racial attitudes are critical for further understanding in this field and should be encouraged to yield better measurements and information about the racial attitudes of groups other than the traditionally studied attitudes of whites toward blacks as well as variation within groups.[1] Research in this area is further enhanced by considerations of the consequences for the life chances of affected populations and efforts to include attitudes in explanations of various types of racial inequality. (The role of attitudes in racial inequality is best represented in studies of residential segregation. For examples, see Massey and Denton [1993], Farley, Steeh, Krysan, Jackson, and Reeves [1994], Zubrinsky and Bobo [1996].)

It is this relation between the existence of racial attitudes and disadvantaged outcomes that makes this an area of concern for scholars of inequality. This chapter, then, focuses on the prevalence of negative attitudes toward African Americans as well as the linkage between these attitudes and negative consequences for African Americans. Inquiry is then made into the attitudes of African Americans toward other African Americans, specifically black employers' attitudes toward black workers and would-be workers. Finally, possible reasons for the variety of attitudes African-American employers have about the people they screen and sometimes hire are explored.

This effort emerges from a much larger research program assessing inequalities in the labor market, especially the disadvantaged position of blacks and, more specifically, of black males. The divergence of labor market outcomes of African Americans from other racial and ethnic groups has been an important question in research on inequality. The literature has produced many explanations for this employment and wage gap; among the most plausible are those that invoke structural causes — for instance, economic transformation, the accompanying spatial reorganization of employment, and labor market segmentation. Another possible explanation is that employers prefer others over blacks in their workforces. Although not ignoring structural forces, this analysis focuses on employers' attitudes and preferences and how this might influence their utilization of black workers. It stresses the importance of employers' racial attitudes in the employment process and briefly reviews findings that show the negative consequences these attitudes have for black employment. The existing literature does not differentiate among employers, but rather tends to assume that they all belong to the majority group. The truth is, of course, that African Americans are also involved in the hiring process, both as owners and as managers; indeed, there is some evidence that, arguably because of equal employment legislation, they are disproportionately represented in human resource positions (Sokoloff 1992; Collins in press). Yet black employers' attitudes toward black workers remain unexamined.

In an effort to redress that lacunae, in-depth interviews with 14 black employers in Chicago and surrounding Cook County are examined. These interviews are a subset of a larger stratified, random sample of 185 employers. The original sample was stratified by industry, size, and location and represented the employment opportunities available to Cook County residents. Characteristics of the subset of black employers itself are, however, revealing (see Table 10.1) and suggest that the structural causes of racial inequality — especially spatial mismatch and racial segregation within jobs — merit the attention they receive. For instance, even though less than 10 percent of the sample is made up of black employers, either owners in their own right or managers of white-owned firms, only one of these was associated with a firm located in the suburbs. Yet the entire sample was evenly divided among inner city, other city areas (which included the central business district, known as "the Loop"), and suburbs. Five of the six black-owned firms in the sample were located in the inner city, while one was located in the Loop. The remaining eight African-American respondents were at some level of personnel management in white-owned firms. Of these, four were in the inner city, three were in the Loop, and only one was in the suburbs. These facts reinforce previous findings that show the interaction of race and space: For many, "inner city" connotes black while "suburb" connotes white (Kirschenman & Neckerman 1991), lending credence to space as a dimension or cause of inequality (Wilson 1987; Holzer 1991; Tilly, Moss, & Kirschenman 1996).

Racial segregation within occupations and jobs has been scrutinized as a cause of wage disparity. Recent research reinforces past findings that when African Americans work in segregated workplaces, they earn less than their counterparts who work in integrated workplaces (Browne, Hewitt, Tigges, & Green 1996). Indeed, this subsample shows that the only firm that did not have between 50 and 100 percent black representation in the sample job was the firm located in the suburb, which had 15 percent black representation. ("Sample job" refers to the modal job at the firm that did not require education beyond high school.) Indeed, five firms had 100 percent black representation, one had 98 percent, and most of the remainder had more than 75 percent black representation.[2] Not only do these results indicate extreme levels of racial segregation within workplaces, but also support research that shows African Americans are far more likely to supervise workers of their own race than workers of other races (Bobo & Suh 1996).

Pursuing questions of inequality along social cleavages is particularly important given the polarization of the economy — growth at the top and at the bottom. The economic transformation occurring across advanced industrialized societies is not affecting populations randomly but is having more deleterious effects on the already disadvantaged — women and minorities. Furthermore, the changing economy brought with it the dramatic loss of manufacturing jobs, a traditional avenue of mobility for lower skilled males, and the expansion of low-paying, dead-end service jobs, historically seen as the domain of lower skilled females. These

TABLE 10.1
Sample Characteristics

Ownership	Respondent Position	Location	Industry	Sample Job	Percent Black in Firm	Percent Black in Job
Black	Owner	Inner city	Retail	Sales clerk	100	100
Black	Owner	Inner city	Retail	Sales clerk	55	75
Black	Owner	Inner city	Wholesale	Warehouse-delivery	90	100
Black	Owner	Inner city	Manufacturing-retail	Sales clerk	96	100
Black	Owner	Downtown	Services	Clerical	54	80
Black	Human resources manager	Inner city	Manufacturing	Packer	98	98
White	Supervisor	Inner city	Services	Security Officer	65	65
White	Manager	Inner city	Restaurant	Counter worker	100	100
White	Personnel director	Inner city	Manufacturing	Paint filler	refused*	refused
Nonprofit	Administrative assistant	Inner city	Services	Secretary	33	58
White	Assistant personnel manager	Downtown	FIRE: Insurance	File clerk	50	missing†
White	Manager of employee benefits	Downtown	Manufacturing	Receptionist	10	100
Publicly owned	Director of employment and staff manager	Downtown	Utilities	Customer service representative	15	50
White	Personnel manager	Suburb	Retail	Baggers	15	15

*Interviewer observations report that, with the exception of the respondent, only whites were seen on the location.
†Respondent noted that all applicants for these jobs were young and black.

changes undoubtedly contribute to the rising racial gap in both employment rates and wages witnessed since the early 1970s. (For a review of this literature, see Moss and Tilly [1993].)

In addition to the transformation of the industrial and occupational structure, other changes in the economy have inspired different skill requirements — that is, the replacement of a production-driven economy with a consumption-driven economy means that employers give new precedence to soft skills or the types of skills or qualities that have more to do with communication and personal interaction than with what is learned in school (Kirschenman 1992; Moss & Tilly 1996). The qualities that employers desire may have more to do with cultural biases (for example, unaccented English and the ability to pay deference to high-end consumers) than skills that can be attained through education and training. Indeed, soft skills or cultural biases may actually be class, race, or gender biased. Moreover, these skills or traits are not easily measured objectively, but are judged subjectively. This situation makes it critical to understand how social distinctions of race, class, and gender become loaded with meaning and play into employers' decision-making processes.

Suggesting the danger of employing subjective methods to evaluate subjective characteristics is research finding that firms that rely less on subjective methods (such as the job interview) in the hiring process and more on objective means (such as administering a skills test) have higher representations of black workers in their firms (Neckerman & Kirschenman 1991). The effect that employers' attitudes might have on inequality in the labor market becomes clear when this combination of desirable subjective qualities being subjectively evaluated is considered in conjunction with the prevalence of negative stereotypes about African Americans, especially poor black men (Anderson 1990; Kirschenman & Neckerman 1991). To illustrate, it is not plausible that the white employer who told us that black males are "lazy and dishonest, more prone to street culture" gets rid of those stereotypes while conducting a job interview with a black man to fill a position that requires being able to "present a pleasing image of the company" — especially if that employer is "look(ing) at him with a more finely tuned eye," which is how another employer told us he scrutinizes his black male applicants compared to others.

The notion that the economy has an increased demand for skills that are based in race, class, and gender biases suggests that already existing inequalities along these dimensions could be exacerbated as attitude-laden employers, the critical mediating link between macroeconomic forces and job opportunities, make hiring decisions. William Julius Wilson has already taught us how a changing economy combined with sociopolitical events created a bifurcated black class structure and the beginnings of a black urban underclass (1978). Moreover, one could argue that today's polarized social structure has widened this gap, providing content for stereotypes and negative attitudes toward the most disadvantaged — poor African-American men. A logical next step would be to conclude that this class divide within the black community has also produced perceptual divisions and structured different attitudes, depending on where one is situated in the social hierarchy.

Earlier research on employers' attitudes, including my own, treated employers as monolithic with respect to their status in various socially defined groups. This chapter now attempts to redress that by closely examining the attitudes of African-American employers toward African-American workers. This will allow me to discern variation from the attitudes of the dominant group and call attention to the role of class in the formation of attitudes. It is unlikely that black employers are exempt from economic forces that encourage demand for soft skills or that they are immune to cultural biases as they assess their potential workers, although these biases will likely be based in class or gender rather than race.

DATA

Most of the analyses in this chapter are based on 14 structured, in-depth interviews with African-American employers in the Chicago area, although they also rely on and extensively report research based on the entire set of 185 employer interviews. The sample was stratified by location, industry, and size; firms were randomly sampled in proportion to the distribution of employment in Cook County, with inner-city firms being oversampled. As no comprehensive list exists of Chicago-area employers, the sampling frame was assembled from two directories of Illinois businesses, supplemented with the telephone book for categories of firms underrepresented in the business directories. The field period lasted from July 1988 to March 1989, and yielded a completion rate of 46 percent.

Given our focus on employment opportunities, the purpose of the design was to yield a sample that approximately matched the distribution of employment in Cook County. For instance, if five percent of Cook County jobs were in large, inner-city manufacturing firms, then five percent of the interviews should be in large, inner-city manufacturing firms. The sample necessarily underrepresents small firms, but does so in order to gain a more representative picture of employment opportunities. In terms of industry and size, the completed sample's weighted distribution, indeed, roughly approximates the distribution of employment in Cook County. Only about 22 percent of employers we contacted refused to take part, but constrained resources prevented us from pursuing all potential respondents who were willing to be interviewed. Midway through the field period, we set a minimum 40 percent completion rate in all industry-by-location categories, and stopped pursuing unresolved cases in categories with completion rates higher than 40 percent. Response rates by industry, firm size, and location were monitored, and special efforts were made to pursue cases in categories with low completion rates.

Our initial contacts and the majority of interviews themselves were conducted with the highest ranking official at the sampled establishment. The interviewers were not matched by race with the respondents. All of the interviewers were non-Hispanic white; 8.5 percent of the respondents were black, 1.5 percent were Hispanic, and the remainder were non-Hispanic white. Among the subset of black respondents more extensively analyzed in this chapter, half were women and half were men.

The interviews were taped and transcribed. Item nonresponse varied depending on the sensitivity and factual difficulty of the question, with most resulting from lack of knowledge rather than refusal to answer. In addition, the length and detail of responses to open-ended questions varied widely. Answers to these questions were examined in the context of each case.

Much of the interview focused on the "sample job," defined as the most typical entry-level position in the firm's modal nonprofessional, nonmanagerial, and nontechnical occupational category — sales, clerical, skilled, semiskilled, unskilled, or service. Because we sampled firms by industry and size, we do not have a random sample of entry-level jobs; however, when we compared the occupational distribution of our sample jobs to that of Cook County (excluding professional, managerial, and technical categories), we found that the two distributions were quite similar.

The interview schedule included both closed- and open-ended questions about employers' hiring and recruitment practices and their perceptions of Chicago's labor force and business climate. We asked several questions that bear on issues of racial and gender bias in addition to closed-ended questions about the race and ethnicity of employees in the sample job. Additionally, in the context of a general discussion of the quality of the workforce and of inner-city problems, we asked employers to comment on the high unemployment rates of inner-city black men and women; on whether these two populations might experience the labor market differently; and on any differences they saw between immigrant and native-born workers and among black, white, and Hispanic workers.

Some limitations of these data constrain the following analysis. First, we did not ask employers to make gender comparisons within other racial or ethnic groups; thus, I cannot address distinctions employers might also have drawn between, for instance, white women and white men. Furthermore, although we asked about the racial and ethnic make-up of employees in the firm and in the sample job, we did not ask about the gender representation within each racial or ethnic group. Thus, except in cases where the sample job is both race- and sex-segregated, it is not possible to determine whether hiring patterns conform to employers' gendered perceptions. Finally, the subset of African-American employers extensively analyzed in this chapter is essentially an opportunity sample — that is, the firm fell into our sample and the respondent happened to be black. (This sample subset is further described in the introduction and in Table 10.1.) Yet, with the exception of underrepresentation of black employers in the suburbs, it is a diverse sample and fairly represents the dimensions of the entire sample according to the three strata we sampled on — industry, size, and location (inner city and other parts of the city). (As noted earlier, this lack of black employers in the suburbs likely represents reality.) Importantly, these are very rich data that allow us not only to examine white employers' attitudes toward blacks but also to move beyond the generalizations and stereotypes of the dominant group by studying black employers' attitudes.

Employers' Attitudes toward Black Workers

The possibility that black workers' disadvantaged position in the labor market is, at least in part, the result of discrimination has usually been arrived at indirectly. Social scientists analyze the differences in wages or employment among different racial and ethnic groups, then interpret as discrimination what remains unexplained after education and experience are controlled (for a recent example, see Cancio, Evans, and Maume [1996]). Even then it is a matter of the researchers' perspective because this residual is just as likely to be interpreted as the result of individuals within the disadvantaged group failing to expend adequate effort as it would be the result of employers' discriminatory treatment of this same group. Moreover, although racial inequalities in the labor market had rarely been examined at the firm level, the recent emergence of these types of studies significantly expands our understanding of the role of race in the hiring process. (For some examples, see Braddock and McPartland [1987]; Turner, Fix, and Struyk [1991]; Holzer [1996]; and Moss and Tilly [1996].)

In an earlier analysis of the Chicago-area data (Kirschenman & Neckerman 1991), we demonstrated that white employers of low-wage workers readily use race as a marker of worker productivity and rely on their racial attitudes when making hiring decisions. It was not only racial attitudes that were found to matter, however; attitudes about class status, space or residence, and gender served to refine employers' negative racial attitudes and were called upon as they sorted through the labor pool. The way each of these interactions operated against poor, inner-city, black males was well documented. Thus we argued that efforts to explain black males' extraordinarily low labor market participation rates cannot ignore white employers' attitudes toward these workers. Whether these attitudes are based on experience, media images, or the experiences of others, their existence strongly indicates that the "demonization" of the black male has succeeded.

In this chapter, I turn to an equally important question: How do black employers' attitudes toward black workers affect hiring decisions. A few references have indicated that African-American employers also categorize black workers negatively, especially with respect to class. An in-depth examination of these employers suggests that the bifurcated black class structure gives black employers cause to also categorize and refine while they make hiring judgments. As I turn to those data, I attempt to understand variation within that group — that is, it is not as simple as a monolithic black middle class having adopted the discourse of the dominant culture and joined in their white counterparts' negative portrayals of black workers.

Black Employers' Attitudes toward Black Workers

As noted, research on racial attitudes has tradionally focused on the attitudes of the majority group toward the minority group. Only recently has systematic data become available to explore the racial attitudes of blacks toward whites (Schuman, Steeh, & Bobo 1985). With the exception of some work showing that blacks have a more favorable impression of their racial group than of other racial groups (Schuman, Steeh, & Bobo 1985), we have not had the means to examine more fully blacks' attitudes toward other blacks and how these compare to those held by the dominant group.

The prevailing assumption is that racial groups agree on various issues that show up on the public agenda. This notion of a cohesive black opinion does not take into account class differences within the African-American population, particularly the differences one would expect to emerge with the bifurcation of the black class structure (Wilson 1978; Grant, Oliver, & James 1996; see Chapter 11 in this volume). Class distinctions are important for this analysis because employers are assumed to bear a higher class status than the low-skilled, low-wage laborers they are screening and hiring.

Generally, black employers cast a critical eye on their black workers, often echoing many of the generalizations made by their white counterparts. There are vast differences, however, in the rates at which they hire blacks (as indicated in Table 10.1, the workforces of black employers are disproportionately black). Furthermore, nearly all black employers tempered negative characterizations of black workers with structural reasoning. (This is similar to differences in black and white reasoning found by other scholars [Kluegel & Smith 1986].) That is, rather than attribute perceived deficiencies in black workers to individual faults, they were much more likely to credit the effects of historical oppression. Additionally, many articulated the deleterious effects of macroeconomic changes on employment opportunities for black residents of Chicago.

Some white employers also provided similar explanations for "problems among inner-city workers," but they more readily and uncritically invoked racial stereotypes — then refined these stereotypes with additional stereotypes about class, space, and gender. Different experiences caused the typical black employer, then, to start the cognitive process with less "taken-for-grantedness" but then — similar to white employers — called upon other categories to distinguish among the low-skilled black workforce. Indeed, because these employers hire black workers at disproportionately high rates and value the same soft skills required by their counterparts in the majority group, they rely heavily on class, space, and gender distinctions during the sorting process. Unlike some white employers who only drew the primary distinction on the basis of race and then proceeded to avoid those from the nonfavored group, black employers (with the possible exception of one) have succeeded in selecting black workers. Nonetheless, as with white employers, the particular way black employers utilize the interactions of race with class, space, and gender to screen for the skills they need militates against the poor, those who reside in the inner city, and men. Indeed, the only firms with overrepresentations of black men were a warehouse/delivery company and a security firm that required literacy in English. This corresponds to the finding that the only blue-collar jobs in the city that had higher representations of blacks than Hispanics were those that required mathematics, literacy skills, or both (Kirschenman & Neckerman 1991).

In addition to drawing out the themes detailed in the study of white employers, more attention is given to the structural position of these employers, especially the degree of autonomy they have as employers. This type of analysis informs interpretations of the employers' remarks but also lends to diminishing the assumption that the black middle class is a monolithic group with similar perceptions and attitudes. On the basis of their comments about black workers, these respondents may be categorized into three groups: those who rather uncritically shared the dominant group's negative views, those who attributed discrimination for problems among black workers, and those who made strong class distinctions — both in the way they sorted the labor force and in efforts they made to point out differences between themselves and the workers they hired. There is, as with any typology, overlap in these categories: With one exception, each black employer acknowledged the existence of discrimination but varied in the emphasis they gave unequal treatment;

several employers who emphasized discrimination also recognized class differences.

Beyond class distinctions, gender and space matter to these employers. Indeed, in this chapter only general attention is paid to gender distinctions made by these employers because, with the exception of one, each drew sharp differences between men and women in the labor market. Their firms' overrepresentation of black women compared to black men are evidence of their preferences on this dimension. Finally, although used by some to sort through job applicants, space was a less important category for these employers, undoubtedly because many of these firms were actually located in the inner city. Assuming these employers relied on a local labor pool, space would not be a viable screening device.

Generalizations about black workers approaching those made by white employers dominate the comments made by three employers, each in very different positions with respect to the autonomy they exercised. When asked what role discrimination played in the difficulties African Americans faced in the labor market, the office manager who assisted in hiring clerical workers told us what the white male owner of this software company told her to tell us:

Very . . . I'm going to have to say very important, very important, because it seems now . . . just like here . . . (the owner) asked me to mention this. We are an equal opportunity employer and it seems like lately, every time a minority is dismissed from the company, they haunt us. They come with the E.E.O.C., it's like, what is happening? But, everybody feels like they're being discriminated on. I'm not saying we award big damages. . . . So where does it all end? A company tries to be fair, a gentleman is dismissed, a good year later. . . . Yes, it's very important.

This comment provides evidence of two, not mutually exclusive, phenomena: The manager has bought into critiques of affirmative action found in the dominant discourse or does not have enough autonomy to develop her own perspective. Incidentally, while the sample job for which she hired had 100 percent black representation, the entire firm had only 10 percent.

More complicated evidence of these phenomena is provided by careful analysis of the comments made by the director of personnel for a large white-owned manufacturing company located in the inner city. (This is the same firm that refused our request for a demographic profile, but only white workers were observed, as described in note 2.) They experienced low turnover, which they attributed to being a good place to work, describing themselves as "the last of the big spenders on the south side of Chicago." The interview was sheduled with the director of personnel at the site, but when the interview was conducted he was joined by his supervisor, the director of personnel for the entire regional division. The interviewer's notes are informative, providing the following record:

I had the sense that (the regional director) was there to make sure (the site director) didn't give out the wrong kind of information. He was suspicious at first, didn't know some questions and unwilling to guess. Rapport improved when we moved to open-ended section. (The site director)'s conservative views made it easier for (the regional director) to express his own view in what could otherwise have been an uncomfortable situation. I think (the regional director) was genuinely interested in what (the site director) had to say on subjects he probably wouldn't have felt comfortable asking about himself.

In addition to making an association between class and space, some indication of the effects of the white supervisor's presence on the main respondent are in this answer to a question about how many of their workers were from Chicago: "I couldn't give you a percent. People move around all the time. You can hire them in Chicago and they move in the suburbs 'cause they be making so much money off of us. I was living in Chicago and I made so much money — thanks to him — that I moved in the suburbs." When asked about why there might be such high unemployment rates among black workers, the white respondent thought "a lot of it has to do with attitude among the workers. Whether they want to work or not." His black colleague agreed, but also revealed his ambivalence,

Suspect(ing) that to a large degree one becomes suppressed after a while in terms of the system, but there are jobs around. You know, you have the same dilemma around even people that aren't in that system. You know jobs go vacant. . . . Again, it gets back to an attitudinal thing. I don't think that, certainly you know, where I come from which is probably a different perspective from (the regional director). . . . I would think that it would be fairly easy to get crushed by the system in your spirit, but it would take for a lot of people just getting that first, getting out of that, getting going and I think that's a lot of individual will power.

More evidence that the black respondent was not being completely intimidated into giving only answers his boss would approve of is the conversation surrounding possible effects of welfare. When asked about these, the supervisor said, "Well, I'd like to hear what (the site director) has to say before I give you my opinion." The site director then proceeded to say that he thought a welfare system, if managed correctly, was needed for those who were unable to work. His superior then elaborated his view of welfare as a dependency trap; however, the site director then changed his tune somewhat when the discussion focused on the labor market difficulties of black males. He said it was due to "Attitude. Poor attitude. I'm very vocal on that. They lazy, a lot of them. You know, when you trapped, you realize you're trapped, but if you don't try to do some-thing about it yourself, then you'll always be trapped. If you get into a welfare mode, then you becomes a slave. And if that's what you want to be, so be it as an individual, but I don't want to be a slave. I'm going to work. It's an attitude problem, that's all I can tell you. And I've known. . . . I been around them. I know what's happening."

Indeed, the white respondent expresses more tolerance at this point, agreeing that some people have attitude problems but that some people do need help to get out of disadvantaged neighborhoods. His colleague reminds us that he came from a bad neighborhood, but he realized that he had to make the first step. He elaborates, "We used to the give away pro-gram. You know, that time's out now, the 60s is over, the 70s over, you got to do something for yourself. And that's the way I feel and I get into real trouble with my people in my communities, too, when I talk this way, but they got to hear the truth sooner or later."

He continues his negative appraisal of black men by contrasting them with their female counterparts, who are more favorably assessed: "They're getting way ahead of the black man. Yes, they are. I think they're beginning to see the real side of life. They know that they're not going to be taken care of, for the most part, you know a lot of situations where women, black women especially, have had children without a man being there in the household and they know they gotta get out and make it for themself."

The manager of an all-black workforce at a white-owned fast-food restaurant in the inner city noted that he experienced lots of turnover "because they feel the work is a little bit too hard," but had little difficul-ty hiring workers "in the Chicago market because you got so many peo-ple you can choose from to do your work." Ironically, he also perceived ample opportunity for job seekers:

If people want to work they can. There are a lot of jobs out there, you know. The main thing you hear, I been looking for a job for two years or a year and I haven't been able to find one. And I know some people working two, some even three jobs. I figure if these people can find jobs, what's the deal, you know? If you don't want to work, you'll never find a job. If you want to work, you'll find a job tomor-row, basically, if you've got the right attitude about working. I mean, I'm work-ing to better myself, not, you know. . . . I'm working my butt off and I'm not get-ting paid enough, instead of like that.

In addition to believing that getting a job is a matter of personal respon-sibility, we see here the beginnings of an effort to distinguish himself from others. Later in the interview, this respondent further elaborated his dim view of his workers' work ethic and related it back to turnover issues. He said, "People really just don't want to work. . . . I feel if you find a job, why not keep that job? Why become a part of the high turnover rate that plagues the inner cities? All your large inner cities basically have the same thing, you know, as far as turnover rate. All of them are very high. Nobody wants to work hard for what they accomplish. Everybody's looking for an easier way." This same respondent had a more positive view of black women, however: "Most inner-city, black women, I feel, the majority of them want to work, you know, to change their life style." Finally, he did believe that discrimination contributed "maybe a small percentage" to the employment problems of black workers: "That threat, it's always present."

Although nearly all black employers attributed the status of black workers in the Chicago labor market in part to discrimination, three employers relied almost exclusively on discriminatory treatment of African Americans to explain their problems getting jobs. Two respondents, both owners with nearly 100 percent black workforces (one firm had one Hispanic worker), explicitly linked discrimination with perceived lower productivity. That is, because of repeated disappointments in the labor market resulting from unfair treatment, blacks — especially males — eventually give up. Representatives of the third company, a large utility, posited that black males suffered from discrimination in two specific ways, through access to training programs where they might acquire job skills and through access to unskilled jobs for which they would be qualified.

Both respondents who owned their own companies, a liquor store and a warehouse/retail supply, had no trouble finding staff "because of the high unemployment among blacks." Furthermore, both held dim views of the state of race relations in the city and in the nation; with respect to the obstacles businesses face in the city, both noted crime — as did many of their white counterparts — but paid much more attention to racism. One said, "Well, race relations is a big problem. Get back the leadership, you know. To me, it's race problems. To me, it's race relations out in the city. Most racist city, I think, in America. . . . And the white politician don't want to cooperate with the black leadership." The other, in a similar context, said, "America's got to turn it, it's got to turn it, it's got to turn around itself. It's got to make a moral decision. Well, in the first place, now we're going more like a South Africa . . . apartheid." They were consistent in carrying this rationale into the labor market. This last respondent also noted that "We have people who come into this inner city and operate businesses here and don't employ blacks. People make their living from the community, but don't give back to the community." He did believe that welfare destroyed incentive for blacks and whites, but singled out black males as having "adopted some of the devil-may-care attitudes or lack of work ethic because some of them have been subjected to such menial wages and working conditions that they feel they'd be just as well off on welfare." The respondent, also in the context of discussing obstacles to business, shifted easily to relating employment problems to discrimination. Talking about the lack of a consumer base in the inner city, he said, "Well, the people in this area, I would say 40, 50 percent of them is out of work. There's only the General Assistance. Big problem for the city of Chicago amongst the black people, though, you understand. I say he's the first one to be fired and the last one to be hired." This discriminatory treatment, combined with serious job shortages, meant that "they get disgusted, after a while they don't care. They try hard, but they ain't got no jobs." He strenuously reemphasized this argument later in the interview when asked why black males might experience difficulty finding jobs: "Well, that's why they have hard times, they're no jobs for them. They're the first that you fire and the last to be hired." The interviewer asks, "And why do you think they are the last to be hired and the first to be fired?" Without pause, he replies, "Because they black. So much hatred in this country. You have a sickness: you hate a person because he black. That's what you find in this world. They don't want you to have nothing."

Like the earlier cases presented, these two male respondents concluded the situation was different for black women. One said, "Well, they got a better chance than the black men as far as getting hired." The other believed that "the black female, she has a desire. . . . I think a greater desire to produce good work, better work habits because the black woman has always been the backbone of the family as best as she can. And she, as a result, she's probably a little bit more of a stable work person than the black male."

One could argue that these two respondents presented their case for discrimination so strongly because they were confident of their own employment situation, both being business owners. Perhaps their perspective was also related to their notice of race relations in the wider society, especially that between politics and business. Discrimination, however, was also invoked as a major explanatory factor for labor market difficulties during an interview conducted with two black women in personnel management at a large utility company that had a 50 percent black, mostly female, workforce. They posited discrimination both as an indirect cause and a direct cause of unemployment for black males, perceiving a more favorable situation for black females. One observed that black males failed in the labor market because, as a group, they lack the basic skills required for available jobs; the other contended that the majority of job training programs are for women to prepare them for clerical work, "so there aren't even training programs for black men." Discrimination compounds the problem for black males: They may not have many skills, but they are not represented in unskilled jobs. This respondent noted a large construction site located near a predominantly black area of the city that had very few black male construction workers. She concluded that even workers in unskilled jobs do not reflect the demographic makeup of Chicago.

Class entered black employers' discourse in various ways, but they primarily used class to distinguish themselves from the black workers they scrutinized during the hiring process — as in the first two cases examined in this section, to explain perceived differences in worker productivity and to describe how they assessed productivity among low-skilled black workers by correlating class with the perceived possession of soft skills. Black employers presumed this perceived gap in soft skills caused members of the majority to avoid these workers, but they also admitted to screening on class markers. Indeed, because most of the black employers hired disproportionately large numbers of black workers, it is reasonable to conclude that they used class markers extensively to distinguish among an otherwise homogeneous workforce — at least with respect to race, which, for white employers, was the primary distinction.

The remarks of a black female employer of clerical workers for a non-profit legal assistance firm recall earlier findings that employers looked for middle-class signals when hiring for this occupation (Kirschenman & Neckerman 1991). Communication skills were very important to her but not necessarily among "the excessively liberal management staff we have here." Like white employers who were concerned that racial and ethnic diversity may cause conflict in the workplace, this respondent noted how the interaction of race and class led to conflict. She commented on "the cultural fears of white men that run businesses" and wondered if that fear might arise "from never socializing with them." She noted an "awkwardness when black attorneys are hired. Things seem to be a lot more comfortable socially when blacks are not on the same social level."

Discrimination entered the picture, as she said, "insidiously": Black attorneys are given the less complex cases initially. She joined her colleagues across the city when she extended her belief that "black women have an easier time than black men getting hired." According to her, black men are frequently portrayed as shiftless, not wanting to work, not having a work ethic, and "these are all stereotypes they have to overcome or prove are not part of their life." She continued that she faces obstacles but not to the degree that a black male would; consequently, "it's difficult to be a black man being looked at condescendingly and seeing females doing better." Moreover, because this nonprofit agency is located in the inner city, she noted among the obstacles to doing business there was "racism" among their service providers. For instance, they had difficulty getting people to come repair their office equipment because of their location. Furthermore, they had to screen their job applicants very well "to tell people what it is like here. We're very honest, so that we don't get people who take the job and then are terrified of being in some of these communities and/or because of Chicago being the most racist city in the U.S., and living in little racial clusters, that they understand the racial mix of the places where we are as well."

The black female owner of an ice cream manufacturing and retail concern explicitly drew class distinctions among her entirely black low-skilled workforce and described how this led to conflict in the workplace. She gave jobs to some young people "who had been exposed to middle class values" through a program sponsored by wealthy people, but she concluded that, although they were better workers because they were more outgoing, "things don't work out unless your whole staff is like that." On the other hand, she worried about hiring youth from the inner city for retail jobs because they are not used to seeing large amounts of money, and they are tempted to steal. She said,

And I can almost tell a project kid when we get 'em. You can tell 'em by the way they look at the cash register. They've just never seen that kind of money before. We can have a good day, with $1200 to $2000 a day sales and when they see that much money . . . when you hit that drawer and you look up at their eyes and the way they look at it, you can tell. But there are some really good people who come out of the projects, I mean really great. I don't want to stereotype them. But, I would hesitate because I know that they're not used to seeing the money and are more prone to steal.

Speaking more generally, she also invoked the presence of a "gendered" discrimination: "I think it's the perception by employers — black men just have a bad reputation." Although she questioned black men's "ambition," she believed that many received a "bum rap," and "women have protected them because they have the jobs." She argued that black women were taught by their mothers to be independent; that translated into their better work ethic — however, she concluded that, overall, the work ethic of whites was superior to that of blacks.

Two respondents in personnel management — one man and one woman — at a large black-owned manufacturer in the inner city that employed 98 percent black workers (80 percent of whom are women) called attention to class differences as they interact with space. With respect to hiring people who lived in poor neighborhoods, the male respondent said, "we take 'em," but he continued that "if I had to go to Robert Taylor Homes [a large high-rise public-housing development] and meet someone, I'm not going to go in there." He also noted a gap between the black middle class and the poor in the community, using class and space to refine race: "The middle class blacks think they're more like those in the white community and they move to the suburbs."

Suggesting that these employers used soft skills to distinguish among applicants, his colleague said that she primarily looked at "appearance, how the applicant presents him or herself, whether the applicant is respectful." In answer to the interviewer's probe for specifics, she said the applicant should "dress appropriately, i.e., not wear shorts, and should be quiet, nice, polite, and easy spoken."

Having drawn a relation between inner-city residence, attendance at public schools, and a poorly qualified workforce, these two respondents also emphasized discrimination as a prominent cause of unemployment. One noted that "once black kids graduate from high school, they have nowhere to go. There are not even summer jobs. There's no work for them. It's hard to get." Discrimination was the main reason: "I don't think all our people are dumb or stupid." Both noted that a lot of people are afraid of black men, while the male respondent gave content to the stereo- type, "Every black male is on drugs, steals, drinks, pimps, and is slow- witted." The female respondent echoed the gendered distinction that nearly all her counterparts made: "whites aren't afraid of black women because black women have been part of their households for a long time — as the white man's mistress, as the mother of his children, as domes- tics, as cooks in restaurants, and as office cleaners." She added that although these were menial jobs, it meant that women were able to adopt some of white people's ways. Significantly, this again calls our attention to — if not class — at least shared cultures and may be referring to those "middle class values and behaviors" she and many employers seek in their workers. This linkage of "white people's ways" and black women is more discursive evidence for the argument that links the desire for soft skills with disadvantage for black males.

An owner of a jewelry store in the inner city called dramatic attention to class when asked what type of qualities he looked for in a worker. His reply was "A person who doesn't need a job." Puzzled, the interviewer asks, "That's what you're looking for?" He answered, "That's what we usually try to hire. People that don't need the job." He further explained to the still-confused interviewer, "Because they will tend to be a little more honest. Most of the people that live in the neighborhoods and areas where my stores are at need the job. They are low income, and so, conse- quently, they're under more pressure and there's more of a tendency to be dishonest, because of the pressure."

In addition to recognizing the importance of class, this respondent also held individuals accountable for the employment problems in the black community. He first related employment issues to poor schools, but:

You know, it's a case where if you say that poor schools are because of discrimi- nation, I don't think that's the basic reason. I think it's that people who live in the community, even though they're poor, are not involved in the educational process, don't demand from the system a better quality product, production, stu- dents aren't able to learn, I mean they don't force the system to work for them. So I mean that . . . you can't blame that on prejudice. But the ultimate product that comes through the door is someone who's not capable of performing up to the level that his counterpart is that comes from a majority area. So, I mean, I don't know whether you call it prejudice, but you know the end result is that you've got a person who has minimal skills.

This same interviewee, however, invoked discriminatory treatment, especially of black males. Companies with good jobs "don't generally offer jobs to black males because they feel threatened by males, and not as threatened from a minority female." So once again, the notion that black males are more disadvantaged, especially that they are more likely to experience discrimination, emerges: "They [black women] have more advantage, they have a better opportunity to get a job." He then linked this lack of access to good jobs to differences in work ethic and attitudes to work:

I don't perceive a difference between black work ethic and white work ethic in the United States. What I do perceive is a difference in the attitude when people go to work for different types of companies. In other words, if I took a minority worker or a white worker and I started them to work for AT&T, they would both approach the job, I think, in like manner. If I took one black worker and put him in AT&T, and one white worker, and put him in [my jewelry store], there would be a difference in their attitudes, the reason being is that when a person goes to work for a large company, they can envision in their minds promotional opportunities, success, I mean the American dream being fulfilled. When they go to work for a small company, you see limited advancement, and that dream potential is not there. So consequently they would tend to give less because they feel like there's less chance of getting a return on that that they're giving.

Given the emphasis clerical employers put on soft skills, we are not surprised by the attention to class made by the black female president of a business college that specializes in training and then placing secretaries. She recalled, "I had an employer once say to me, 'You know, I really like the applicant you sent, but she kept pronouncing ask as "ax." That just grated me so badly, because she was going to be on my phone and I couldn't tolerate hearing, "May I ax who's calling?"' Now those things, in and of themselves, that shouldn't be such a big deal, but it is a big deal. And it's all those kinds of things that are cues that turn off people and on either side of the table, you don't know what it is. And I think when you come out of certain environments, you bring with you the trappings of those environments. If you could live in that community and still present the image that that person expects to see you could live there, I don't think he would care." Thus, the appropriate class signals or ability to display desirable soft skills could lessen the negative effects of space and race.

This business owner conflated cultural differences with class and distinguished those from racial differences, arguing that "the value set is interchangeable between middle-class blacks and white American values, but there are fewer black people that have middle-class values because there's lots of unemployment and misery in the black community." She added that with so many people disadvantaged economically, "there is bizarre behavior and it creates a different set of values."

Consistent with her counterparts, this respondent also singled out the plight of black men. She linked culture, class, and race when she noted that "black and white men don't speak the same language. Black men feel the need to assert themselves in an environment that has battered them." Consequently, she figured that white male employers hired less threatening black males, even if they were not necessarily the smartest or the most capable — they were deemed the most manageable. Furthermore, she believed that these same employers were more willing to cope with black women, who are perceived as less threatening.

The personnel manager of a security firm thought that discrimination existed but that "it cannot be used as a crutch." During hiring, he was concerned with basic personal interaction skills: "good clean hygiene, a person who can speak, don't appear to be grumpy or discontented or disenchanted with work you're trying to get them to do." Whether "the person says, 'yes, sir,' 'no, sir,' you know, the type of language they use, like slang or they're using profane language. . . . That's very important." A "good common sense of proper etiquette" tells him how applicants are going to act with the client, reminding us of the importance of the perceived tastes of customers. If this employer's workers did not share "middle-class culture," they should at least pay it deference.

This respondent also drew strong gender differences: Black males have been irresponsible, and, consequently, employers have learned that women are more reliable.

And a lot of company owners and factory owners with these women's . . . with these factory jobs saw some things. Whereas a man would take off two days or three days off of work or he'll miss on a Monday 'cause he done went out and partied all over the weekend and then got drunk. The woman was at work, she was there on time, she worked a little harder because she was afraid of losing her job knowing what she had to take care of at home, so she worked a little faster, and a little harder. And when these bosses started looking around and seeing a good job the woman has done and here, Joe Blow comes back, says he wants his job back, she's a better employee. Are you going to give Joe Blow his job back? No, buddy. You're out. And it's the same way with the professional field. A lot of men who would have been bankers or whatever else. It's been a great fast change.

He concludes that this is partly the result of a "lack of role models for males because there are no working fathers in the house."

Among the qualities sought by a black assistant personnel manager at a large insurance company when hiring file clerks were "communication skills, ability to work under minimal supervision, someone who's promotable, good analytical abilities, someone preferably with personality. . . . And the reason for that is we do, at some point, if this person goes on to other positions, there's a lot of client contact. And we like people that are phone people, people that can meet and mingle or interface with clients and not have a problem doing so." These traits become important if the worker were to be promoted to a position where customer interaction became a daily task; they are less important to the "back of the office" jobs filled by entry-level file clerks, further reinforcing the significance of soft skills and their potential race, class, and gender biases.

Fifty percent of this respondent's entry-level file clerks are black, two-thirds of these are women, and most are young (25 or under). This manager sorted through her labor pool according to whether people attended city or suburban schools, favorably selecting those who attended the latter. She implicitly, then, used space distinctions to separate desirable workers from the less desirable, even though "I'm a graduate of the Chicago public school system and that's . . . it's unfortunate. I don't mean to imply that everybody coming out of the Chicago public schools are poor." She also attributed the exodus of Chicago business to the suburbs to this negative view of city schools. She regretted that the perception is that the Chicago public schools are mostly black and the children lack reading, writing, and social skills; however, she thought there was some truth to the perception. Indeed, her screening tactics likely emerged from this perception.

This respondent further distinguished black males: "Some of it is due to the fact that they don't have the proper skills, but, for those that do have the proper skills some of it is, unfortunately, prejudice . . . unfortunately. I think that there is a real insecurity among white males to deal with black males. They would rather deal with a black female than a black male. And that's unfortunate, especially for those black males that are qualified and have the skills."

This respondent's white female supervisor was interviewed earlier; indeed, when the interview was completed, she suggested that her assistant might "offer a different and interesting perspective" and should also be interviewed. They offered contrasting opinions. The white respondent believed that blacks were more inclined to leave their jobs, were more likely to lie about absenteeism, and more likely to have problems with attendance. Moreover, discrimination was not an issue because the company looks for the most qualified applicant. In contrast, the black respondent linked any racial differences in productivity to discrimination, describing its self-fullfilling prophecy effects. She thought there were some differences between the way some blacks and whites worked, but

"I'm not saying that blacks don't work hard. I think that many times because they don't have the right skills to get ahead and they feel that they've been passed over due to discrimination on the basis of color as opposed to skills, that they have a tendency not to work as hard as they should because they just simply think, 'Well, they're not going to promote me anyway because I'm black and therefore I'm not going to work hard.' And that's a self-defeating attitude."

The personnel manager of a suburban grocery store, the only black respondent located in the suburbs, was looking for someone "who's not afraid of hard work," has "excellent interpersonal skills" to relate with customers as well as coworkers, and has a neat appearance. Those desired qualities, again, recall the "soft skills" or traits associated with manageable workforces and middle-class customers' tastes. Consistent with the spatial mismatch hypothesis, this suburban employer is the only black respondent who faced labor shortages:

We don't really have an employment problem in the city of Chicago, where we have our problem is in terms of our suburban stores and I think you'll find that some of your unskilled workers in the city are finding it very difficult to reach those jobs in the suburban areas because of lack of transportation. I think it's the . . . with the reduced . . . with the reduction in the employment work force it has helped affirmative action because you . . . most of the people that desire work are your blacks and minorities and as employers go to recruit, quite naturally they're beginning to look upon the blacks which means it's an increase for them, but it's unskilled labor.

Unfortunately, this respondent found it difficult to hire such workers because of perceived race, class, and cultural differences in the work ethic. He said,

I think there's some difference, but I don't think. . . . See I think that if you looked at a certain segment of each race population you're going to find that they're going to have a high work ethic in each segment of that community. There's going to be that that's going to be low. I think blacks, for the most part, it's because of their cultural upbringing. Sometimes there's a lot of resistance in terms of wanting to do things because they haven't been taught. You know, just in terms of how to interview for a job because they've been culturally deprived for so many years, it's just basically a knowledge factor. They are not totally aware in terms of how to go about finding a job or doing a job.

Furthermore, this respondent made gendered distinctions and explicitly related these to culture: "I think that's really the culture. I think that a lot of the black males look at some of the jobs that they feel are beneath their dignity to work and rather than accept any job, they'd rather stay out of employment rolls. Yet, you have your females and that's evident in our city stores . . . that you have more females applying for jobs than the males. I think it's something in terms of the way the black male feels about their particular role in society."

Although the stores, especially in the city, could "hire all the females that they need," what they really needed were "some males because you do recognize there are physical differences between males and females and a lot of times you can't ask a female to lift a 50 pound bag of salt." But "they would feel that they would want to do something better instead of getting in something and working toward it."

Finally, the respondent thought that discrimination "plays a part," but reflecting his position as a suburban employer faced with a shortage of low-wage workers, he was

Not so sure right now with the status of people needing people so badly. . . . The interesting thing is that my counterpart in the north areas is very willing to hire anyone because again, it's a very affluent area that he's got stores in and they cannot find anyone to work. I think it's less . . . I think race plays a less role today compared to five years ago and that's only because of the shrinking labor market. If you look at most of your fast food franchises and businesses in the suburban areas, you'll see that I would say that 90 percent of those people are made up of minorities.

Eighty percent of his workforce, however, is white.

The office manager who hired clerical staff for a software company looked for someone very reliable and dependable, with excellent communication skills, an "outgoing personality." Inferring that these soft skills were not widely available in the black community, she believed that high unemployment among blacks was because "they don't have the right skills." For instance, "displaced factory workers have skills that are no longer applicable."

Although black employers share their white counterparts' tendency to categorize, for the most part they hire disproportionately large numbers of black workers, indicating they do not make decisions on the basis of race — the primary distinction drawn by white employers. Rather, like many white employers, black employers used class, space, and gender to sort through their labor pool. Moreover, although many characterized the black labor supply as problematic, they were much more willing to see deficiencies as the result of historical and current discrimination. Nonetheless, some employers did call on individualistic explanations for problems witnessed among the inner-city workforce. Perhaps most striking is the black employers' gendered distinction of the black workforce and the way this operates to the disadvantage of black men.

CONCLUSIONS

Earlier I found that white employers in Chicago readily generalized about racial and ethnic differences in the labor supply and did not hesitate to use race as a marker of productivity. These generalizations included negative portrayals of Chicago workers, especially African-American workers. Social distinctions based on class, space, and gender were used as additional signals of desirability. These distinctions interacted with negative racial attitudes in ways that ultimately served to limit job opportunities for poor black men who live in the inner city.

The negative characteristics employers associated with black men — unstable, uncooperative, dishonest, and uneducated — stand in direct contrast to the types of qualities employers say they are looking for in their workers — dependability, strong work ethic, cooperativeness, communications skills, and personality. The transformation of the economy has not been neutral, but rather has increased employers' demand for these "soft skills," which, arguably, are race, class, and gender biased. Additionally, the economy has widened already existing inequalities between blacks and whites, but also within the black population — making it more likely that the qualities proxied by race (behavioral and attitudinal attributes) are likely to be observed among the most disadvantaged. In short, poor black men's structural exclusion from the economy makes them an easy target for demonization; one employer offered justification for his negative portrayal of black men, saying, "Go look in the jails."

Black employers seek profits as owners and seek job security as managers in this same economy. Most black employers hired disproportionately high numbers of black workers, indicating they did not discriminate against black workers generally. Rather, black employers called attention to the heterogeneity within the black population. Like their white counterparts, these employers also used class, space, and gender to distinguish among black workers. Although most black employers did not attribute perceived skill deficiences to personal responsibility, some did use recruiting and hiring practices that would disadvantage poor inner-city black men. Specifically, black employers recognized that productivity is not an individual trait, but rather is embedded in class-based social relations. Class differences have become very important to black employers precisely because race is so important to the wider society to which they strive — that is, black employers practice classism in an effort to accommodate to racism. This situation is probably especially true when race is used to mark skills that are really attitudes: The "bad attitudes" of black men are the result of antagonistic relations between employers and workers, among coworkers, and between clients and workers. The increased reliance on discrimination and characterizations of the dominant group's demonization of black men indicate that black employers fully recognize the self-fullfilling effect of discrimination.

NOTES

This research is based on data collected under the auspices of the Urban Poverty and Family Structure project directed by William Julius Wilson of Harvard University. This project received funding from the Ford Foundation, The Rockefeller Foundation, the Joyce Foundation, the Carnegie Corporation, the Lloyd A. Fry Foundation, the William T. Grant Foundation, the Spencer Foundation, the Woods Charitable Foundation, the Chicago Community Trust, the Institute for Research on Poverty, and the U.S. Department of Health and Human Services. Their support is gratefully acknowledged. Thank you to Sherry Russ Lee for providing valuable insights and able research assistance on this chapter.

Thanks to Daniel Breslau, Judy Mintz, Kathryn Neckerman, Lori Sparzo, and Loic Wacquant, who helped conduct the interviews.

1.   The current work of Lawrence Bobo and his colleagues is exemplary in this regard.

2.   One employer refused to give a demographic profile of his firm, but observations recorded by the interviewer are suggestive: "All workers I saw were white except (the respondent). You had to be buzzed into the office lobby by a secretary who could look through her window and see who was there. I was buzzed through without any questions, as was a white man in a business suit. A young black man and woman came to the door, and instead of buzzing the secretary opened the window and asked what their business was. They were directed to the hiring office which had another outside door. The white man said to me, 'They really keep 'em out, don't they?'"

11

Fifty Years after Myrdal: Blacks' Racial Policy Attitudes in the 1990s

Steven A. Tuch, Lee Sigelman, and Jack K. Martin

Half a century has passed since the publication of Gunnar Myrdal's monumental two-volume work, *An American Dilemma: The Negro Problem and Modern Democracy* (1944). Myrdal painted an agonizing portrait of the pervasiveness of racially prejudiced attitudes and discriminatory practices in U.S. life; perhaps, though, his most important contribution lay not in the descriptive detail he amassed concerning these conditions (Bobo, 1993) but in the compelling new interpretive context he provided for understanding racial prejudice and discrimination. Central to this context was the paradox posed by the coexistence of race-based social, economic, and political inequality, on the one hand, and the cherished U.S. cultural values of freedom and equality, on the other hand. By highlighting this deeply rooted contradiction, Myrdal did much to inform and advance the efforts of civil rights activists, jurists, policy-makers, and others concerned with ameliorating racial disadvantage.

The decades since the publication of *An American Dilemma* have witnessed a dramatic decline in white Americans' overt expressions of antiblack and anti-integrationist sentiments (Greeley & Sheatsley, 1971; Hyman & Sheatsley, 1956, 1964; Jaynes & Williams, 1989; Schuman, Steeh, & Bobo, 1985; Sheatsley, 1966; Taylor, Sheatsley, & Greeley, 1978). In recent years, though, this liberalizing trend appears to have moderated. According to some analysts, white racism persists today but finds expression, not in traditional beliefs about racial inferiority but rather in a new, more subtle language of racial antipathy that emphasizes blacks' ostensibly illegitimate demands for changing the status quo (Sears, 1988) or their failure to endorse "mainstream" social values (See & Wilson, 1988; see also Chapter 3 in this volume). Most whites now voice strong support for general principles of racial equality but look askance at specific programs designed to reduce race-based disadvantage, such as admissions and hiring quotas. This is the so-called principle-implementation gap, the causes and consequences of which have been subjects of heated debate (for example, Kinder, 1986; Sniderman & Tetlock, 1986; Tuch & Hughes, 1996a, 1996b).

Though still incomplete, our understanding of the factors that shape whites' views on racial policy issues far outstrips our understanding of the factors that shape blacks' views on these issues. Indeed, data on blacks' policy views have traditionally been missing in action from the policy debate. In the words of A. Wade Smith (1987, p. 441), "The attitudes white Americans hold toward their black counterparts probably comprise the longest running topic in public opinion research. Yet until recently black Americans — long the minority group most identified with 'racial matters' in the United States — were virtually invisible to serious students of American values" (see also Sigelman & Welch, 1991; Walton, 1985). Because most researchers have employed data from national surveys with severely restricted black subsamples, it has proven difficult to examine attitudinal differentiation among blacks. Thus, as Smith (1987, p. 441) recognized, the false impression has arisen that black Americans all think alike about these issues — an impression that impedes our understanding of blacks' views on racial issues in general and on policy issues in particular.

RACE-TARGETED POLICIES AND
THE BLACK MIDDLE CLASS

In this chapter, we explore the attitudes of black Americans — and middle-class black Americans in particular — toward policies designed to ameliorate racial disadvantage. We address two key issues. First, how supportive are blacks of race-targeted policies? Race-targeted policies are initiatives, typically but not necessarily by the federal government, explicitly intended to combat racial discrimination and reduce racial inequality. Those who study attitudes toward race-targeted policies often distinguish between compensatory programs, such as job training and special education, which are designed to help members of disadvantaged groups compete more effectively in the workplace, and preferential treatment, such as admissions and hiring quotas (for example, Lipset & Schneider, 1978). Prior research has established that most whites and most blacks support the former (Bobo & Kluegel, 1993; Sigelman & Welch, 1991). On the other hand, most whites reject programs they view as according preferential treatment on the basis of group membership because, in their view, such programs violate fundamental principles of fairness. Many blacks seem to agree with them, but the evidence is far less reliable.

In exploring blacks' attitudes toward race-targeted policies that span the broad spectrum between the extremes of compensatory action and preferential treatment, we pay special attention to middle-class blacks. In recent years, much has been said about what many see as the increasing social and economic polarization of the black community occasioned by the concurrent swelling of the black middle class and entrapment in poverty of the great mass of ghetto blacks (see especially Wilson, 1987). Is this socioeconomic differentiation fostering political cleavages among blacks? According to one school of thought, a conservative black middle class whose objective class interests are closely tied to those of middle-class whites is emerging. These common class interests, it is argued, predispose middle-class blacks to adopt perspectives and behaviors generally associated with whites similarly situated in the class structure rather than with lower-class and working-class blacks. Others argue, however, that blacks — as members of a historically subordinated group — are likely to maintain their sense of group identification in spite of increasing economic fragmentation. According to this view, black political interests and perspectives continue to cross class lines. It follows that in contrast to middle-class whites, who exhibit strong class ties, middle-class blacks are likely to identify common interests with their racial rather than their class peers.

Several attempts have been made to gauge how much blacks' views on policy issues reflect their class standing (Dawson, 1994; Gilliam & Whitby, 1989; Jackman & Jackman, 1983; Seltzer & Smith, 1985; Smith & Seltzer, 1992; Tate, 1993; Walton, 1985; Welch & Combs, 1985; Welch & Foster, 1987). Unfortunately, only rarely have these studies focused on attitudes toward race-targeted policies, and no study has focused on attitudes toward a broad array of such policies. In what follows, we merge data from two series of omnibus national opinion surveys — the 1987, 1988, 1989, 1990, 1991, and 1993 General Social Surveys (GSS) and the 1988, 1990, and 1992 American National Election Studies (ANES) — to enable analysis of blacks' appraisals of a substantially wider variety of questions about race-targeted policies than have been considered in any previous study. (The GSS was not conducted in 1992 and the ANES is conducted in even-numbered years.)

RACIAL DIFFERENCES IN SUPPORT OF RACE-TARGETED POLICIES

Table 11.1 shows how black interviewees and white interviewees in the 1987–93 GSS and the 1988–92 ANES responded to eight questions about race-targeted policies. On the first of these questions, which appeared in the GSS, interviewees were asked whether too much, about the right amount, or too little money is being spent on assistance to blacks. Their responses indicate that a wide gulf separates blacks from whites on this issue: Eight out of 10 blacks but only 1 white in 4 said that too little is being spent on assistance to blacks, whereas 1 white in 4 but only 1 black in 40 said that too much is being spent for this purpose. Black-white differences of comparable magnitude cropped up on the second question, which is the ANES version of the same item. Here, about 7 blacks in 10 but fewer than 2 whites in 10 expressed support for increased federal spending on programs that assist blacks.

TABLE 11.1
Blacks' and Whites' Opinions on Racial Policy Issues
(in percent)

	Blacks	Whites
1. We are faced with many problems in this country, none of which can be solved easily or inexpensively. I'm going to name some of these problems, and for each one I'd like you to tell me whether you think we're spending too much money on it, too little money, or about the right amount. Are we spending too much, too little, or about the right amount on assistance to blacks?		
Too little	80.8	25.6
About right	16.8	50.4
Too much	2.3	23.9
N	475	3,754
2. Should federal spending programs that assist blacks be increased, decreased, or kept about the same?		
Increased	69.5	18.4
Kept the same	28.8	56.5
Decreased	1.7	25.2
N	691	4,321
3. Some people think that blacks have been discriminated against for so long that the government has a special obligation to improve their living standard. Others believe that the government should not be giving special treatment to blacks. Where would you place yourself on this scale?		
Government should help	36.6	5.5
	17.6	9.4
	31.9	29.9
	6.3	20.1
No special treatment	7.6	35.1
N	432	3,470

	Blacks	Whites

4. Some people feel that the government should make every effort to improve the social and economic positions of blacks. Others feel that the government should not make any special effort to help blacks because they should help themselves. Where would you place yourself on this scale, or haven't you thought much about this?

Government should help	28.9	4.0
	11.0	5.1
	9.3	11.4
	23.7	26.0
	0.8	16.5
	7.6	15.9
Blacks help themselves	9.8	21.2
N	655	4,088

5. Irish, Italian, Jewish, and many other minorities overcame prejudice and worked their way up. Blacks should do the same without any special favors.

Agree strongly	19.5	39.3
Agree somewhat	26.9	35.1
Neither	12.1	9.6
Disagree somewhat	17.9	12.6
Disagree strongly	23.6	3.4
N	513	3,492

6. Some people feel that if black people are not getting fair treatment in jobs, the government in Washington ought to see to it that they do. Others feel that it is not the federal government's business. Have you had enough interest in this question to favor one side over the other?

Should intervene	91.1	50.9
Should not intervene	8.9	49.1
N	316	1,780

7. Some people say that, because of past discrimination, blacks should be given preference in hiring and promotion. Others say that such preference in hiring and promotion of blacks is wrong because it gives blacks advantages they haven't earned. What about your opinion — are you for or against preferential hiring for blacks?

Strongly favor	53.4	6.2
Favor	10.1	7.9
Oppose	14.9	18.3
Strongly oppose	21.6	67.6
N	476	3,379

	Blacks	Whites

8. Some people say that, because of past discrimination, it is sometimes necessary for colleges and universities to reserve openings for black students. Others oppose quotas because they say quotas give blacks advantages they
haven't earned. What is your opinion — are you for or against quotas to
admit black students?

	Blacks	Whites
Strongly favor	64.4	11.7
Favor	12.3	15.4
Oppose	8.5	22.4
Strongly oppose	14.8	50.6
N	481	3,296

Sources: Items 1 and 3 are from the National Opinion Research Center's 1987–1993 General
Social Surveys (Davis & Smith, 1993). Items 2 and 4–8 are from the Institute for Social
Research's 1988, 1990, and 1992 American National Election Studies (Miller, 1993). Both
sets of surveys are based on full-probability sampling designs and are representative of
the noninstitutionalized adult population of the continental United States.

The third and fourth items, taken from the GSS and the ANES, respectively, asked about the necessity for special assistance for blacks. On the
first version of this question, 54 percent of the black interviewees placed
themselves on the "government should help" side of the scale and only 14
percent on the "no special treatment" side, but these percentages were
almost exactly reversed among white interviewees. On the second version, black-white differences are somewhat less extreme, probably
because this question invoked black self-help as a counterpoise to special
efforts to help blacks; given that symbolically potent stimulus, more than
27 percent of black interviewees took a stand against special government
efforts to help blacks.

The self-help motif also figured prominently in the fifth item, which
solicited agreement or disagreement with the proposition that blacks, like
earlier minority groups, should work their way up "without any special
favors." More blacks agreed (46 percent) than disagreed (42 percent) with
this notion, although agreement was much more widespread among
whites (74 percent) and disagreement correspondingly lower (16 percent).

In contrast to the first five items, each of which asked in some way
about a race-targeted policy without specifically describing the policy, the
sixth, seventh, and eighth items were more specific. Of all eight items considered here, the sixth, which asked whether the federal government
should intervene to ensure that blacks receive fair treatment in employment, seems closest to traditional U.S. conceptions of equal opportunity
and most distant from notions of preferential treatment. It thus occasions

no great surprise to observe that white interviewees were more likely to express support for race-targeted policy in response to this question than to any of the seven others. Even so, only 51 percent of whites said that federal intervention was warranted, with 49 percent disagreeing. Their disagreement might, to some extent, have stemmed from specific objections to federal, as opposed to state or local, intervention (Kuklinski & Parent, 1981; Margolis & Haque, 1981); whatever its sources, it contrasts sharply with the clear-cut consensus among blacks, 91 percent of whom considered federal intervention warranted to ensure that blacks are accorded fair treatment in employment.

The seventh and eighth items focused on two of the most controversial applications of race-targeting in public policy — racial preferences in hiring and promotion decisions and the use of racial quotas in college admissions. Both blacks and whites were somewhat more positively disposed toward admissions quotas than they were toward preferential hiring and promotion. In both cases, however, blacks were far more supportive than whites were, with 63 percent of blacks but only 14 percent of whites endorsing preferential hiring and promotion, and 77 percent of blacks but only 27 percent of whites approving of the use of quotas in college admissions.

Across the eight items considered here, two broad patterns stand out. The first and most obvious is simply that blacks were much more likely than whites to support race-targeted policies. This is by no means a novel finding, but as far as we know, it has not previously been documented for such a wide variety of race-targeted policies. Second, blacks were by no means homogeneous in their support of race-targeted policies. To be sure, as many as nine blacks in ten expressed support for some of these policies, but on other questions, the split between positive and negative responses was much more evenly balanced. Especially on policies about which there was fairly widespread disagreement among blacks, the question now becomes whether such disagreement was structured along class lines. That is, can we observe a clear class imprint on blacks' evaluations of race-targeted policies, with middle-class blacks being less likely than other blacks to support such policies?

CLASS DIFFERENCES IN BLACKS' SUPPORT
OF RACE-TARGETED POLICIES

In Table 11.2 we reconsider the same eight survey items examined in Table 11.1, this time by distinguishing middle class from other blacks and whites.[1] On the first two items in the table, both of which pertained to support for government spending on programs for blacks, we see only faint hints of any class fissure among blacks in support for race-targeted policies — differences of only three or four percentage points between middle-class and other blacks, well within the bounds of sampling error. Nor do the responses of middle-class blacks stand out on the third and fourth questions, which asked about the appropriateness of special help for blacks. On the third item, the balance of positive and negative responses was almost identical for middle-class and other blacks, with a slightly higher percentage of the former than the latter expressing a

TABLE 11.2
Social Class Differences in Blacks' and Whites' Opinions on Racial Policy Issues

(in percent)

	Blacks		Whites	
	Middle Class	Others	Middle Class	Others
1. We are faced with many problems in this country, none of which can be solved easily or inexpensively. I'm going to name some of these problems, and for each one I'd like you to tell me whether you think we're spending too much money on it, too little money, or about the right amount. Are we spending too much, too little, or about the right amount on assistance to blacks?				
Too little	78.9	81.4	27.2	24.6
About right	17.5	16.6	54.4	47.9
Too much	3.5	1.9	18.4	27.4
N	114	361	1,447	2,307
2. Should federal spending programs that assist blacks be increased, decreased, or kept about the same?				
Increased	67.2	69.9	18.8	18.1
Kept the same	29.5	28.6	57.2	56.0
Decreased	3.3	1.4	24.0	25.9
N	122	569	1,661	2,660
3. Some people think that blacks have been discriminated against for so long that the government has a special obligation to improve their living standard. Others believe that the government should not be giving special treatment to blacks. Where would you place yourself on this scale?				
Government should help	34.9	37.3	5.6	5.5
	15.8	18.1	10.5	8.7
	37.3	30.4	30.7	29.4
	5.7	6.2	24.5	17.4
No special treatment	6.3	8.0	28.8	39.0
N	99	333	1,321	2,149

	Blacks		Whites	
	Middle Class	**Others**	**Middle Class**	**Others**

4. Some people feel that the government should make every effort to improve the social and economic positions of blacks. Others feel that the government should not make any special effort to help blacks because they should help themselves. Where would you place yourself on this scale, or haven't you thought much about this?

	Blacks		Whites	
	Middle Class	Others	Middle Class	Others
Government should help	22.1	30.4	3.2	4.6
	13.1	10.5	5.3	5.0
	13.9	8.3	14.1	9.5
	28.7	22.5	27.1	25.2
	10.7	9.6	17.7	15.6
	6.6	7.9	16.5	15.5
Blacks help themselves	4.9	10.9	16.0	24.6
N	122	533	1,629	2,459

5. Irish, Italian, Jewish, and many other minorities overcame prejudice and worked their way up. Blacks should do the same without any special favors.

	Blacks		Whites	
	Middle Class	Others	Middle Class	Others
Agree strongly	12.8	21.0	32.3	43.8
Agree somewhat	23.4	27.7	35.7	34.7
Neither	6.4	13.4	9.5	9.7
Disagree somewhat	17.0	18.1	17.0	9.7
Disagree strongly	40.4	19.8	5.5	2.0
N	94	419	1,389	2,103

6. Some people feel that if black people are not getting fair treatment in jobs, the government in Washington ought to see to it that they do. Others feel that it is not the federal government's business. Have you had enough interest in this question to favor one side over the other?

	Blacks		Whites	
	Middle Class	Others	Middle Class	Others
Should intervene	91.0	91.2	53.8	48.8
Should not intervene	9.0	8.8	46.2	51.6
N	67	249	821	959

7. Some people say that, because of past discrimination, blacks should be given preference in hiring and promotion. Others say that such preference in hiring and promotion of blacks is wrong because it gives blacks advantages they haven't earned. What about your opinion — are you for or against preferential hiring for blacks?

	Blacks		Whites	
	Middle Class	Others	Middle Class	Others
Strongly favor	42.0	55.9	5.3	6.9
Favor	9.1	10.3	8.5	7.4
Oppose	23.9	12.9	19.2	17.8
Strongly oppose	25.0	20.9	67.1	67.9
N	88	388	1,352	2,027

	Blacks		Whites	
	Middle Class	Others	Middle Class	Others

8. Some people say that because of past discrimination it is sometimes necessary for colleges and universities to reserve openings for black students. Others oppose quotas because they say quotas give blacks advantages they haven't earned. What is your opinion — are you for or against quotas to admit black students?

	Blacks		Whites	
	Middle Class	Others	Middle Class	Others
Strongly favor	60.9	65.2	11.0	12.1
Favor	13.8	11.9	16.0	14.9
Oppose	11.5	7.9	22.9	22.0
Strongly oppose	13.8	15.0	50.0	51.0
N	87	394	1,331	1,985

Sources: Items 1 and 3 are from the National Opinion Research Center's 1987–1993 General Social Surveys (Davis & Smith, 1993). Items 2 and 4–8 are from the Institute for Social Research's 1988, 1990, and 1992 American National Election Studies (Miller, 1993). Both sets of surveys are based on full-probability sampling designs and are representative of the noninstitutionalized adult population of the continental United States.

noncommittal view. On the fourth item, the percentage of middle-class and other blacks who were positively oriented toward race-targeted programs (categories 1 through 3) was again virtually identical, but middle-class blacks were slightly less attracted than other blacks (by 22 percent to 28 percent) to the black self-help end of the continuum (categories 5 through 7).

Responses to the fourth item hinted at a warmer embrace of black self-help among working-class and lower-class blacks than can be found in the black middle class. This came through much more clearly in responses to the fifth item, on which 57 percent of middle-class blacks but only 38 percent of other blacks registered their disagreement with the suggestion that blacks, like many other minorities before them, should work their way up without any special favors. This is the first clear class-based differential we have observed in blacks' responses, and, intriguingly, middle-class blacks are less likely to endorse this notion than their lower-class and working-class counterparts.

On the sixth item, which called for agreement or disagreement that the federal government should intervene in cases of unfair job treatment of blacks, identical percentages of middle-class and other blacks endorsed government action. On the seventh item, however, a class-based differential emerged in support of racial preferences in hiring and promotion; this time it was lower-class and working-class blacks who took a more positive view of a race-targeted policy, with 51 percent of the black middle class, but 66 percent of other blacks endorsing such a policy. With the data at hand, it is difficult to know how to account for this difference. It could be that most middle-class black respondents rose through their own individual efforts and were thus ill disposed toward letting other blacks take what they perceived to be the easy way out; however, the responses of members of the black middle class to questions about other race-targeted policies — and especially to the fifth question — do not seem very consistent with such a mind-set. Although this matter warrants much closer scrutiny, it is worth speculating that middle-class blacks have had greater firsthand experience than lower-class or working-class blacks with preferential hiring and promotion programs and are thus more keenly attuned to some of the negative effects such programs can have on their intended beneficiaries (see, for example, Coate & Loury, 1993; Summers, 1991).

Finally, the gap between middle-class and other blacks in support of preferential hiring and promotion was not matched by any class-based differential in support of racial quotas in college admissions, with 75 percent of middle-class blacks and 77 percent of other blacks expressing support for such quotas.

On six of the eight items considered here, then, we observed little or no difference in the views of middle-class and other blacks toward race-targeted policies. On one of the two remaining items, middle-class blacks were more supportive of a race-targeted policy; on the other item, they were less so. Overall, these comparisons are hardly indicative of any consistent or appreciable class-based differential in blacks' attitudes.

CONCLUSION

In each policy area examined here, blacks were more favorable than whites, often substantially so, toward federal government intervention to ameliorate racial inequality. From a self-interest point of view, this is hardly surprising. More unexpected, perhaps, is our failure, in analyses of class differences among blacks on these policies, to uncover any consistent evidence of a deep political divide between middle-class and other blacks. Indeed, we observed hardly any evidence of political divide, deep or shallow, between middle-class blacks and lower-class or working-class blacks. Despite earlier indications that middle-class blacks have adopted attitudes and behaviors similar in some respects to those of middle-class whites (see, for example, Smith & Seltzer, 1992), no such class-based attitudinal configuration joining middle-class blacks and whites has surfaced here. Race, not class, is the primary determinant of the views of both whites and blacks on race-targeted policies. Class appears to play little, if any, role.

This is not to say that blacks are united in their support of race-targeted policies because, as we have seen, that is simply not the case. Black disunity on these issues does not, for the most part, pit the emerging black middle class against the persisting black lower and working classes.

Why is this so? That is, why is there so little differentiation between the policy views of middle-class and other blacks? One contributing factor is undoubtedly that the overrepresentation of middle-class blacks in public sector occupations and the dependence of many lower-class blacks on government assistance creates a natural coalition based on common economic interests that cross class lines (Welch & Combs, 1985) — a coalition that naturally tends to favor governmentally based approaches to dealing with the problems that continue to beset blacks. More generally, though, blacks tend to retain a strong sense of solidarity with other blacks, even after they have achieved middle-class status and moved to the suburbs (Bledsoe, Welch, Sigelman, & Combs, 1994). Many members of the black middle class were not born into the black middle class, and their basic political orientations may be more reflective of the circumstances in which they were raised than of the circumstances in which they live. It is also true that middle-class blacks continue to feel disadvantaged relative to middle-class whites, particularly in the workplace. There is ample evidence that many successful black managers and professionals perceive themselves as targets of continuing discrimination at work and elsewhere (see, for example, Feagin, 1991), and such perceptions cannot help but reinforce racial identification rather than foster class identification with whites. Moreover, like Jews and members of other historically subordinated groups, blacks are likely to maintain their strong sense of group identification in spite of increasing economic fragmentation. It follows that in contrast to middle-class whites, who exhibit strong class ties, middle-class blacks tend to identify common interests with their racial, rather than their class, peers.

NOTE

1. Most work in this area has used education or income as proxy measures of class. Such measures require the selection of arbitrary education and income cutting points to differentiate classes. We measure class in terms of a less arbitrary occupation-based classification, defining members of the middle class as incumbents of the "managerial and professional specialty occupations" category of the 1980 Census occupational classification, plus nonclerical incumbents of the "technical, sales, and administrative support occupations" category (codes 003 through 259).

References

Abelson, R. P., D. R. Kinder, M. D. Peters, and S. T. Fiske. 1982. "Affective and Semantic Components in Political Person Perception." *Journal of Personality and Social Psychology 42*, 619–630.

Abramson, H. 1973. *Ethnic Diversity in Catholic America*. New York: Wiley.

Alba, R. D. 1990. *Ethnic Identity: The Transformation of White America*. New Haven, CT: Yale University Press.

Alba, R. D., and M. B. Chamlin. 1983. "A Preliminary Examination of Ethnic Identification among Whites." *American Sociological Review 48*, 240–247.

Allport, G. W. 1954. *The Nature of Prejudice*. Reading, MA: Addison-Wesley.

America: Trends and Interpretations. Cambridge, MA: Harvard University Press.

Anderson, E. 1990. *Streetwise: Race, Class and Change in an Urban Community*. Chicago: University of Chicago Press.

Apostle, R. A., C. Y. Glock, T. Piazza, and M. Suelzle. 1983. *The Anatomy of Racial Attitudes*. Berkeley: University of California Press.

Ardrey, S. C., and W. E. Nelson. 1990. "The Maturation of Black Political Power: The Case of Cleveland." *PS 23*, 148–151.

Arian, A., A. S. Goldberg, J. H. Mollenkopf, and E. T. Rogowsky. 1991. *Changing New York City Politics*. New York: Routledge.

Ashmore, R. D., and F. K. Del Boca. 1981. "Conceptual Approaches to Stereotypes and Stereotyping." In D. L. Hamilton (Ed.), *Processes in Stereotyping and Human Behavior* (pp. 1–35). Hillsdale, NJ: Erlbaum.

Barker, L. J. 1987. "Ronald Reagan, Jesse Jackson, and the 1984 Presidential Election: The Continuing American Dilemma of Race." In M. B. Preston, L. J. Henderson, Jr., and P. L. Puryear (Eds.), *The New Black Politics: The Search for Political Power* (2d ed.) (pp. 29–44). New York: Longman.

Becker, G. S. 1957. *The Economics of Discrimination.* Chicago: University of Chicago Press.

Becker, J. F., and E. E. Heaton, Jr. 1967. "The Election of Senator Edward W. Brooke." *Public Opinion Quarterly 31*, 346–358.

Bell, E. L., T. C. Denton, and S. Nkomo. 1993. "Women of Color in Management: Toward an Inclusive Analysis." In E. Fagenson (Ed.), *Women in Management: Trends, Issues and Challenges in Managerial Diversity* (pp. 105–130). Newbury Park, CA: Sage Publications.

Bernard, J. 1951. "The Conceptualization of Intergroup Relations with Special Reference to Conflict." *Social Forces 19*, 243–251.

Blalock, H. M., Jr. 1967. *Toward a Theory of Minority-Group Relations.* New York: Wiley.

Blalock, H. M., Jr. 1957. "Percent Non-White and Discrimination in the South." *American Sociological Review 22*, 667–682.

Blauner, R. A. 1989. *Black Lives, White Lives: Three Decades of Race Relations in America.* Berkeley: University of California Press.

Blauner, R. A. 1972. Racial Oppression in America. New York: Harper & Row.

Bledsoe, T., S. Welch, L. Sigelman, and M. Combs. 1994. *Suburbanization, Residential Integration, and Racial Solidarity among African Americans.* Paper presented at the annual meeting of the Midwest Political Science Association, Chicago.

Bloom, J. M. 1987. *Class, Race, and the Civil Rights Movement.* Bloomington: Indiana University Press.

Blumer, H. 1958. "Race Prejudice as a Sense of Group Position." *Pacific Sociological Review 1*, 3–7.

Bobo, L. 1993. *From Jim Crow Racism to Laissez Faire Racism: The Transformation of Racial Attitudes in the United States.* Paper presented at the Conference on Racial Attitudes, University of Georgia, Athens.

Bobo, L. 1988a. "Attitudes toward the Black Political Movement: Trends, Meaning and Effects on Racial Policy Preferences." *Social Psychology Quarterly 51*, 287–302.

Bobo, L., 1988b. "Group Conflict, Prejudice, and the Paradox of Contemporary Racial Attitudes." In P. A. Katz and D. A. Taylor (Eds.), *Eliminating Racism: Profiles in Controversy* (pp. 85–114). New York: Plenum.

Bobo, L. 1983. "Whites' Opposition to Busing: Symbolic Racism or Realistic Group Conflict?" *Journal of Personality and Social Psychology 45*, 1196–1210.

Bobo, L., and V. L. Hutchings. 1996. "Perceptions of Racial Group Competition: Extending Blumer's Theory of Group Position to a Multiracial Social Context." *American Sociological Review 61*, 951–972.

Bobo, L., and J. Kluegel. 1993. "Opposition to Race-Targeting: Self-Interest, Stratification Ideology, or Racial Attitudes?" *American Sociological Review 58*, 443–464.

Bobo, L., and J. R. Kluegel. 1991, August. *Whites' Stereotypes, Social Distance, and Perceived Discrimination Toward Blacks, Hispanics and Asians: Toward a Multiethnic Framework.* Paper presented at the 86th Annual Meeting of the American Sociological Association, Cincinnati.

Bobo, L., and R. A. Smith. 1994. "Anti-Poverty Policy, Affirmative Action, and Racial Attitudes." In S. Danziger, G. Sandefur, and D. Weinberg (Eds.),

Confronting Poverty: Prescriptions for Change (pp. 365–395). Cambridge, MA: Harvard University Press and the Russell Sage Foundation.

Bobo, L., and S. A. Suh. 1996. *Racial Attitudes and Power in the Workplace: Do the Haves Differ From the Have Nots?* Paper presented at the Conference of the Multi-city Study of Urban Inequality, Russell Sage Foundation, New York.

Bobo, L., and S. A. Suh. 1995. "Surveying Racial Discrimination: Analyses from a Multiethnic Labor Market." Working paper #75, Russell Sage Foundation, New York.

Bobo, L., and C. L. Zubrinsky. 1996. "Attitudes on Residential Integration: Perceived Status Differences, Mere In-group Preference, or Racial Prejudice?" *Social Forces 74*, 999–1025.

Bobo, L., C. L. Zubrinsky, J. H. Johnson, Jr., and M. L. Oliver. 1994. "Public Opinion Before and After a Spring of Discontent." In M. Baldassare (Ed.), *The Los Angeles Riots: Lessons for the Urban Future* (pp. 103–133). Boulder, CO: Westview Press.

Bogardus, E. S. 1959. *Social Distance.* Yellow Springs, OH: Antioch Press.

Bonacich, E. 1972. "A Theory of Ethnic Antagonism: The Split Labor Market." *American Sociological Review 37*, 447–559.

Bonacich, E., and J. Modell. 1980. *The Economic Basis of Ethnic Solidarity: Small Business in the Japanese American Community.* Berkeley: University of California Press.

Bound, J., and R. B. Freeman. 1992. "What Went Wrong? The Erosion of Relative Earnings and Employment Among Young Black Men in the 1980s." *Quarterly Journal of Economics 107*, 201–232.

Braddock, J. H., and J. M. McPartland. 1987. "How Minorities Continue to be Excluded from Equal Employment Opportunities: Research on Labor Markets and Institutional Barriers." *Journal of Social Issues 43*, 5–39.

Braverman, H. 1974. *Labor and Monopoly Capital: The Degradation of Work in the Twentieth Century.* New York: Monthly Review Press.

Brink, W., and L. Harris. 1966. *Black and White: A Study of U.S. Racial Attitudes Today.* New York: Simon and Schuster.

Brown, D. L., and G. V. Fuguitt. 1972. "Percent Non-White and Racial Disparity in Non-Metropolitan Cities in the South." *Social Science Quarterly 53*, 574–582.

Browne, I., C. Hewitt, L. Tigges, and G. Green. 1996. "Segregated Jobs, Segregated Communities and Wages among African Americans." Unpublished manuscript.

Browning, R. P., D. R. Marshall, and D. H. Tabb. 1984. *Protest Is Not Enough: The Struggle of Blacks and Hispanics for Equality in Urban Politics.* Berkeley: University of California Press.

Byrne, B. 1989. A Primer of LISREL. New York: Springer-Verlag.

Cancio, A. S., T. D. Evans, and D. J. Maume, Jr. 1996. "Reconsidering the Declining Significance of Race: Racial Differences in Early Career Wages." *American Sociological Review 61*(4), 541–556.

Carter, S. L. 1991. *Reflections of an Affirmative Action Baby.* New York: Basic Books.

Chafets, Ze'ev. 1990. *Devil's Night and Other True Tales of Detroit.* New York: Random House.

Chandler, R. 1972. *Public Opinion: Changing Attitudes on Contemporary Political and Social Issues.* New York: R. R. Bowker.

Chesler, M. A. 1976. "Contemporary Sociological Theories of Racism." In P. A. Katz (Ed.), *Towards the Elimination of Racism*. New York: Pergamon.

Citrin, J., D. P. Green, and D. O. Sears. 1990. "White Reactions to Black Candidates: When Does Race Matter?" *Public Opinion Quarterly 54*, 74–96.

Coate, S., and G. C. Loury. 1993. "Will Affirmative Action Policies Eliminate Negative Stereotypes?" *American Economic Review 83*, 1220–1240.

Colasanto, D., and L. Williams. 1987. "The Changing Dynamics of Race and Class." *Public Opinion 9*, 50–54.

Collins, S. M. In press. *Dancing on a Bubble: The Rise and Fall of a Black Middle Class*. Philadelphia: Temple University Press.

Colton, E. O. 1989. *The Jackson Phenomenon: The Man, the Power, the Message*. New York: Doubleday.

Crotty, W. 1989. "Jesse Jackson's Campaign: Constituency Attitudes and Political Outcomes." In L. J. Barker and R. W. Walters (Eds.), *Jesse Jackson's 1984 Presidential Campaign: Challenge and Change in American Politics* (pp. 57–95). Urbana: University of Illinois Press.

Cummings, S., and C. W. Pinnel III. 1978. "Racial Double Standards of Morality in a Small Southern Community: Another Look at Myrdal's American Dilemma." *Journal of Black Studies 9*, 67–86.

Danziger, S., and P. Gottschalk. 1995. *America Unequal*. Cambridge, MA: Harvard University Press.

Darden, J. 1984. "Black Political Underrepresentation in Majority Black Places." *Journal of Black Studies 15*, 101–116.

Davis, D. W. 1996. "White Americans' Opposition to Racial Policies: Where are the Political Explanations?" *Social Science Quarterly 77*, 746–750.

Davis, J., and T. W. Smith. 1993. *General Social Surveys, 1972–1993*. Chicago: National Opinion Research Center.

Davis, J. A., and T. W. Smith. 1991. *General Social Surveys, 1972–1990*. Chicago: National Opinion Research Center .

Davis, J. A., and T. W. Smith. 1990. *General Social Surveys, 1972–1990*. Chicago: National Opinion Research Center.

Davis, J. A., and T. W. Smith. 1987. *General Social Surveys, 1972–1987: Cumulative Codebook*. Chicago: National Opinion Research Center.

Dawson, M. C. 1994. *Behind the Mule: Race and Class in African-American Politics*. Princeton, NJ: Princeton University Press.

Denton, N. A. 1994. "Are African Americans Still Hypersegregated in 1990?" In R. Bullard, C. Lee, and J. E. Grigsby (Eds.), *Residential Apartheid: The American Legacy* (pp. 49–81). Los Angeles: UCLA Center for Afro American Studies.

de Tocqueville, A. 1966 [1835]. *Democracy in America*. New York: Harper & Row.

Devine, P. G. 1989. "Stereotypes and Prejudice: Their Automatic and Controlled Components." *Journal of Personality and Social Psychology 56*, 5–18.

Diamond, J. B. 1996. "Parent Involvement in Shared Decision-Making: Barriers to Democratic Participation in Urban Elementary Schools." Presented to the Race and Urban Poverty Workshop, The University of Chicago and Northwestern University, Department of Sociology.

Dijker, A. J. M. 1987. "Emotional Reactions to Ethnic Minorities." *European Journal of Social Psychology 17*, 305–325.

Dovidio, J. F., J. Mann, and S. L. Gaertner. 1989. "Resistance to Affirmative Action: The Implications of Aversive Racism." In F. Blanchard and F. Crosby (Eds.), *Affirmative Action in Perspective* (pp. 83–102). New York: Springer-Verlag.

Drake, S. C., and H. Clayton. 1945. *Black Metropolis.* New York: Harcourt, Brace, Jovanovich.

D'Souza, D. 1995. *The End of Racism.* New York: The Free Press.

Du Bois, W.E.B. 1961 [1903]. *The Souls of Black Folk.* Greenwich, CT: Fawcett.

Duncan, O. D. 1968. "Inheritance of Poverty or Inheritance of Race?" In D. P. Moynihan (Ed.), *On Understanding Poverty* (pp. 85–110). New York: Basic Books.

Edwards, K., and W. von Hippel. 1995. "Hearts and Minds: The Priority of Affective Versus Cognitive Factors in Person Perception." *Personality and Social Psychology Bulletin 21,* 996–1011.

Esses, V. M., G. Haddock, and M. P. Zanna. 1993. "Values, Stereotypes, and Emotions as Determinants of Intergroup Attitudes." In D. M. Mackie and D. L. Hamilton (Eds.), *Affect, Cognition, and Stereotyping: Interactive Processes in Group Perception* (pp. 137–166). San Diego, CA: Academic Press.

Farley, R. 1984. *Blacks and Whites: Narrowing the Gap?* Cambridge, MA: Harvard University Press.

Farley, R., and W. H. Frey. 1994. "Changes in the Segregation of Whites From Blacks During the 1980s: Small Steps Toward a More Integrated Society." *American Sociological Review 59,* 23–25.

Farley, R., C. Steeh, M. Krysan, T. Jackson, and K. Reeves. 1994. "Stereotypes and Segregation: Neighborhoods in the Detroit Area." *American Journal of Sociology 100,* 750–780.

Feagin, J. R. 1991. "The Continuing Significance of Race: Antiblack Discrimination in Public Places." *American Sociological Review 56,* 101–116.

Feagin, J. R., and M. P. Sikes. 1994. *Living with Racism: The Black Middle Class Experience.* Boston: Beacon Press.

Ferguson, R. 1993. "New Evidence on the Growing Value of Skill and Consequences for Racial Disparity and Returns to Schooling." Unpublished manuscript. Harvard University.

Fernandez, J. P. 1986. *Black Managers in White Corporations.* New York: John Wiley.

Firebaugh, G., and K. E. Davis. 1988. "Trends in Antiblack Prejudice, 1972–1984: Region and Cohort Effects." *American Journal of Sociology 94,* 251–272.

Fossett, M. S., and J. Keicolt. 1989. "The Relative Size of Minority Populations and White Racial Attitudes." *Social Science Quarterly 70,* 820–835.

Frazier, E. F. 1949. *The Negro in the United States.* New York: MacMillan.

Fredrickson, G. M. 1971. *The Black Image in the White Mind: The Debate on Afro-American Character and Destiny, 1817–1914.* New York: Harper & Row.

Frijda, N. H. 1986. *The Emotions.* Cambridge: Cambridge University Press.

Frijda, N. H., P. Kuipers, and E. Schure. 1989. "Relations among Emotion, Appraisal, and Emotional Action Readiness." *Journal of Personality and Social Psychology 57,* 212–228.

Gans, H. J. 1979. "Symbolic Ethnicity: The Future of Ethnic Groups and Cultures in America." *Ethnic and Racial Studies 2,* 1–20.

Gates, H. L., Jr. 1996. "The Charmer." *New Yorker* (April 29–May 6), 116–131.

Gilliam, F. D., Jr., and K. J. Whitby. 1989. "Race, Class, and Attitudes toward Social Welfare Spending: An Ethclass Interpretation." *Social Science Quarterly 70*, 88–100.

Glaser, J. M. 1994. "Back to the Black Belt: Racial Environment and White Racial Attitudes in the South." *Journal of Politics 56*, 21–41.

Glazer, N., and D. P. Moynihan. 1970. *Beyond the Melting Pot*, 2d ed. Cambridge, MA: MIT Press.

Glenn, N. D., and J. L. Simmons. 1967. "Are Regional Cultural Differences Diminishing?" *Public Opinion Quarterly 31*, 176–193.

Gordon, M. M. 1981. "Models of Pluralism, The New American Dilemma." *Annals of the American Academy of Political and Social Sciences 454*, 178–188.

Gordon, M. M. 1964. *Assimilation in American Life*. New York: Oxford University Press.

Grant, D., M. Oliver, and A. James. 1996. "African Americans: Social and Economic Bifurcation." In R. Waldinger and M. Bozorgmehr (Eds.), *Ethnic Los Angeles*. New York: Russell Sage Press.

Greeley, A. 1974. *Ethnicity in the United States: A Preliminary Reconnaissance*. New York: Wiley.

Greeley, A. M., and P.B. Sheatsley. 1971. "Attitudes toward Racial Integration." *Scientific American 225*, 596–604.

Gurin, P., S. Hatchett, and J. S. Jackson. 1989. *Hope and Independence: Blacks' Response to Electoral and Party Politics*. New York: Russell Sage Foundation.

Gusfield, J. R. 1963. *Symbolic Crusade: Status Politics and the American Temperance Movement*. Urbana: University of Illinois Press.

Hahn, H., D. Klingman, and H. Pachon. 1976. "Cleavages, Coalitions and the Black Candidate: The Los Angeles Mayoralty Elections of 1969 and 1973." *Western Political Quarterly 29*, 521–530.

Hamilton, C. V. 1977. "De-racialization: Examination of a Political Strategy." *First World* (March–April), 3–5.

Hamilton, D. L. (Ed.). 1981. *Cognitive Processes in Stereotyping and Intergroup Behavior*. Hillsdale, NJ: Erlbaum.

Harris, J. F. 1991. "Wilder Presidential Campaign Would Focus on What He Hasn't Done." *Washington Post* (August 25), B1, B5.

Hauser, R. M. 1993a. "The Decline in College Entry among African Americans: Findings in Search of Explanations." In P. M. Sniderman, P. E. Tetlock, and E. G. Carmines (Eds.), *Prejudice, Politics, and the American Dilemma* (pp. 271–306). Stanford, CA.: Stanford University Press.

Hauser, R. M. 1993b. "Trends in College Entry among Whites, Blacks, and Hispanics." In C. T. Clotfelter and M. Rothschild (Eds.), *Studies of Supply and Demand in Higher Education* (pp. 61–104). Chicago: University of Chicago Press.

Hauser, R. M., and D. K. Anderson. 1991. "Post-High School Plans and Aspirations of Black and White High School Seniors: 1976–86." *Sociology of Education 64*, 263–277.

Hechter, M. 1975. *Internal Colonialism*. Berkeley: University of California Press.

Herring, C. 1989. "Convergence, Polarization, or What?: Racially Based Changes in Attitudes and Outlooks, 1964–1984." *Sociological Quarterly 30*, 267–281.

Herring, C., and S. M. Collins. 1995. "Retreat From Equal Opportunity? The Case of Affirmative Action." In M. P. Smith and J. Feagin (Eds.), *The Bubbling Cauldron* (pp. 163–181). Minneapolis: University of Minnesota Press.

Herrnstein, R. J., and C. Murray. 1994. *The Bell Curve: Intelligence and Class Structure in American Life.* New York: Free Press.

Holzer, H. J. 1996. *What Employers Want: Job Prospects for Less-Educated Workers.* New York: Russell Sage Foundation.

Holzer, H. J. 1991. "The Spatial Mismatch Hypothesis: What Has the Evidence Shown?" *Urban Studies 28*(1), 105–122.

Hudson, W. T., and W. D. Broadnax. 1982. "Equal Employment Opportunity as Public Policy." *Public Personnel Management 11*, 268–276.

Hurwitz, J., and M. Peffley. 1987. "How Are Foreign Policy Attitudes Structured? A Hierarchical Model." *American Political Science Review 81*, 1099–1120.

Hyman, H. H., and P. B. Sheatsley. 1964. "Attitudes toward Desegregation." *Scientific American 211*, 16–23.

Hyman, H. H., and P. B. Sheatsley. 1956. "Attitudes on Integration." *Scientific American 195*, 35–39.

Jackman, M. R. 1996. "Individualism, Self-Interest, and White Racism." *Social Science Quarterly 77*, 760–767.

Jackman, M. R. 1994. *The Velvet Glove.* Berkeley: University of California Press.

Jackman, M. R. 1981. "Education and Policy Commitment to Racial Integration." *American Journal of Political Science 25*, 256–269.

Jackman, M. R. 1978. "General and Applied Tolerance: Does Education Increase Commitment to Racial Integration?" *American Journal of Political Science 22*, 302–324.

Jackman, M., and R. Jackman. 1983. *Class Awareness in the United States.* Berkeley: University of California Press.

Jackman, M. R., and M. J. Muha. 1984. "Education and Intergroup Attitudes: Moral Enlightenment, Superficial Democratic Commitment, or Ideological Refinement?" *American Sociological Review 49*, 751–769.

Jackman, M. R., and M. S. Senter. 1983. "Different Therefore Unequal: Beliefs about Trait Differences Between Groups of Unequal Status." *Research in Social Stratification and Mobility 2*, 309–336.

Jackson, W. E. 1994. "Discrimination in Mortgage Lending Markets as Rational Economic Behavior: Theory, Evidence, and Public Policy." In M. E. Lashley and M. N. Jackson (Eds.), *African Americans and the New Policy Consensus: Retreat of the Liberal State* (pp. 157–178). Westport, CT: Greenwood Press.

Jacobson, C. K. 1985. "Resistance to Affirmative Action: Self-Interest or Racism?" *Journal of Conflict Resolution 29*, 306–329.

Jaynes, G. D. 1990. "The Labor Market Status of Black Americans, 1939–1985." *Journal of Economic Perspectives 4*, 9–24.

Jaynes, G. D., and R. M. Williams, Jr. (Eds.). 1989. *A Common Destiny: Blacks and American Society.* Washington, DC: National Academy Press.

Jones, E. W. 1986. "Black Managers: The Dream Deferred." *Harvard Business Review* (May–June), 84–93.

Jordan, W. 1968. *White over Black: American Attitudes Toward the Negro, 1550–1812.* New York: W. W. Norton.

Joreskog, K. G., and D. Sorbom. 1989. *LISREL 7 User's Reference Guide*. Mooresville, IN: Scientific Software.

Kanter, R. M. 1993. *Men and Women of the Corporation*. New York: Basic Books.

Kasarda, J. D. 1985. "Urban Change and Minority Opportunities." In P. E. Peterson (Ed.), *The New Urban Reality*. Washington, DC: Brookings Institution.

Kasarda, J., H. Hughes, and M. Irwin. 1991. "Demographic and Economic Restructuring in the South." In J. S. Himes (Ed.), *The South Moves Into its Future*. Tuscaloosa: University of Alabama Press.

Kasinitz, P., and J. Rosenberg. 1994. "Missing the Connection: Social Isolation and Employment on the Brooklyn Waterfront." Working Paper. New York: Michael Harrington Center for Democratic Values and Social Change, Queens College, City University of New York.

Katz, I. 1991. "Gordon Allport's The Nature of Prejudice." *Political Psychology 12*, 125–157.

Katz, I., and D. C. Glass. 1979. "An Ambivalence-Amplification Theory of Behavior toward the Stigmatized." In W. G. Austin and S. Worchel (Eds.), *The Social Psychology of Intergroup Relations* (pp. 55–70). Monterey, CA: Brooks/Cole.

Katz, I., and R. G. Hass. 1988. "Racial Ambivalence and American Value Conflict: Correlational and Priming Studies of Dual Cognitive Structures." *Journal of Personality and Social Psychology 55*, 893–905.

Katz, I., J. Wackenhut, and R. G. Hass. 1986. "Racial Ambivalence, Value Duality, and Behavior." In J. F. Dovidio, and S. L. Gaertner (Eds.), *Prejudice, Discrimination, and Racism* (pp. 35–60). New York: Academic Press.

Kellogg, S. 1990. "Exploring Diversity in Middle-Class Families: The Symbolism of American Ethnic Identity." *Social Science History 14*, 27–41.

Kinder, D. R. 1986. "The Continuing American Dilemma: White Resistance to Racial Change 40 Years After Myrdal." *Journal of Social Issues 42*, 151–171.

Kinder, D. R., and L. Sanders. 1996. *Divided by Color*. Chicago: University of Chicago Press.

Kinder, D. R., and L. M. Sanders. 1987. *Pluralistic Foundations of American Opinion on Race*. Paper presented at the Annual Meeting of the American Political Science Association, Chicago, September 3–6.

Kinder, D. R., and D. O. Sears. 1981. "Prejudice and Politics: Symbolic Racism versus Racial Threats to the Good Life." *Journal of Personality and Social Psychology 40*, 414–431.

Kirschenman, J. 1996. "Skill Requirements and Employers' Gendered Perceptions of African-American Workers." Unpublished manuscript. University of Chicago.

Kirschenman, J. 1992. *Race and Skills in Low-wage Labor Markets*. Paper presented to the Race, Poverty and Social Policy Workshop, Center for Urban Affairs and Policy Research, Northwestern University and the Center for the Study of Urban Inequality, University of Chicago.

Kirschenman, J. 1991. *Gender Within Race in the Labor Market*. Paper presented at the Urban Poverty and Family Life Conference, University of Chicago.

Kirschenman, J., P. Moss, and C. Tilly. 1995. "The Pre-employment Interview as a Group-Specific Barrier: Evidence from Quantitative and Qualitative Employer Surveys." Working Paper. Russell Sage Foundation, New York, October.

Kirschenman, J., and K. M. Neckerman. 1991. "'We'd Love to Hire Them, But...': The Meaning of Race to Employers." In C. Jencks and P. E. Peterson (Eds.), *The Urban Underclass*. Washington, DC: Brookings Institution.

Kleinpenning, G., and L. Hagendoorn. 1993. "Forms of Racism and the Cumulative Dimension of Ethnic Attitudes." *Social Psychology Quarterly 56*, 21–36.

Kluegel, J. R. 1990. "Trends in Whites' Explanations of the Gap in Black-White Socioeconomic Status, 1977–1989." *American Sociological Review 55*, 512–525.

Kluegel, J. R., and L. Bobo. 1993. "Dimensions of Whites' Beliefs about the Black-White Socioeconomic Gap." In P. Sniderman, P. Tetlock, and E. G. Carmines (Eds.), *Prejudice, Politics, and the American Dilemma* (pp. 127–147). Stanford, CA: Stanford University Press.

Kluegel, J. R., and E. R. Smith. 1986. *Beliefs About Inequality: Americans' Views of What Is and What Ought to Be.* New York: Aldine De Gruyter.

Kluegel, J. R., and E. R. Smith. 1983. "Affirmative Action Attitudes: Effects of Self-Interest, Racial Affect, and Stratification Beliefs on Whites' Views." *Social Forces 61*, 797–824.

Kluegel, J. R., and E. R. Smith. 1982. "Whites' Beliefs about Blacks' Opportunity." *American Sociological Review 47*, 518–532.

Kuklinski, J. H., and W. Parent. 1981. "Race and Big Government, Contamination in Measuring Political Attitudes." *Political Methodology 7*, 131–159.

Landry, B. 1987. *The New Black Middle Class.* Berkeley: University of California Press.

Lau, R. R. 1982. "Negativity in Political Perception." *Political Behavior 4*, 353–378.

Leahy, R. L. 1983. "The Child's Construction of Social Inequality: Conclusions." In R. L. Leahy (Ed.), *The Child's Construction of Social Inequality* (pp. 311–328). New York: Academic Press.

Lichter, D. T. 1988. "Racial Difference in Underemployment in American Cities." *American Journal of Sociology 93*, 771–792.

Lieberson, S. 1985. "Unhyphenated Whites in the United States." *Ethnic and Racial Studies 8*, 159–180.

Lieberson, S. 1980. *A Piece of the Pie: Black and White Immigrants Since 1880.* Berkeley: University of California Press.

Lieberson, S., and G. Fuguitt. 1967. "Negro-White Occupational Differences in the Absence of Discrimination." *American Journal of Sociology 73*, 188–200.

Lieberson, S., and M. C. Waters. 1988. *From Many Strands: Ethnic and Racial Groups in Contemporary America.* New York: Russell Sage Foundation.

Lieberson, S., and M. C. Waters. 1986. "Ethnic Groups in Flux: The Changing Ethnic Responses of American Whites." *The Annals of the American Academy 487*, 79–91.

Lipset, S. M., and W. Schneider. 1978. "The Bakke Case: How Would It Be Decided at the Bar of Public Opinion?" *Public Opinion* (March/April), 38–44.

Mackie, D. M., and D. L. Hamilton (Eds.). 1993. *Affect, Cognition, and Stereotyping: Interactive Processes in Group Perception.* San Diego, CA: Academic Press.

Marable, M. 1990. "A New Black Politics." *The Progressive 54*(8), 18–23.

Margolis, M., and K. E. Haque. 1981. "Applied Tolerance or Fear of Government? An Alternative Interpretation of Jackman's Findings." *American Journal of Political Science 25*, 241–255.

Massey, D., A. B. Gross, and M. L. Eggers. 1991. "Segregation, the Concentration of Poverty, and the Life Chances of Individuals." *Social Science Research 20*, 397–420.

Massey, D. S., and N. A. Denton. 1993. *American Apartheid: Segregation and the Making of the Underclass.* Cambridge, MA: Harvard University Press.

Massey, D. S., and N. A. Denton. 1989. "Hypersegregation in U.S. Metropolitan Areas: Black and Hispanic Segregation along Five Dimensions." *Demography 26*, 373–392.

Massey, D. S., and Z. L. Hajnal. 1995. "The Changing Geographic Structure of Black-White Segregation in the United States." *Social Science Quarterly 76*, 527–542.

Mayo, S. C. 1964. "Social Change, Social Movements, and the Disappearing Sectional South." *Social Forces 43*, 1–10.

McAdam, D. 1982. *Political Process and the Development of Black Insurgency, 1930–1970.* Chicago: University of Chicago Press.

McClendon, M. J. 1985. "Racism, Rational Choice, and White Opposition to Racial Change: A Case Study of Busing." *Public Opinion Quarterly 49*, 214–233.

McConahay, J. B. 1986. "Modern Racism, Ambivalence, and The Modern Racism Scale." In S. L. Gaertner and J. Dovidio (Eds.), *Prejudice, Discrimination, and Racism: Theory and Research* (pp. 91–126). New York: Academic Press.

McConahay, J. B. 1982. "Self-Interest Versus Racial Attitudes as Correlates of Anti-Busing Attitudes in Louisville: Is It the Buses or the Blacks?" *Journal of Politics 44*, 692–720.

McConahay, J. B., and J. C. Hough, Jr. 1976. "Symbolic Racism." *Journal of Social Issues 32*, 23–45.

McKinney, J. C., and L. B. Bourque. 1971. "The Changing South: National Incorporation of a Region." *American Sociological Review 36*, 399–411.

Milkman, R., and C. Pullman. 1991. "The Technological Change in an Auto Assembly Plant: The Impact of Worker's Tasks and Skills." *Work and Occupations 18*(2), 123–147.

Miller, W. E. 1992. *American National Election Study.* Ann Arbor, MI: Inter-University Consortium for Political and Social Research.

Miller, W. E. 1990. *American National Election Study.* Ann Arbor, MI: Inter-University Consortium for Political and Social Research.

Miller, W. E. 1989. *American National Election Study, 1988: Pre- and Post-Election Survey.* Codebook for ICPSR Study 9196. Ann Arbor, MI: Inter-University Consortium for Political and Social Research.

Miller, W. E. 1987. *American National Election Study, 1986: Post-Election Survey.* Codebook for ICPSR Study 8678. Ann Arbor, MI: Inter-University Consortium for Political and Social Research.

Miller, W. E., D. R. Kinder, and S. J. Rosenstone. 1993. *American National Election Study, 1992: Post-Election Survey [Enhanced with 1990 and 1991 Data].* Codebook for ICPSR Study 6067. Ann Arbor, MI: Inter-University Consortium for Political and Social Research.

Miller, W. E., D. R. Kinder, and S. J. Rosenstone. 1992. *American National Election Study, 1990: Post-Election Survey.* Codebook for ICPSR study 9548. Ann Arbor, MI: Inter-University Consortium for Political and Social Research.

Monteith, M. J., J. R. Zuwerink, and P. G. Devine. 1994. "Prejudice and Prejudice Reduction: Classic Challenges, Contemporary Approaches." In P. G. Devine, D. L. Hamilton, and T. M. Ostrom, (Eds.), *Social Cognition: Impact on Social Psychology* (pp. 323–346). San Diego, CA: Academic Press.

Morris, A. 1984. *The Origins of the Civil Rights Movement: Black Communities Organizing for Change.* New York: The Free Press.

Morris, A. 1981. "Black Southern Students Sit-in Movement: An Analysis of Internal Organization." *American Sociological Review 46,* 744–767.

Morris, L., and L. F. Williams. 1989. "The Coalition at the End of the Rainbow: The 1984 Jackson Campaign." In L. J. Barker and R. W. Walters (Eds.), *Jesse Jackson's 1984 Presidential Campaign: Challenge and Change in American Politics* (pp. 227–248). Urbana: University of Illinois Press.

Morrison, A. M., and M. A. Von Glinow. 1990. "Women and Minorities in Management." *American Psychologist 45,* 200–208.

Moss, P., and C. Tilly. 1996. "Soft Skills and Race: An Investigation of Black Men's Employment Problems." *Work and Occupations 23,* 252–276.

Moss, P., and C. Tilly. 1993. *Why Aren't Employers Hiring More Black Men? Final Report.* New York: Social Science Research Council, Committee for Research on the Urban Underclass.

Myrdal, G. 1944. *An American Dilemma: The Negro Problem and Modern Democracy.* New York: Random House.

Neckerman, K. M., and J. Kirschenman. 1991. "Hiring Strategies, Racial Bias, and Inner-city Workers." *Social Problems 38*(4), 801–815.

Neidert, L. J., and R. Farley. 1985. "Assimilation in the United States: An Analysis of Ethnic and Generation Differences in Status and Achievement." *American Sociological Review 50,* 840–850.

Nelson, W. E., Jr. 1987. "Cleveland: The Evolution of Black Political Power." In M. Preston, L. J. Henderson, Jr., and P. Puryear (Eds.), *The Search for Political Power* (pp. 172–199). New York: Longman.

Niemi, R. G., J. Mueller, and T. W. Smith. 1989. *Trends in Public Opinion: A Compendium of Survey Data.* New York: Greenwood Press.

Oliver, M. L., and T. M. Shapiro. 1995. *Black Wealth, White Wealth: A New Perspective on Racial Inequality.* New York: Routledge.

Page, H. F. 1990. "Lessons of the Jackson Campaign: Discursive Strategies of Symbolic Control and Cultural Capitalization." In L. Morris (Ed.), *The Social and Political Implications of the 1984 Jesse Jackson Presidential Campaign* (pp. 135–156). New York: Praeger.

Pearce, D. M. 1979. "Gatekeepers and Homeseekers: Institutional Patterns in Racial Steering." *Social Problems 26,* 325–342.

Peffley, M. A., and J. Hurwitz. 1985. "A Hierarchical Model of Attitude Constraint." *American Journal of Political Science 29,* 871–890.

Perry, H. L. 1991. "Deracialization as an Analytical Construct in American Urban Politics." *Urban Affairs Quarterly 27,* 181–191.

Pettigrew, T. F. 1997. "Generalized Intergroup Contact Effects on Prejudice." *Personality and Social Psychology Bulletin 23,* 173–185.

Pettigrew, T. F. 1991. "Normative Theory in Intergroup Relations: Explaining Both Harmony and Conflict." *Psychology and Developing Societies 3,* 3–16.

Pettigrew, T. F. 1985. "New Black-White Patterns: How Best to Conceptualize Them?" *Annual Review of Sociology 11*, 329–346.

Pettigrew, T. F. 1982. "Prejudice." In S. Thernstrom, A. Orlov, and O. Handlin (Eds.), *Dimensions of Ethnicity* (pp. 1–29). Cambridge, MA.: Belknap.

Pettigrew, T. F., and R. W. Meertens. 1995. Subtle and Blatant Prejudice in Western Europe. *European Journal of Social Psychology 25*, 57–75.

Piore, M. J., and C. F. Sabel. 1984. *The Second Industrial Divide: Possibilities of Prosperity*. New York: Basic Books.

Preston, M. 1989. "The 1984 Presidential Primary Campaign: Who Voted for Jesse Jackson and Why." In L. J. Barker and R. W. Walters (Eds.), *Jesse Jackson's 1984 Presidential Campaign: Challenge and Change in American Politics* (pp. 129–146). Urbana: University of Illinois Press.

Quillian, L. 1995. "Prejudice as a Response to Perceived Group Threat: Population Composition and Anti-Immigrant and Racial Prejudice in Europe." *American Sociological Review 60*, 586–611.

Rabb, E., and S. Martin Lipset. 1962. "The Prejudiced Society." In E. Rabb (Ed.), *American Race Relations Today* (pp. 29–55). New York: Doubleday.

Reed, A. L., Jr. 1986. *The Jesse Jackson Phenomenon*. New Haven, CT: Yale University Press.

Reed, J. S. 1991. "New South or No South: Regional Culture in 2036." In J. S. Himes (Ed.), *The South Moves Into its Future: Studies in the Analysis and Prediction of Social Change* (pp. 225–235). Tuscaloosa: University of Alabama Press.

Reed, J. S. 1986. *The Enduring South: Subcultural Persistence in a Mass Society* (Rev. ed.). Chapel Hill: University of North Carolina Press.

Reed, J. S. 1983. *Southerners: The Social Psychology of Sectionalism*. Chapel Hill: University of North Carolina Press.

Reed, J. S., and M. Black. 1985. "How Southerners Gave Up Jim Crow." *New Perspectives 17*, 15–19.

Reed, J. S., J. Kohls, and C. Hanchette. 1990. "The Dissolution of Dixie and the Changing Shape of the South." *Social Forces 69*, 221–233.

Reissman, L. 1965. "Urbanization in the South." In J. McKinney and E. Thompson (Eds.), *The South in Continuity and Change*. Durham, NC: Duke University Press.

Roseman, I. J. 1984. "Cognitive Determinants of Emotion: A Structural Theory." In P. Shaver (Ed.), *Review of Personality and Social Psychology* (Vol. 5). Beverly Hills, CA: Sage.

Roth, B. M. 1990. "Social Psychology's Racism." *The Public Interest 98*, 26–36.

Ryan, W. 1976. *Blaming the Victim*. New York: Vintage.

Scherer, K. R. 1988. "Cognitive Antecedents of Emotion." In V. Hamilton, G. H. Bower, and N. H. Frijda (Eds.), *Cognitive Perspectives on Emotion and Motivation* (pp. 89–126). Dordrecht: Kluwer.

Schuman, H. 1971. "Free Will and Determinism in Beliefs about Race." In N. C. Yetman and C. H. Steele (Eds.), *Majority and Minority: The Dynamics of Racial and Ethnic Relations*. Boston: Allyn and Bacon.

Schuman, H., and L. Bobo. 1988. "Survey-Based Experiments on White Racial Attitudes Toward Residential Integration." *American Journal of Sociology 94*, 273–299.

Schuman, H., and S. Presser. 1981. *Questions and Answers in Attitude Surveys*. New York: Academic Press.

Schuman, H., C. Steeh, and L. Bobo. 1985. *Racial Attitudes in America: Trends and Interpretations*. Cambridge, MA: Harvard University Press.

Sears, D., L. Huddy, and L. G. Schatter. 1984. "A Schematic Variant of Symbolic Politics Theory as Applied to Racial and Gender Equality." In R. R. Lau and D. Sears (Eds.), *Political Cognition: The 19th Annual Carnegie Symposium on Cognition*. Hillsdale, NJ: Erlbaum.

Sears, D. O. 1988. "Symbolic Racism." In P. A. Katz and D. A. Taylor (Eds.), *Eliminating Racism: Profiles in Controversy* (pp. 53–84). New York: Plenum.

Sears, D. O. 1983. "A Person Positivity Bias." *Journal of Personality and Social Psychology 44*, 233–250.

Sears, D. O. 1975. "Political Socialization." In F. I. Greenstein and N.W. Polsby, (Eds.), *Handbook of Political Science*, Volume 2: *Micropolitical Theory* (pp. 93–154). Reading, MA: Addison-Wesley.

Sears, D. O., and H. M. Allen, Jr. 1984. "The Trajectory of Local Desegregation Controversies and Whites' Opposition to Busing." In N. Miller and M. B. Brewer (Eds.), *Groups in Contact: The Psychology of Desegregation* (pp. 123–151). New York: Academic Press.

Sears, D. O., and C. L. Funk. 1991. "The Role of Self-Interest in Social and Political Attitudes." *Advances in Experimental Social Psychology 24*, 1–91.

Sears, D. O., C. P. Hensler, and L. K. Speer. 1979. "Whites Opposition to 'Busing': Self-Interest of Symbolic Politics?" *American Political Science Review 73*, 369–384.

Sears, D. O., and T. Jessor. 1996. "Whites' Racial Policy Attitudes: The Role of White Racism." *Social Science Quarterly 77*, 751–759.

Sears, D. O., and D. R. Kinder. 1985. "Whites Opposition to Busing: On Conceptualizing and Operationalizing Group Conflict." *Journal of Personality and Social Psychology 48*, 1141–1147.

Sears, D. O., and D. R. Kinder. 1971. "Racial Tensions and Voting Behavior in Los Angeles." In W. Z. Hirsch (Ed.), *Los Angeles: Viability and Prospects for Metropolitan Leadership*. New York: Praeger.

See, K. O., and W. J. Wilson. 1988. "Race and Ethnicity." In N. Smelser (Ed.), *Handbook of Sociology* (pp. 223–242). Newbury Park, CA: Sage.

Seltzer, R., and R. C. Smith. 1985. "Race and Ideology." *Phylon 46*, 98–105.

Sheatsley, P. B. 1966. "White Attitudes toward the Negro." *Daedalus 95*, 217–238.

Shexnider, A. J. 1990. "The Politics of Pragmatism: An Analysis of the 1989 Gubernatorial Election in Virginia." *PS 23*, 154–156.

Siegel, P. M. 1970. "On the Cost of Being Negro." In E. O. Laumann, P. M. Siegel, and R. W. Hodge (Eds.), *The Logic of Social Hierarchies* (pp. 727–743). Chicago: Markham.

Sigelman, L., and S. Welch. 1991. *Black Americans' Views of Racial Inequality: The Dream Deferred*. New York: Cambridge University Press.

Simmons, R. G., and M. Rosenberg. 1971. "Functions of Children's Perceptions of the Stratification System." *American Sociological Review 36*, 235–249.

Smith, A. W. 1987. "Problems and Progress in the Measurement of Black Public Opinion." *American Behavioral Scientist 30*, 441–455.

Smith, A. W. 1981. "Racial Tolerance as a Function of Group Position." *American Sociological Review 46*, 558–573.

Smith, E. R. 1993. "Social Identity and Social Emotions: Toward New Conceptions of Prejudice." In D. M. Mackie and D. L. Hamilton (Eds.), *Affect, Cognition, and Stereotyping: Interactive Processes in Group Perception* (pp. 297–315). San Diego, CA: Academic Press.

Smith, H., T. F. Pettigrew, and L. Vega. 1996. "Relative Deprivation: A Conceptual Critique and Meta-Analysis." Unpublished manuscript.

Smith, R. C. 1992. "'Politics' Is Not Enough: The Institutionalization of the African American Freedom Movement." In R. C. Gomes and L. F. Williams (Eds.), *From Exclusion to Inclusion: The Long Struggle for African American Political Power* (pp. 97–126). Westport, CT: Greenwood Press.

Smith, R. C. 1990a. "From Insurgency toward Inclusion: The Jackson Campaigns of 1984 and 1988." In L. Morris (Ed.), *The Social and Political Implications of the 1984 Jesse Jackson Presidential Campaign* (pp. 215–230). Westport, CT: Praeger.

Smith, R. C. 1990b. "Recent Elections and Black Politics: The Maturation or Death of Black Politics?" *PS 23*, 160–163.

Smith, R. C. 1981. "Black Power and the Transformation from Protest to Politics." *Political Science Quarterly 96*, 431–443.

Smith, R.C., and R. Seltzer. 1992. *Race, Class, and Culture: A Study in Afro-American Mass Opinion*. Albany, NY: State University of New York Press.

Smith, T. W. 1985. "The Subjectivity of Ethnicity." In C. F. Turner and E. Martin (Eds.), *Surveying Subjective Phenomena* (pp. 117–128). New York: Russell Sage.

Smith, T. W. 1980. "Ethnic Measurement and Identification." *Ethnicity 7*, 78–95.

Smith, T. W., and P. B. Sheatsley. 1984. "American Attitudes toward Race Relations." *Public Opinion* (October/November), 14–15, 50–53.

Sniderman, P. M., and M. G. Hagen. 1985. *Race and Inequality: A Study in American Values*. Chatham, NJ.: Chatham House Press.

Sniderman, P. M., and T. Piazza. 1993. *The Scar of Race*. Cambridge, MA: Harvard University Press.

Sniderman, P. M., and P. E. Tetlock. 1986a. "Reflections on American Racism." *Journal of Social Issues 42*, 173–187.

Sniderman, P. M., and P. E. Tetlock. 1986b. "Symbolic Racism: Problems of Motive Attribution in Political Analysis." *Journal of Social Issues 42*, 129–150.

Sokoloff, N. 1992. *Black Women and White Women in the Professions*. New York: Routledge.

Stangor, C., L. A. Sullivan, and T. E. Ford. 1991. "Affective and Cognitive Determinants of Prejudice." *Social Cognition 9*, 359–380.

Starr, P. 1992. "Civil Reconstruction: What to do Without Affirmative Action." *The American Prospect* (Winter), 7–16.

Steady, F. C. 1981. *The Black Woman Cross-Culturally*. Cambridge, MA: Schenkman Publishing.

Steeh, C., and M. Krysan. 1996. "Affirmative Action and the Public, 1970–1995." *Public Opinion Quarterly 60*, 128–158.

Steeh, C., and H. Schuman. 1992. "Young White Adults: Did Racial Attitudes Change in the 1980s?" *American Journal of Sociology 98*, 340–367.

Steinberg, S. 1981. *The Ethnic Myth: Race, Ethnicity and Class in America*. Boston: Beacon Press.

Stoker, L. 1996. "Understanding Differences in Whites' Opinions Across Racial Policies." *Social Science Quarterly 77*, 768–777.

Summers, R. J. 1991. The Influence of Affirmative Action on Perceptions of a Beneficiary's Qualifications." *Journal of Applied Social Psychology 21*, 1265–1276.

Taeuber, K. E., and A. F. Taeuber. 1965. *Negroes in Cities: Residential Segregation and Neighborhood Change*. Chicago: Aldine.

Tate, K. 1993. *From Protest to Politics: The New Black Voters in American Elections*. Cambridge, MA: Harvard University Press.

Taylor, D. G., P. B. Sheatsley, and A. M. Greeley. 1978. "Attitudes toward Racial Integration." *Scientific American 238*, 42–51.

Taylor, M. C. 1995. "White Backlash to Workplace Affirmative Action." *Social Forces 73*, 1385–1414.

Tienda, M., and H. Stier. 1991. "Joblessness and Shiftlessness: Labor Force Activity in Chicago's Inner City." In C. Jencks and P. E. Peterson (Eds.), *The Urban Underclass*. Washington, DC: Brookings Institution.

Tilly, C., P. Moss, and J. Kirschenman. 1996. *Space as a Signal, Space as a Barrier: How Employers Map and Use Space in Four Metropolitan Labor Markets*. Paper presented to the Annual Meeting of the American Sociological Association, New York.

Torney-Purta, J. 1983. "The Development of Views about the Role of Social Institutions in Redressing Inequality and Promoting Human Rights." In R. L. Leahy (Ed.), *The Child's Construction of Social Inequality* (pp. 287–310). New York: Academic Press.

Tuch, S. A. 1987. "Urbanism, Region, and Tolerance Revisited: The Case of Racial Prejudice." *American Sociological Review 52*, 504–510.

Tuch, S. A., and M. Hughes. 1996a. "Whites' Racial Policy Attitudes." *Social Science Quarterly 77*, 723–745.

Tuch, S. A., and M. Hughes. 1996b. "Whites' Opposition to Race-Targeted Policies: One Cause of Many?" *Social Science Quarterly 77*, 778–788.

Turner, J., and R. Singleton. 1978. "A Theory of Ethnic Oppression: Toward a Reintegration of Cultural and Structural Concepts in Ethnic Relations Theory." *Social Forces 56*, 1001–1018.

Turner, J. C., M. A. Hogg, P. J. Oakes, and S. D. Reicher. 1987. *Rediscovering the Social Group: A Self-Categorization Theory*. Oxford: Blackwell.

Turner, M. A. 1992. "Discrimination in Urban Housing Markets: Lessons from Fair Housing Audits." *Housing Policy Debates 3*, 185–215.

Turner, M. A., M. Fix, and R. J. Struyk. 1991. *Opportunities Denied, Opportunities Diminished: Racial Discrimination in Hiring*. Washington, DC: Urban Institute Press.

Wajcman, J. 1991. "Patriarchy, Technology and Conceptions of Skill." *Work and Occupations 18*(1), 29–45.

Waldinger, R., and T. Bailey. 1991. "The Continuing Significance of Race: Racial Conflict and Racial Discrimination in Construction." *Politics and Society 19*, 291–323.

Walters, R. W. 1981. "The Challenge of Black Leadership: An Analysis of the Problem of Strategy Shift." *Urban League Review 5*, 77–88.

Walton, H. 1985. *Invisible Politics: Black Political Behavior.* Albany: State University of New York Press.

Waters, M. C. 1990. *Ethnic Options: Choosing Identities in America.* Berkeley: University of California Press.

Weber, L., and E. Higgenbotham. 1995. *Perceptions of Workplace Discrimination Among Black and White Professional-Managerial Women.* Memphis, TN: University of Memphis, Center for Research on Women.

Weiss, K. 1997. "UC Law Schools' New Rules Cost Minorities Spots." *The Los Angeles Times,* May 15, p. A1.

Welch, S., and M. Combs. 1985. "Intraracial Differences in Attitudes Among Blacks: Class Cleavage or Consensus?" *Phylon 46,* 91–97.

Welch, S., and L. S. Foster. 1987. "Class and Conservatism in the Black Community." *American Politics Quarterly 4,* 445–470.

Westie, F. 1965. "The American Dilemma: An Empirical Test." *American Sociological Review 30,* 527–538.

White, J. 1990. *Black Leadership in America: From Booker T. Washington to Jesse Jackson,* 2d ed. New York: Longman.

Williams, L. F. 1990. "White/Black Perceptions of the Electability of Black Political Candidates." In L. J. Barker (Ed.), *Black Electoral Politics* (pp. 45–64). New Brunswick, NJ: Transaction Publishers.

Williams, R. M., Jr. 1964. *Strangers Next Door: Ethnic Relations in American Communities.* Englewood Cliffs, NJ: Prentice Hall.

Wills, G. 1988. "New Votuhs." *New York Review of Books,* August 18.

Wilson, C. A., J. H. Lewis, and C. Herring. 1991. *The 1991 Civil Rights Act: Restoring Basic Protections.* Chicago: Urban League.

Wilson, T. C. 1996. "Cohort and Prejudice: Whites' Attitudes Toward Blacks, Hispanics, Jews, and Asians." *Public Opinion Quarterly 60,* 253–274.

Wilson, W. J. 1987. *The Truly Disadvantaged.* Chicago: University of Chicago Press.

Wilson, W. J. 1978. *The Declining Significance of Race: Blacks and Changing American Institutions.* Chicago: University of Chicago Press.

Wilson, W. J. 1973. *Power, Racism, and Privilege: Race Relations in Theoretical and Sociohistorical Perspectives.* New York: The Free Press.

Yancey, D. 1988. *When Hell Froze Over: The Untold Story of Doug Wilder. A Black Politician's Rise to Power in the South.* Roanoke, VA: Taylor Publishing.

Yinger, J. M. 1996. *Closed Doors, Opportunities Lost: The Continuing Costs of Housing Discrimination.* New York: Russell Sage Foundation.

Yinger, J. M. 1985. "Ethnicity." *Annual Review of Sociology 11,* 151–180.

Yinger, J. M. 1983. "Ethnicity and Social Change: The Interaction of Structural, Cultural, and Personality Factors." *Ethnic and Racial Studies 6,* 395–409.

Yoder, J. D. 1991. "Rethinking Tokenism: Looking Beyond Numbers." *Gender and Society 5*(2), 178–192.

Zanna, M. P., G. Haddock, and V. M. Esses. 1990. "The Determinants of Prejudice." Presented at Society of Experimental Social Psychology, Buffalo, NY.

Zubrinsky, C. L., and L. Bobo. 1996. "Prismatic Metropolis: Race and Residential Segregation in the City of the Angels." *Social Science Research 25,* 335–374.

Zweigenhaft, R. L., and G. W. Domhoff. 1991. *Blacks in the White Establishment?: A Study of Race and Class in America.* New Haven, CT: Yale University Press.

Index

About the Contributors

CHARLES AMISSAH is Assistant Professor in the Department of Sociology at Hampton University. His research interests include stratification and inequality, immigration, and race and ethnicity.

E. M. BECK is Professor of Sociology and Head of the Department of Sociology at the University of Georgia. His interest is in the political economy of racial violence, in particular the relationship between economic changes in the status of the white lower class and violence against blacks. His current research focuses on the economic and organizational factors associated with contemporary racial violence in the South. He has authored 50 papers published in sociological and social science journals.

LAWRENCE BOBO is Professor of Sociology and Afro-American Studies at Harvard University. He was a Visiting Scholar at the Russell Sage Foundation in 1995–96. His research interests include race and ethnic relations, public opinion, and social psychology, with a special emphasis on the dynamics of racial attitudes in the United States. Bobo is coauthor of *Racial Attitudes in America: Trends and Interpretations* (with Howard Schuman and Charlotte Steeh).

JAMES E. COVERDILL is Assistant Professor of Sociology at the University of Georgia. His main areas of interest are work, organizations, and inequality. Recent papers explore how work experiences shape gender-role attitudes and the risk and resolution of premarital conceptions. His current research focuses on the matching of people and jobs through personal contacts and private employment agencies.

CEDRIC HERRING is Professor in the Department of Sociology and the Institute of Government and Public Affairs at the University of Illinois at Chicago. He is also Interim Director of the Institute for Research on Race and Comparative Public Policy. Herring has published more than 35 journal articles and book chapters on political sociology, labor force issues and social policy, stratification and inequality, and the sociology of black Americans. He is the author of *Splitting the Middle: Political Alienation, Acquiescence, and Activism* and is the editor of *African Americans and the Public Agenda: The Paradoxes of Public Policy* and *Empowerment in Chicago: Grassroots Participation in Economic Development and Poverty Alleviation.*

MICHAEL HUGHES is Professor of Sociology at Virginia Polytechnic Institute and State University. His early research focused on social integration and well-being and included studies of crowding and living alone. His current research includes racial attitudes; ethnic and racial identity (and their link to individual self-concept); psychiatric epidemiology, with particular attention to the issues of race, class, gender, and marital status differences in mental disorder; posttraumatic stress disorder; and the correlates and consequences of rape. Recent publications include studies of mental disorder, drug dependence, posttraumatic stress disorder, whites' racial attitudes, socialization and racial identity among African Americans, self-esteem and personal efficacy among African Americans, and African Americans' quality of life.

JOLEEN KIRSCHENMAN has worked extensively in the areas of race and poverty, especially with respect to inequality in urban labor markets. Much of this work has focused on the role of employers and their attitudes and practices toward minorities, particularly black men. In addition to noting the significance of racial distinction, her work also attends to class, spatial, and gender inequalities. Among her publications is the widely cited article (with Kathryn M. Neckerman), "'We'd Love to Hire Them, But . . .': The Meaning of Race for Employers." She is currently associated with the Multi-City Study of Urban Inequality, a research project conducted by a national consortium of scholars and funded by the Ford and Russell Sage foundations.

JAMES R. KLUEGEL is Professor of Sociology at the University of Illinois at Urbana-Champaign. He continues to collaborate with Lawrence Bobo in work about modern stereotypes and perceptions of opportunity for minorities and women, based on data from the Multi-City Study of Urban Inequality. He also is pursuing comparative work on public opinion about economic and political justice, building upon research reported in his recent coedited book, *Social Justice and Political Change* (1995). He is working with a team completing surveys in Central and Eastern Europe to track change in justice perceptions since the revolutions of 1989.

JACK K. MARTIN is Senior Research Scientist, Adjunct Professor of Sociology, and Director of the Survey Research Center at the University of Georgia. He has received a National Research Service Award from the National Institutes of Health. His current research focuses on the interaction of workplace structures and worker dispositions as this process affects attitudes toward work and off-the-job behavior. He has authored more than 40 articles and chapters on these issues and is collecting data for the last of three national surveys of U.S. workers, examining the impact of job stressors and workgroup characteristics on attitudes and behaviors at work and off the job. He is also Principal Investigator on a grant funded by the National Institute of Alcohol Abuse and Alcoholism for a five-year panel study of factors that place African-American workers at risk for the development of maladaptive drinking behaviors.

THOMAS F. PETTIGREW is Research Professor of Social Psychology at the University of California, Santa Cruz. He is the author of more than 200 publications; his most recent book is *How to Think Like a Social Scientist* (1996). His primary interests are intergroup prejudice and discrimination as well as social psychological theory. Pettigrew has received numerous honors including a Guggenheim Fellowship, the Spivack Fellowship for Race Relations Research, the Kurt Lewin Award, and (with Joanne Martin) the Gorgon Allport Intergroup Research Prize.

LEE SIGELMAN is Professor of Political Science at The George Washington University. He has written extensively in the fields of public opinion and political behavior and (with Susan Welch) is the author of *Black Americans' Views of Racial Inequality: The Dream Deferred* (1991).

A. WADE SMITH was Professor and Head of the Sociology Department at Arizona State University until his death in 1994. He published extensively in the areas of racial and ethnic relations, social change and social indicators, the sociology of education, and survey research.

RYAN A. SMITH is Assistant Professor in the School of Management and Labor Relations at Rutgers University, New Brunswick. His research focuses on group differences in access to job authority and the consequences of job authority for income. He is author of "Race, Income, and Authority at Work: A Cross-Temporal Analysis of Black and White Men, 1972–1994" (1997).

STEVEN A. TUCH is Associate Professor of Sociology at The George Washington University. His research focuses on issues and problems in race relations, social stratification and inequality, and public opinion. He has written extensively on the racial attitudes of whites and African Americans, with a particular focus on the measurement and explanation of over-time trends in these attitudes. In collaboration with Jack K. Martin, he is Co-Principal Investigator on a five-year project, funded by the National Institute of Alcohol Abuse and Alcoholism, to investigate the factors that shape maladaptive alcohol use among African Americans.